THE 100 BEST STOCKS TO OWN FOR UNDER $20

GENE WALDEN

DEARBORN™
A **Kaplan Professional** Company

This publication is designed to provide accurate and authoritative information in regard to the subject matter covered. It is sold with the understanding that the publisher is not engaged in rendering legal, accounting, or other professional service. If legal advice or other expert assistance is required, the services of a competent professional person should be sought.

Editorial Director: Cynthia A. Zigmund
Managing Editor: Jack Kiburz
Interior Design: Lucy Jenkins
Cover Design: Utopia Communications
Typesetting: the dotted i

© 1999 by Dearborn Financial Publishing, Inc.®

Published by Dearborn, a Kaplan Professional Company

Printed in the United States of America

99   00   01   10   9   8   7   6   5   4   3   2

Library of Congress Cataloging-in-Publication Data

Walden, Gene.
   The 100 best stocks to own for under $20 / Gene Walden.
      p.   cm.
   Includes index.
   ISBN 0-7931-3230-4
    1. Small capitalization stocks. I. Title. II. Title: One hundred best stocks to own for under $20.
   HG4971.W35 1999
   332.63'2044—dc21   99-29670
                                           CIP

Contents

Alphabetical Listing of the 100 Best Stocks Under $20

Preface

If I've done my job well, by the time you read this, there will be some stocks in this book that are trading at well over $20 a share. Sorry about that, but that's the nature of the beast. Good stocks in a strong market won't stay under $20 forever. In fact, over time I hope they all grow to over $20. But even at a higher price, most of those stocks should continue to be solid investments with a bright future.

It is also likely that some of the stocks on the list will suddenly disappear as a result of a merger or acquisition. Many of the best small stocks ultimately become buyout targets for larger companies. Fortunately, with a list of 100 stocks, there will still be plenty of other picks from which to choose. (We'll try to keep track of the major changes at our investment research Web site at www.best-100.com. You can use the site free for several months just for asking; see the site for details.)

The world of small stocks is constantly in flux; that's part of the draw of the small stock segment. They're exciting stocks in transition. Get them while they're hot.

Acknowledgments

Typically, this is the part of the book where the author graciously thanks all the people who helped along the way. I'll go a step further here. This book would not have been possible without Randy Royals and Paul Mallon, who initially came up with the idea for the book. Randy, of Target Stores, was looking for a guide that would help small investors get involved in what has been one of the greatest bull markets of this century. Paul, the sales director at Dearborn Financial Publishing, suggested the title, *The 100 Best Stocks to Own for Under $20,* and approached me with the idea. Sometimes you just get lucky.

Also deserving special thanks is Larry Nelson, who, as he has for nearly all of my Best 100 books, worked from start to finish on the project, assisting with the research and fact-gathering, the graphs, the tables, and other key elements of the book. I also want to thank my editors at Dearborn, including Cynthia Zigmund and Jack Kiburz, who did an exceptional job of shaping the book into an attractive, professional, and user-friendly format.

Introduction

There's nothing like a collection of low-priced stocks to stir the speculative juices of investors large and small. Imagine, for instance, buying Microsoft in its infancy in 1987. A $10,000 investment then would have grown to just over $1 million by 1999. A $10,000 bet on Dell Computer in 1989 would have soared to about $2.75 million by 1999. And a $10,000 investment in Cisco Systems in 1990 would have grown to more than $6 million by 1999.

Those three companies represent what is perhaps the best argument for buying small stocks—a relatively small investment can reap extraordinary returns. But you also have to weigh the exceptional success of those three stocks against the hundreds of stocks that were small stocks a decade ago and remain small stocks today.

The fact is, cheap stocks are usually cheap for a reason. According to investing's "efficient market theory," stocks tend to sell for about what they're worth. That's not a knock on small stocks. In fact, there are some very good reasons the stocks featured in this book have been trading for under $20.

By their very nature, small stocks tend to be little-known companies with short histories and uncertain futures. Just a handful are followed by the major Wall Street brokerage houses. Many are involved in technologies or services that we don't understand. There are no household names among these small stocks, and no market darlings. You'll find no Coca-Colas on the list, no Microsofts, and no Home Depots. It truly is a list of no-names.

This should not detract from the investment appeal of these small stocks, however. In fact, those are exactly the traits you want in small stocks—young, up-and-coming companies that have not yet been discovered by the rest of the investing world. The purpose of this book is to identify some of the best fast-growing, unknown, and underappreciated small stocks available today on the U.S. stock market.

For all their risks, the small stocks listed here have some very attractive qualities. They all have a history of strong financial growth, many are in fast-growing technology sectors, and the vast majority appear to be exceptional values relative to the rest of the market. Low- and mid-priced stocks have trailed the overall market since about 1994. So, as prices of the bigger blue chip stocks climbed through the mid- and late-1990s, the lower-priced stock sector remained stagnant. Most of the stocks in this book have had very attractive PE ratios (stock price divided by earnings per share), which is the measure widely used on Wall Street to determine whether a stock is fairly priced relative to other stocks on the market. In very general terms, the lower the PE, the better the bargain. Most of the big blue chip stocks have PEs in the 20 to 40 range, and high-tech companies such as Microsoft and Cisco Systems have PEs even higher. Most of the stocks in this book have been trading well below that level, with PEs in the range of 5 to 20.

Small stocks tend to move in cycles that are independent of the rest of the market. They may be out of favor for several months or years and then suddenly become in vogue as the rest of the market is faltering. When the market's momentum shifts to the smaller stocks, the ride up can be breathtaking.

Despite the uncertainty and volatility of smaller stocks, their average performance over the long term has exceeded not only larger stocks but also every other conventional form of investing. Small stocks of the 20th century have done better than bonds, money markets, oil, gold, silver, real estate, annuities, collectibles, and every other conventional form of investment.

Since 1925, small stocks have provided an average annual return of 12.5 percent, compared with a 10.5 percent return for large stocks. (See chart below.)

Growth of Small Stocks vs. Large Stocks, 1925–1995

	Avg. Annual Growth	Current Value of $1,000 Invested in 1925
Large Stocks	10.5%	$1.14 million
Small Stocks	12.5	4.0 million

The difference has been even more dramatic in recent decades, particularly among stocks with market capitalizations of under $25 million. A $10,000 investment in small stocks at the end of 1951, if held through 1994, would have grown to $29 million, according to a study by James P. O'Shaughnessy, author of *What Works on Wall Street.* That's an annual average return of 20 percent!

Another study by Mark Reinganum of the University of Southern California also showed a dramatic difference in the performance of small stocks versus large stocks during a 17-year period from 1963 through 1980.

Reinganum divided all stocks of the New York Stock Exchange into eight categories from smallest to largest—reassembling the list anew each of the 17 years. As the following chart demonstrates, there was a clear and dramatic correlation between the size of the stock and the rate of growth.

Small Stocks vs. Large Stocks, 1963–1980*
(Listed from largest to smallest stocks)

Avg. Annual Return	1980 Value of $10,000 Invested in 1963
1. 11.8% (largest)	$ 75,000
2. 12.9	88,200
3. 15.1	126,800
4. 15.2	127,000
5. 16.2	139,500
6. 18.5	201,000
7. 17.9	185,000
8. 23.7 (smallest)	452,000

* Based on a study of the stocks of the New York Stock Exchange by Mark Reinganum of the University of Southern California

As the chart demonstrates, for investors interested in explosive growth, smaller stocks clearly offer more potential. But great performance of small stocks *as a group* doesn't necessarily translate into great performance of small stocks on an individual basis. The challenge is finding the stocks that are most likely to live up to that potential.

THE SELECTION PROCESS

With more than 8,000 stocks selling for under $20, paring the list to the "best" 100 was clearly a very daunting undertaking. It did afford me the luxury of being highly selective, and it's a good thing, because the vast majority of those 8,000-plus under-$20 stocks were poor performers with little to offer. Coming up with 100 stocks I really liked—even from this vast universe of choices—was like plucking 100 widely scattered needles from a massive hay stack.

The selection process was a tedious and time-consuming procedure that took several months to complete. I consulted sources, studied research reports, and ran a specially tailored computerized screen of all U.S. stocks of under $20. Specifically, I screened for companies with three-year earnings growth of more than 50 percent, a return on equity of at least 9 percent, a price-to-sales ratio of no more than 10, a solid debt-to-equity ratio, and a market capitalization ranging from $5 million to $3 billion.

That screen trimmed the list from more than 8,000 stocks to about 700 decent prospects. Then I went stock by stock, along with my research associate, Larry Nelson, evaluating all 700 companies and eliminating the ones we didn't feel made the grade. Many were dropped because of inconsistent growth, or because their momentum seemed to be faltering. Others were axed because I didn't feel their products or services could provide sustained growth. For example, several cigar makers had posted some pretty good numbers, but it's my opinion that the growth of that industry is waning. Others were dumped because their company's revenue was tied almost entirely to a single product or service. For instance, a small company called Media Arts has enjoyed outstanding growth for several years, but its entire revenue stream is based on the sale of art work created by a single artist. I could be wrong—the company could continue to thrive as long as the artist is healthy and working—but that's not the kind of enterprise I would care to bet on. In a few cases, I eliminated some stocks with pretty good financial numbers, because there were already several similar companies from the same industry with better numbers on the list.

That exhaustive process narrowed the list down to an even 100 stocks, all with a solid track history and the potential for bigger things to come.

RANKING THE STOCKS

The stocks are ranked from number 1 through 100 based on a 16-point rating system with four key factors:

1. Four-year earnings growth
2. Four-year revenue growth
3. Three-year stock growth
4. Four-year consistency of earnings and revenue growth

The charts below detail the specific break points of my 16-point rating system.

Earnings Growth (Based on Four-Year Returns)

Avg. Annual Return	Points Awarded
10–14%	★
15–19%	★ ★
20–29%	★ ★ ★
30% and above	★ ★ ★ ★

Revenue Growth (Based on Four-Year Returns)

Avg. Annual Return	Points Awarded
15–19%	★
20–24%	★ ★
25–34%	★ ★ ★
35% and above	★ ★ ★ ★

Stock Growth (Based on Three-Year Returns)

Avg. Annual Return	Points Awarded
10–14%	★
15–19%	★ ★
20–29%	★ ★ ★
30% and above	★ ★ ★ ★

Consistency

A stock that has had four consecutive years of increased revenue and earnings per share would earn the maximum of four points. One point is deducted for every time the company did not post an increase in earnings or revenue. For instance, a company with earnings gains three of the past four years and revenue gains all four years would score a three out of four. A company with earnings gains three of the past four years and revenue gains three of the past four years would score just two out of four. A company with earnings gains and revenue gains just two of the past four years would have all four points deducted for a score of zero.

BREAKING TIES

The higher the score, the higher the rank. For stocks with the same score, I evaluated several factors in breaking ties. First I looked at growth momentum. Companies whose revenue and earnings were still growing at a strong clip got the nod over companies that seemed to be losing speed. I also looked at the size of the company, the type of products or services it offered, and its consistency in terms of revenue and earnings growth. The ones that looked the best got the highest ranking.

Don't take my word for it, though. As you browse through this book, try to evaluate each stock based on your own standards and expectations. There are likely to be some big winners on this list, as well as a few big losers. The ability to correctly pick one over the other is part genius, part luck, and part persistence. If at first you don't succeed, just keep trying.

INVESTING IN SMALL STOCKS

Investing in any stock can be risky, and small stocks are no exception. But you can increase your odds by playing the averages. Rather than to invest in one or two small stocks, select five to ten that look promising and invest a little in each. Two or three big winners could keep your entire portfolio on the upswing.

Here's an example: Let's say you buy six stocks, investing $1,000 in each stock. Four stocks remain about the same, and two triple in price. Suddenly your initial $6,000 investment is now worth $10,000—a 67 percent increase. That's the way you need to play the small stock market. Play the averages by picking several stocks that look attractive.

THE SEVEN MYTHS OF SMALL STOCK INVESTING

Investors have some unusual ideas about small stock investing. Here are seven common misconceptions.

1. You can't lose big money on small stocks. You can lose as much on small stocks as you can on any other form of investment. Whatever you invest, you can lose. Consider this: You buy $1,000 worth of a $10 stock— 100 shares in all. At the same time, your friend buys $1,000 worth of a

$100 stock—10 shares in all. Your $10 stock drops $2 to $8 a share just as your friend's $100 stock drops $20 to $80 a share. Who loses the most? Neither. Both of you lost 20 percent—exactly $200. The amount you invest and the percentage the stock gains or loses determine the dollar amount you earn or lose on a stock—not the price of the stock.

2. Low-priced stocks are cheap.   To the eyes of a Wall Street analyst, stock price really has no bearing on whether the stock is cheap or expensive. What matters is PE ratio (stock price divided by earnings per share). A $5 stock with a PE ratio of 50 is much more expensive, in value terms, than a $50 stock with a PE of 5. For a stock with a 50 PE, you are paying $50 for every $1 of earnings. For a 5 PE stock, you're paying $5 for every $1 of earnings. From that perspective, the $5 stock with the 50 PE costs ten times as much as a $50 stock with the 5 PE, even though, on the surface, it would seem to be just the opposite.

3. Buying a small stock mutual fund is the same as buying small stocks. Small stock mutual funds are so broadly diversified—with investments in dozens or hundreds of stocks—that they can avoid some of the volatility that often comes with individual stocks. Small stock funds tend to be safer and more consistent, but even the greatest mutual fund could never approach the returns of a great stock. Good funds may beat the market by a few percentage points, offering returns in a good year of 15 to 30 percent. But a great small stock can grow 100 to 300 percent in a good year.

4. You can't buy big stocks with small dollars.   Some investors are drawn to small stocks because they don't think they can afford big stocks. There's really no difference between buying 100 shares of a $10 stock and 10 shares of $100 stock. The brokerage fee is about the same, and if either stock grows 10 percent, that's a $100 gain. The number of shares you own is irrelevant. Buy the best stocks regardless of price.

5. Double down on small stocks if they drop in price.   The practice of buying a stock down, which is to buy more shares as the price drops, may be a sound policy for investing in established blue chips such as Merck, Bristol-Myers, and Coca-Cola, but it's not always wise with small stocks. When small stocks encounter trouble, they can drop fast and far. Most recover slowly, and some never recover. A friend of mine bought the stock of a company called Statosphere that owns a hotel at the edge of Las Vegas. The stock reached a high of $14, and started dropping. The more it dropped, the more shares my friend bought. Ultimately, the company went into bankruptcy, and the stock dropped to under $1 a share. My friend lost thousands of dollars throwing good money after bad.

6. Always buy and hold for the long term.   Buying stocks you *hope* to hold for the long term is a good policy, but that doesn't mean you should actually *hold* every stock for the long term. Some small stocks aren't worth holding. If you buy a stock because the company's financials are growing quickly, then be prepared to sell if the growth starts to level off. Review your portfolio periodically to see which stocks are doing well and which are going nowhere. When appropriate, weed out the ones that aren't moving.

7. Always sell stocks after a big run-up in price.   Some investors love to take a profit on their winners. They're often the same investors who like to hold onto their losers in hopes of a turnaround. Those investors take the expression "buy low and sell high" too literally. If you always sell your winners and hold your losers, you'll end up with a portfolio of losers. What you want is a portfolio of winners, so keep your winners and dump your losers. Imagine, for instance, the investor who sold Microsoft in 1987 after watching the stock jump 30 percent. A $10,000 investment would have netted a nice $3,000 short-term gain. But if the investor had held the stock instead of selling, it would now be worth over $1 million. Don't settle for chump change. Go for the big win. That's why you're investing in the world of small stocks.

Here's hoping you can cull from this list of small stocks some of the great growth companies of the 21st century.

1

Hauppauge Digital, Inc.

Hauppauge!

91 Cabot Court
Hauppauge, NY 11788
516-434-1600
www.hauppauge.com

Chairman and CEO:
Kenneth Plotkin
President:
Kenneth R. Aupperle

Earnings Growth	★ ★ ★ ★
Revenue Growth	★ ★ ★ ★
Stock Growth	★ ★ ★ ★
Consistency	★ ★ ★ ★
Nasdaq: HAUP	**16 points**

TV on your personal computer is no longer just an idle vision of the future. It's here today, thanks to Hauppauge Digital.

With a Hauppauge WinTV card, you can connect your TV cable directly to your computer. Think of the possibilities—watching Cheers reruns in a resized square in the corner of your monitor while typing out reports, setting up spreadsheets, or surfing the Web.

Based in Hauppauge, New York, the company has a whole line of video-related products designed to be used with computers. In addition to its WinTV product line, Hauppauge also makes the VideoWizard product line to capture and edit videotapes digitally on a PC; the Impact VCB boards used by manufacturers to add video display and Internet video conferencing applications to computers; and the VideoTalk product line used by consumers to do video conferencing over the Internet.

The company markets its products through distributors, computer retailers, and computer manufacturers. Distributors and retailers account for about 85 percent of total sales.

The basic WinTV computer card retails for about $79. The boards were first developed in 1992 and have been refined and expanded a couple of times since. Hauppauge's most advanced TV board is the WinCast/TV model, which has a 125-channel cable-ready TV tuner with automatic channel scan and a video digitizer. The digitizer allows users to capture still and motion video images to hard disk in order to create presentations and to video-conference over the Internet.

Hauppauge's VideoWizard boards can digitize full-frame live video from a video camera or a VCR and store it to the hard disk, so that it can be digitally edited on a PC.

The company's ImpactVCB boards offer a low-cost alternative to digitized video. Designed for PC-based video conferencing and industrial applications, the boards provide live video in a window on the monitor, still image capture, and AVI capture driver.

Hauppauge went public with its initial stock offering in 1995. It has about 60 employees and a market capitalization of about $40 million.

EARNINGS PER SHARE GROWTH ★ ★ ★ ★

Past two years: 388 percent (70 percent per year)

REVENUE GROWTH ★ ★ ★ ★

Past four years: 830 percent (75 percent per year)

STOCK GROWTH ★ ★ ★ ★

Past three years: 208 percent (45 percent per year)
Dollar growth: $10,000 over the past three years would have grown to about $31,000.

CONSISTENCY ★ ★ ★ ★

Increased earnings per share: four of the past four years
Increased revenue: four of the past four years

HAUPPAUGE DIGITAL AT A GLANCE

Fiscal year ended: Sept. 30
Revenue and net income in $ millions

	1994	1995	1996	1997	1998	4-Year Growth Avg. Annual (%)	Total (%)
Revenue ($)	4.2	11.6	14.7	25.6	38.8	75	830
Net income ($)	−1.3	−1.5	0.28	0.986	1.9	60*	578*
Earnings/share ($)	−1.03	−0.64	0.09	0.22	0.44	70*	388*
Avg. PE ratio	—	—	63	20	23	—	—

*Net income and earnings per share growth percentages are for two years.

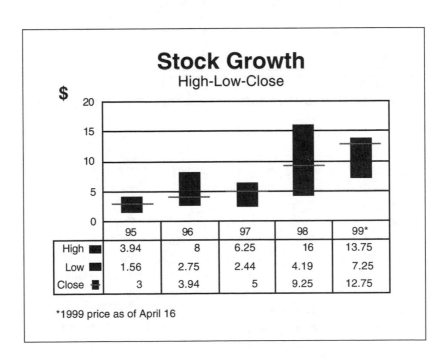

Stock Growth
High-Low-Close

$	95	96	97	98	99*
High	3.94	8	6.25	16	13.75
Low	1.56	2.75	2.44	4.19	7.25
Close	3	3.94	5	9.25	12.75

*1999 price as of April 16

Actrade International, Ltd.

7 Penn Plaza
Suite 422
New York, NY 10001
212-563-1036
www.actrade.com

CEO:
Amos Aharoni

Earnings Growth	★ ★ ★ ★
Revenue Growth	★ ★ ★ ★
Stock Growth	★ ★ ★ ★
Consistency	★ ★ ★ ★
Nasdaq: ACRT	**16 points**

Actrade International helps U.S. companies buy and sell their goods and services on both the domestic and international markets through a series of innovative financial services.

Its leading product is a *trade acceptance draft* (TAD), which helps buyers and sellers expedite payments while limiting credit risk. A TAD is a negotiable note signed by the buyer and made payable to the seller. Once the buyer signs the TAD agreement, it confirms that the goods or services were delivered by the seller and accepted by the buyer. The receivable is converted to an insured financial instrument purchased by Actrade.

The popularity of the TAD program is indicated in the growth of the company's business. Revenues from TADs have grown from about $250,000 in 1993 to $55.5 million in fiscal 1998.

TADs are used by small and large companies alike. TADs eliminate the problem of aging receivables, as well as the cost and personnel time of pursuing collection of past due accounts.

Actrade has recently created a similar instrument used for international trade. The international instrument, which is called a *negotiable international check* (NIC), provides extended credit for importers. For instance, for a U.S. company exporting to a foreign country, the NIC is deducted from the bank account of the buyer. Actrade pays the seller and holds the NIC drafts, assuming the buyer risk for 6 to 12 months. Actrade is careful to deal only with buyers with strong credit standings.

The New York–based operation also has an international trading arm that exports products to the Middle East, South America, Europe, and the Pacific Rim. Actrade provides foreign buyers for products of U.S. companies through Actrade's network of buyers, wholesalers, and distributors. The company also can arrange required export services, including air or sea shipping, inland freight arrangements, and other shipping arrangements. Actrade's leading export products are commercial air-conditioning units and related equipment.

Founded in 1987, Actrade went public with its initial stock offering in 1992. The company has just 35 employees and a market capitalization of $121 million.

EARNINGS PER SHARE GROWTH ★ ★ ★ ★

Past four years: 767 percent (73 percent per year)

REVENUE GROWTH ★ ★ ★ ★

Past four years: 714 percent (68 percent per year)

STOCK GROWTH ★ ★ ★ ★

Past three years: 628 percent (75 percent per year)
Dollar growth: $10,000 over the past three years would have grown to about $73,000.

CONSISTENCY ★ ★ ★ ★

Increased earnings per share: four of the past four years
Increased revenue: four of the past four years

ACTRADE AT A GLANCE

Fiscal year ended: June 30
Revenue and net income in $ millions

	1994	1995	1996	1997	1998	4-Year Growth Avg. Annual (%)	Total (%)
Revenue ($)	12.1	16.4	23.8	43.5	98.5	68	714
Net income ($)	0.254	0.408	0.757	1.9	4.4	104	1,632
Earnings/share ($)	0.06	0.08	0.14	0.28	0.52	73	767
Avg. PE ratio	38	22	36	68	35	—	—

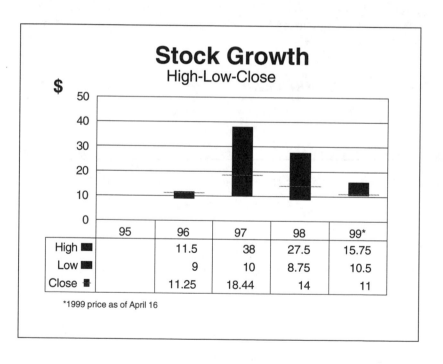

Stock Growth
High-Low-Close

$	95	96	97	98	99*
High ▪		11.5	38	27.5	15.75
Low ▪		9	10	8.75	10.5
Close ▪		11.25	18.44	14	11

*1999 price as of April 16

3
TV Guide, Inc.

7140 South Lewis Avenue
Tulsa, OK 74136
918-488-4000
www.usvg.com

Chairman and CEO:
Anthea Disney
President:
Joe Kiener

Earnings Growth	★ ★ ★ ★
Revenue Growth	★ ★ ★
Stock Growth	★ ★ ★ ★
Consistency	★ ★ ★ ★
Nasdaq: TVGIA	**15 points**

Formerly known as United Video Satellite, the company took the name TV Guide in early 1999 when United Video acquired TV Guide. In addition to its publishing holdings, the firm is a major player in the exploding video communications industry. The company provides satellite-delivered video, audio, data, and program promotion services to cable television systems, direct-to-home satellite dish users, radio stations, and private network users throughout North America.

TV Guide also offers software development and systems integration services to commercial entities, the federal government, and defense related agencies.

In addition to its well-known publication, TV Guide operates in five business segments:

1. *Program promotion and guide services.* The firm supplies cable television systems and other multichannel video programming distribu-

tors on-screen program promotion and guide services, including Prevue Channel and Sneak Prevue.

2. *Direct-to-home satellite services.* Through a joint venture with Superstar/Netlink Group, the company markets satellite entertainment programming to C-band DTH satellite dish owners.

3. *Satellite distribution of video entertainment services.* The company markets and provides a satellite feed for superstations WGN (Chicago), KTLA (Los Angeles), and WPIX (New York) to cable television and other multichannel programming distributors.

4. *Software development and systems integration services.* The firm assists large communications organizations with complex computer needs.

5. *Satellite transmission services for private networks.* The firm provides point-to-multipoint audio and data transmission services via satellite for radio programmers, paging network operators, financial information providers, news services, and other private businesses.

The company that began as United Video Satellite was founded in 1965 and went public with its initial stock offering in 1993. The company has about 1,500 employees and a market capitalization of about $1.5 billion.

EARNINGS PER SHARE GROWTH ★ ★ ★ ★

Past four years: 278 percent (39 percent per year)

REVENUE GROWTH ★ ★ ★

Past four years: 204 percent (33 percent per year)

STOCK GROWTH ★ ★ ★ ★

Past three years: 250 percent (52 percent per year)
Dollar growth: $10,000 over the past three years would have grown to $35,000.

CONSISTENCY ★ ★ ★ ★

Increased earnings per share: four of the past four years
Increased revenue: four of the past four years

TV GUIDE AT A GLANCE

Fiscal year ended: Dec. 31
Revenue and net income in $ millions

	1994	1995	1996	1997	1998	Avg. Annual (%)	Total (%)
						4-Year Growth	
Revenue ($)	196.7	262.9	437.2	507.6	598.4	33	204
Net income ($)	16.3	23.4	39.8	63.5	79.4	48	387
Earnings/share ($)	0.23	0.32	0.42	0.62	0.87	39	278
Avg. PE ratio	19	22	22	18	22	—	—

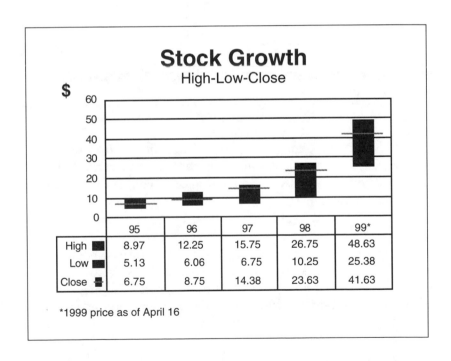

Stock Growth
High-Low-Close

	95	96	97	98	99*
High	8.97	12.25	15.75	26.75	48.63
Low	5.13	6.06	6.75	10.25	25.38
Close	6.75	8.75	14.38	23.63	41.63

*1999 price as of April 16

Melita International Corp.

5051 Peachtree Corners Circle
Norcross, GA 30092
770-239-4330
www.melita.com

Chairman and CEO:
Aleksander Szlam

Earnings Growth	★ ★ ★ ★
Revenue Growth	★ ★ ★ ★
Stock Growth	★ ★ ★
Consistency	★ ★ ★ ★
Nasdaq: MELI	**15 points**

That steady stream of dinnerhour phone solicitations—from everyone from brokers and insurance agents to credit card companies and long distance phone companies—may be an annoyance to you, but it's big business to Melita International.

Melita makes software and related products designed to help make life easier for telemarketing services, retailers, brokers, credit card companies, phone companies, and other organizations that use outbound or inbound telephone contacts to sell their products or services. Melita's products help organize phone bank activity, automate customer contacts (no dialing for the solicitors), and guide the sales agent through the solicitation contact.

The Norcross, Georgia operation's leading product is PhoneFrame Explorer, an integrated package of software applications and hardware that provides a broad range of telecommunications applications.

Components of PhoneFrame Explorer include the Universal Telephony Platform, which provides call analysis and media management; the Universal Server, which is used to manage calling list data, call attempts, contact history, agent profiles, call processing, and agent supervision activity; and Magellan, which uses graphic user interfaces to guide telephone agents through conversations.

Melita markets its products through a direct sales force of about 100 sales representatives throughout the United States, Canada, Mexico, and the United Kingdom. It also does business in nearly 30 other countries through its outside distribution network.

The company's leading customers are in the financial services, retail, media, communications, and service bureau industries.

In addition to its line of products, the firm provides some service and support for its customers, including maintenance, installation, training, custom applications, and consulting.

Melita was founded in 1983 by Aleksander Szlam, who still serves as chairman and CEO. The firm went public with its initial stock offering in 1997. Melita has about 325 employees and a market capitalization of about $285 million.

EARNINGS PER SHARE GROWTH ★ ★ ★ ★

Past four years: 508 percent (57 percent per year)

REVENUE GROWTH ★ ★ ★ ★

Past four years: 243 percent (37 percent per year)

STOCK GROWTH ★ ★ ★

Past one year: 118 percent
Dollar growth: $10,000 over the past year would have grown to about $22,000.

CONSISTENCY ★ ★ ★ ★

Increased earnings per share: four of the past four years
Increased revenue: four of the past four years

MELITA INTERNATIONAL AT A GLANCE

Fiscal year ended: Dec. 31
Revenue and net income in $ millions

	1994	1995	1996	1997	1998	4-Year Growth Avg. Annual (%)	Total (%)
Revenue ($)	27.2	35.3	47.5	65.8	93.4	37	243
Net income ($)	1.51	2.96	4.78	7.61	11.7	68	675
Earnings/share ($)	0.12	0.24	0.39	0.55	0.73	57	508
Avg. PE ratio	—	—	—	19	20	—	—

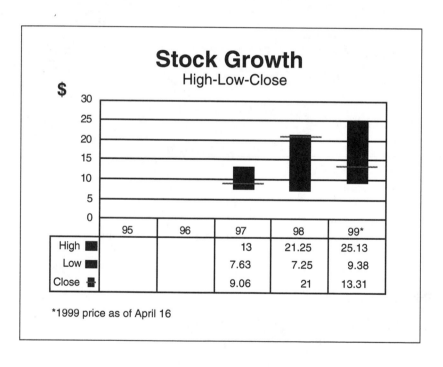

Stock Growth
High-Low-Close

$

	95	96	97	98	99*
High			13	21.25	25.13
Low			7.63	7.25	9.38
Close			9.06	21	13.31

*1999 price as of April 16

AmeriCredit Corp.

200 Bailey Avenue
Fort Worth, TX 76107-1220
817-332-7000
www.chasemellon.com

Chairman and CEO:
Clifton H. Morris, Jr.
President:
Michael R. Barrington

Earnings Growth	★ ★ ★ ★
Revenue Growth	★ ★ ★ ★
Stock Growth	★ ★ ★
Consistency	★ ★ ★
NYSE: ACF	**14 points**

AmeriCredit is an indirect automobile finance company that purchases loans made by franchised and select independent auto dealers to their customers. The firm focuses primarily on dealers of late model used cars, and to a lesser extent on new car dealers.

The Ft. Worth, Texas operation targets consumers who may have trouble obtaining loans from traditional sources because of limited credit histories or prior credit difficulties. Because its customers are higher risk borrowers, the company charges a higher rate of interest on loans than traditional auto financing sources.

Because it is an indirect lender, AmeriCredit focuses its marketing efforts on auto dealerships—primarily used car dealers. AmeriCredit prefers to finance late model, low mileage used cars. The firm purchased contracts from more than 9,000 dealerships during fiscal 1998.

AmeriCredit markets its financing program to dealers through a broad network of branch offices. Branch office personnel are responsible for the solicitation, enrollment, and education of new dealers. The firm has more than 130 branch offices throughout the United States.

In selecting car dealers to solicit, AmeriCredit analyzes the dealer's operating history and reputation in the marketplace. Once its loans are approved, the company collects and processes consumer payments, responds to consumer inquiries, and contacts consumers who are delinquent in their payments. AmeriCredit also monitors insurance coverage of the financed vehicle, and for those who fail to make their loan payments handles the repossession and resale of the automobile.

Through its AmeriCredit Mortgage Services division, the company also originates and acquires nonprime mortgage loans through a network of mortgage brokers. The firm sells its mortgage loans and related servicing rights in the wholesale markets.

AmeriCredit was founded in 1986. It has about 1,500 employees and a market capitalization of about $760 million.

EARNINGS PER SHARE GROWTH   ★ ★ ★ ★

Past four years: 1,163 percent (88 percent per year)

REVENUE GROWTH   ★ ★ ★ ★

Past four years: 1,333 percent (93 percent per year)

STOCK GROWTH   ★ ★ ★

Past three years: 102 percent (26 percent per year)
Dollar growth: $10,000 over the past three years would have grown to about $20,000.

CONSISTENCY   ★ ★ ★

Increased earnings per share: three of the past four years
Increased revenue: four of the past four years

AMERICREDIT AT A GLANCE

Fiscal year ended: June 30
Revenue and net income in $ millions

	1994	1995	1996	1997	1998	4-Year Growth Avg. Annual (%)	4-Year Growth Total (%)
Revenue ($)	15.9	33.1	80.9	137.7	227.9	93	1,333
Net income ($)	5.07	28.9	21.6	38.7	60.7	82	1,097
Earnings/share ($)	0.08	0.48	0.38	0.67	1.01	88	1,163
Avg. PE ratio	42	12	21	18	13	—	—

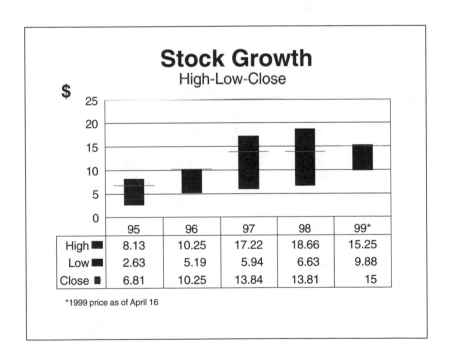

Stock Growth
High-Low-Close

	95	96	97	98	99*
High	8.13	10.25	17.22	18.66	15.25
Low	2.63	5.19	5.94	6.63	9.88
Close	6.81	10.25	13.84	13.81	15

*1999 price as of April 16

Richton International Corporation

767 5th Avenue
New York, NY 10153
212-751-1445

Chairman and CEO:
Fred R. Sullivan

Earnings Growth	★ ★ ★ ★
Revenue Growth	★ ★ ★
Stock Growth	★ ★ ★ ★
Consistency	★ ★ ★ ★
AMEX: RHT	**15 points**

Let it rain. But if it doesn't rain, there's always Richton.

Richton International, through its Century Supply subsidiary, is the nation's largest wholesale distributor of sprinkler irrigation systems. It sells systems and related products from more than 60 suppliers, including Rain Bird, Hunter, Irritrol, and Legacy. Century is a distributor for all of the leading manufacturers of turf irrigation equipment in the United States.

The Madison, New Jersey operation has about 65 branch offices in about 20 states, primarily in the East, South, and Midwest. Its primary customers are irrigation and landscape contractors who install irrigation systems for commercial, residential, and golf course watering systems.

In all, the company sells to a customer base of more than 12,000 contractors. The firm has begun to expand to other regions of the country through strategic acquisitions of smaller regional irrigation system suppliers.

Richton supplements its sales business with some related services, including design assistance, training seminars, and incentive programs.

The bulk of Richton's revenue is derived from irrigation sales. The company also sells outdoor lighting and decorative fountain equipment through its Century Supply subsidiary.

In addition to its irrigation distribution business, Richton recently acquired CBE Technologies, which is a systems integrator providing network consulting, design, and installation; network management and related support; technical services outsourcing; comprehensive hardware maintenance; and equipment sales.

CBE serves as an authorized service and warranty center for most leading PC and printer manufacturers, including IBM, Compaq, Hewlett-Packard, Apple, and many others. The company has offices in Boston, New York, Los Angeles, and Portland, Maine.

Richton International has about 425 employees and a market capitalization of about $25 million.

EARNINGS PER SHARE GROWTH ★ ★ ★ ★

Past four years: 194 percent (31 percent per year)

REVENUE GROWTH ★ ★ ★

Past four years: 194 percent (31 percent per year)

STOCK GROWTH ★ ★ ★ ★

Past three years: 170 percent (40 percent per year)
Dollar growth: $10,000 over the past three years would have grown to $27,000.

CONSISTENCY ★ ★ ★ ★

Increased earnings per share: four of the past four years
Increased revenue: four of the past four years

RICHTON INTERNATIONAL AT A GLANCE

Fiscal year ended: Dec. 31
Revenue and net income in $ millions

	1994	1995	1996	1997	1998	4-Year Growth Avg. Annual (%)	Total (%)
Revenue ($)	50.3	66.7	87.8	106.5	147.9	31	194
Net income ($)	1.0	1.37	1.77	2.29	3.53	37	253
Earnings/share ($)	0.34	0.47	0.60	0.78	1.00	31	194
Avg. PE ratio	13	7	7	7	9	—	—

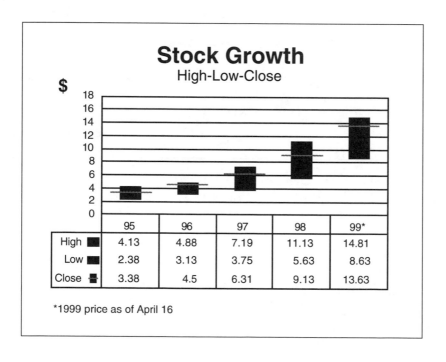

Stock Growth
High-Low-Close

	95	96	97	98	99*
High	4.13	4.88	7.19	11.13	14.81
Low	2.38	3.13	3.75	5.63	8.63
Close	3.38	4.5	6.31	9.13	13.63

*1999 price as of April 16

TSR, Inc.

TSR Consulting Services, Inc.

400 Oser Avenue
Hauppauge, NY 11788
516-231-0333

Chairman, President, and CEO:
Joseph F. Hughes

Earnings Growth	★ ★ ★ ★
Revenue Growth	★ ★ ★
Stock Growth	★ ★ ★ ★
Consistency	★ ★ ★ ★
Nasdaq: TSRI	**15 points**

TSR helps companies with a wide range of technical projects and with Y2K compliance.

TSR works with a number of Fortune 1000 companies who face the ongoing problem of maintaining and improving the service level of their increasingly complex information systems. TSR's consultants work with its client company's in-house personnel to help solve technical problems and keep computer systems up-to-date.

The Hauppauge, New York operation has consulting specialists in a wide range of technical areas, including mainframe and midrange computer operations, personal computers and client server support, voice and data communications, and help desk support. The company provides software development and applications re-engineering services for its corporate clients. TSR can fulfill nearly any application or systems program project.

TSR's consultants can work on both short-term projects and long-term projects that may take several months to implement. Most of the major projects in which TSR is involved range from three months to a year to complete.

The company also addresses the Y2K challenge with a software product called Catch/21. It automates, to a significant extent, the conversion process for applications that may not interpret dates after the year 1999. Catch/21 can solve the Y2K problem on IBM and a wide range of other computer applications.

Most of the firm's revenue comes from its technology staffing business. The company maintains a database of more than 35,000 technical personnel with a wide range of skills. TSR keeps about 20 recruiters on staff full-time to recruit, interview, and test prospective consultants.

TSR markets its services through full-time account executives who are responsible for customers in their assigned areas. In all, TSR provides staffing services for well over 100 corporate clients.

TSR was founded in 1969. The company has about 400 employees and a market capitalization of about $66 million.

EARNINGS PER SHARE GROWTH   ★ ★ ★ ★

Past four years: 625 percent (64 percent per year)

REVENUE GROWTH   ★ ★ ★

Past four years: 221 percent (34 percent per year)

STOCK GROWTH   ★ ★ ★ ★

Past three years: 692 percent (99 percent per year)
Dollar growth: $10,000 over the past three years would have grown to about $79,000.

CONSISTENCY   ★ ★ ★ ★

Increased earnings per share: four of the past four years
Increased revenue: four of the past four years

TSR AT A GLANCE

Fiscal year ended: May 31
Revenue and net income in $ millions

	1994	1995	1996	1997	1998	4-Year Growth Avg. Annual (%)	4-Year Growth Total (%)
Revenue ($)	21.9	26.7	31.8	49.7	70.4	34	221
Net income ($)	0.500	0.801	0.964	1.8	3.4	63	580
Earnings/share ($)	0.08	0.13	0.16	0.31	0.58	64	625
Avg. PE ratio	10	12	43	22	22	—	—

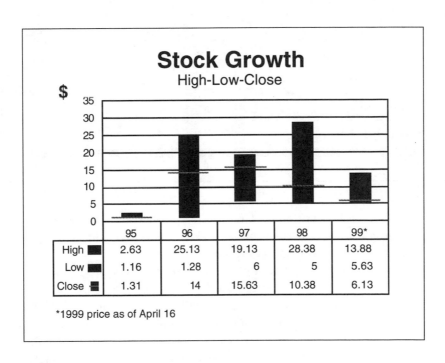

Stock Growth
High-Low-Close

$					
	95	96	97	98	99*
High	2.63	25.13	19.13	28.38	13.88
Low	1.16	1.28	6	5	5.63
Close	1.31	14	15.63	10.38	6.13

*1999 price as of April 16

8
Interstate National Dealer Services, Inc.

333 Earle Ovington Boulevard
Mitchel Field, NY 11553
516-228-8600
www.inds.com

Chairman and CEO:
Chester J. Luby
President:
Cindy H. Luby

Earnings Growth	★ ★ ★ ★
Revenue Growth	★ ★ ★ ★
Stock Growth	★ ★ ★ ★
Consistency	★ ★ ★
Nasdaq: ISTN	**15 points**

Interstate National Dealer Services administers service contracts and warranties for new and used motor vehicles and recreational vehicles, as well as some watercraft, motorcycles, and other vehicles.

The Mitchel Field, New York operation offers a variety of vehicle service contracts and warranty programs, which vehicle dealers provide for customers to cover the cost of repairs. Typically service contracts involve an agreement between Interstate and the car dealer in which Interstate helps the dealer cover the cost of servicing new or used cars. Under the agreements, Interstate obtains insurance coverage to cover the dealer's liability for claims under its service contracts and assists the dealer and purchaser with the processing of claims. (Vehicle service contracts supplement, or are in place of, manufacturers' warranties and provide a variety of extended coverage options—typically ranging from three months to seven years—offered for sale by dealers to vehicle purchasers.)

Interstate markets its service contracts through its nationwide sales force of about 100 independent sales agents. They sell primarily to dealers but also to leasing companies, finance companies, and other service contract marketers.

Under the agreements, vehicle dealers pay a net rate for each service contract or warranty they sell. The payment includes an administrative fee for Interstate, insurance premiums and fees for the insurance underwriter, and a claim reserve to be placed in an interest-bearing loss reserve account maintained for the contract purchaser. The net rate for service contracts can range from about $75 to more than $3,000 per contract. On average, the cost is about $360 for a new car, $400 for a used car, and $500 for a recreational vehicle.

Interstate had traditionally focused on warranties for new cars, but over the past few years it has shifted more of its business to used cars. It also has done an increasing number of service contracts for recreational vehicles.

Interstate was founded in 1981 and went public with its initial stock offering in 1994. The company has about 90 employees and a market capitalization of about $50 million.

EARNINGS PER SHARE GROWTH ★ ★ ★ ★

Past four years: 482 percent (55 percent per year)

REVENUE GROWTH ★ ★ ★ ★

Past four years: 501 percent (57 percent per year)

STOCK GROWTH ★ ★ ★ ★

Past three years: 791 percent (108 percent per year)
Dollar growth: $10,000 over the past three years would have grown to about $89,000.

CONSISTENCY ★ ★ ★

Increased earnings per share: three of the past four years
Increased revenue: four of the past four years

INTERSTATE NATIONAL DEALER SERVICES AT A GLANCE

Fiscal year ended: Oct. 31
Revenue and net income in $ millions

	1994	1995	1996	1997	1998	4-Year Growth Avg. Annual (%)	Total (%)
Revenue ($)	8.2	13.7	21.3	37.9	49.3	57	501
Net income ($)	0.274	0.339	0.963	2.1	3.3	86	1,106
Earnings/share ($)	0.11	0.10	0.28	0.52	0.64	55	482
Avg. PE ratio	35	18	13	16	13	—	—

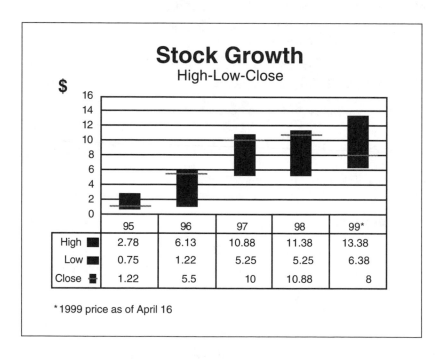

Stock Growth
High-Low-Close

	95	96	97	98	99*
High	2.78	6.13	10.88	11.38	13.38
Low	0.75	1.22	5.25	5.25	6.38
Close	1.22	5.5	10	10.88	8

*1999 price as of April 16

Gentex Corporation

GENTEX
CORPORATION

600 North Centennial Street
Zeeland, MI 49464
616-772-1800
www.gentex.com

Chairman and CEO:
Fred T. Bauer

Earnings Growth	★ ★ ★ ★
Revenue Growth	★ ★ ★
Stock Growth	★ ★ ★ ★
Consistency	★ ★ ★ ★
Nasdaq: GNTX	**15 points**

Gentex has built its business around the rearview mirror. The company manufactures interior and exterior vehicle mirrors using an electrochromic technology that enables the mirrors to cut headlight glare by darkening automatically. The company also manufactures an exterior mirror—the Night Vision Safety Mirror Sub-Assembly—which works as a complete glare-control system along with the Gentex interior mirror.

Its specialty mirrors are standard equipment on all Cadillacs, Oldsmobiles, Lexuses, Lincolns, and Rolls Royces. They're also offered as an option for many other models of U.S. and foreign vehicles.

The Zeeland, Michigan operation was founded in 1974 to manufacture residential smoke detectors, a product line that has since evolved into a more sophisticated group of commercial fire protection products. Gentex plunged into the rearview mirror market in 1982 with the introduction of its first glare-control mirror.

Sales of the specialty rearview mirrors has continued to grow, with the company expanding into new markets. In 1997, the Big Three U.S. automakers began placing the special mirrors on pickup trucks and sport/utility vehicles. Interior mirror sales grew from 1.8 million mirrors in 1995 to 2.4 million in 1996 to 2.8 million in 1997. Sales of exterior mirrors grew from 417,000 in 1995 to 1.1 million in 1997.

Rearview mirror sales account for about 89 percent of the company's annual revenue.

Fire protection products account for the other 11 percent of sales. The firm makes smoke detectors and signaling devices for hotels, hospitals, office complexes, and industrial facilities. Its detectors are less prone to false alarms and quicker to detect slow, smoldering fires because they have special sensors designed to detect and identify dangerous smoke particles.

The company manufactures more than 60 different smoke detector models and more than 160 different models of signaling devices.

Founded in 1974, Gentex has about 1,250 employees and a market capitalization of about $1.8 billion.

EARNINGS PER SHARE GROWTH   ★ ★ ★ ★

Past four years: 183 percent (30 percent per year)

REVENUE GROWTH   ★ ★ ★

Past four years: 148 percent (25 percent per year)

STOCK GROWTH   ★ ★ ★ ★

Past three years: 263 percent (53 percent per year)
Dollar growth: $10,000 over the past three years would have grown to about $36,000.

CONSISTENCY   ★ ★ ★ ★

Increased earnings per share: four of the past four years
Increased revenue: four of the past four years

GENTEX AT A GLANCE

Fiscal year ended: Dec. 31
Revenue and net income in $ millions

	1994	1995	1996	1997	1998	4-Year Growth Avg. Annual (%)	4-Year Growth Total (%)
Revenue ($)	89.8	111.6	148.7	186.3	222.3	25	148
Net income ($)	16.5	18.9	24.0	35.2	50.3	33	205
Earnings/share ($)	0.24	0.29	0.35	0.51	0.68	30	183
Avg. PE ratio	28	19	27	22	24	—	—

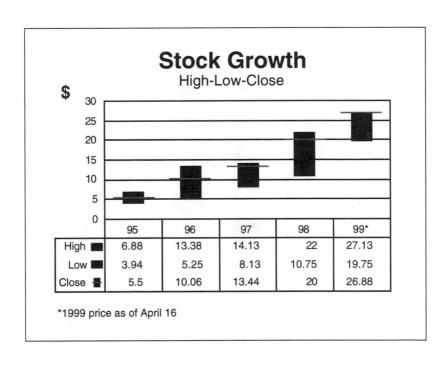

Stock Growth
High-Low-Close

$

	95	96	97	98	99*
High	6.88	13.38	14.13	22	27.13
Low	3.94	5.25	8.13	10.75	19.75
Close	5.5	10.06	13.44	20	26.88

*1999 price as of April 16

10
MYR Group, Inc.

MYR GROUP INC

1701 West Golf Road
Tower 3, Suite 1012
Rolling Meadows, IL 60008
847-290-1891
www.myrgroup.com

Chairman and CEO:
C. M. Brennan
President:
W. S. Skibitsky

Earnings Growth	★ ★ ★ ★
Revenue Growth	★ ★ ★ ★
Stock Growth	★ ★ ★
Consistency	★ ★ ★ ★
NYSE: MYR	**15 points**

MYR Group installs phone lines, power lines, and traffic signals and handles a variety of other construction services for electric utilities, telecommunications providers, industrial operations, and government agencies.

Electric utilities make up the largest share of the company's client base, accounting for about 43 percent of MYR's total revenue.

The Rolling Meadows, Illinois holding company operates through seven regional subsidiaries. The company is involved in the construction and maintenance of electric transmission lines, substations, distribution systems, and lighting systems for electric utilities.

It also provides construction services for the telecommunications market, including installation of foundations and towers for PCS wireless communication installations and fiber-optic and copper communications installation for the transmission of voice, data, and video. MYR also installs telecommunications and teledata services, including computer networks, telephones, and video, voice, data, security, and fire alarm systems.

MYR rarely handles the design and specifications for its projects, relying instead on designs prepared by its clients. Once the design stage is completed, however, the company steps in to provide the project management, labor, and equipment to complete the project.

MYR offers an extensive line of "inside" electric construction and maintenance services for the commercial and industrial markets. The firm handles electrical installation projects at airports, hospitals, hotels and casinos, arenas and convention centers, and manufacturing and processing facilities.

Through its Power Piping subsidiary, the company also provides mechanical construction and maintenance services for the steel industry, electric utility industry, chemical industry, food processors, and other industrial customers in the eastern United States.

It also installs traffic signals, streetlights, and traffic management systems for local and regional government transportation agencies.

MYR was founded in 1891. The firm has about 4,000 employees and a market capitalization of about $66 million.

EARNINGS PER SHARE GROWTH ★ ★ ★ ★

Past four years: 186 percent (30 percent per year)

REVENUE GROWTH ★ ★ ★ ★

Past four years: 429 percent (52 percent per year)

STOCK GROWTH ★ ★ ★

Past three years: 80 percent (22 percent per year)
Dollar growth: $10,000 over the past three years would have grown to $18,000.

CONSISTENCY ★ ★ ★ ★

Increased earnings per share: four of the past four years
Increased revenue: four of the past four years

MYR GROUP AT A GLANCE

Fiscal year ended: Dec. 31
Revenue and net income in $ millions

	1994	1995	1996	1997	1998	4-Year Growth Avg. Annual (%)	Total (%)
Revenue ($)	86.8	267	310.6	431.3	459.3	52	429
Net income ($)	2.33	3.43	3.97	5.95	7.89	35	239
Earnings/share ($)	0.42	0.65	0.74	1.09	1.20	30	186
Avg. PE ratio	13	9	9	10	11	—	—

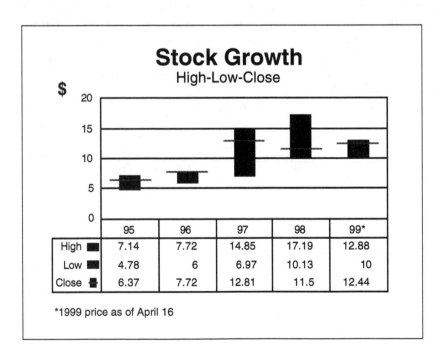

Stock Growth
High-Low-Close

	95	96	97	98	99*
High	7.14	7.72	14.85	17.19	12.88
Low	4.78	6	6.97	10.13	10
Close	6.37	7.72	12.81	11.5	12.44

*1999 price as of April 16

11
Technology Solutions Company

205 North Michigan Avenue
Suite 1500
Chicago, IL 60601
312-228-4500
www.techsol.com

Chairman:
William Waltrip
President and CEO:
John Kohler

Earnings Growth	★ ★ ★ ★
Revenue Growth	★ ★ ★ ★
Stock Growth	★ ★ ★
Consistency	★ ★ ★ ★
Nasdaq: TSCC	**15 points**

Technology Solutions Company (TSC) is a high-end consulting company that helps corporations get the maximum benefit from their personnel and their computer and communications systems.

The company provides professional services worldwide to clients in a wide range of industries, including financial services, communications, manufacturing, health care, and technology.

The Chicago-based operation has worked with more than 600 companies, including Aetna, Cigna, Cisco Systems, ConAgra, The Prudential, Pepsico, Pfizer, MCI, Ameritech, Whirlpool, and the Chicago Board of Trade. Most of its clients have annual revenue in the range of $500 million to $5 billion.

The company's consultants address a broad range of information technology and management issues. They can help companies identify areas of their business that would benefit the most from computer technology, and they offer feasibility studies, business case justification, business process redesign and reengineering, benchmarking and best practices evaluations, project management, systems design, hardware and software selection, programming, implementation, and training.

TSC's business services include business strategic planning, value-based customer segmentation analysis, and marketing research and analysis.

The company has offices throughout the United States, as well as international offices in Columbia, Germany, England, Mexico, France, Chile, Australia, Canada, and Switzerland.

Generally, the company assigns a senior level project manager to supervise each of its major projects. In most cases, the project manager is a TSC vice president with about 20 years of experience in the business. TSC consultants help the client companies develop a customer relationship strategy, assess their current information technology strategy, and help design and set up an information technology system tailored to the unique needs of the company.

TSC has about 1,600 employees and a market capitalization of about $400 million.

EARNINGS PER SHARE GROWTH   ★ ★ ★ ★

Past three years: 391 percent (70 percent per year)

REVENUE GROWTH   ★ ★ ★ ★

Past four years: 411 percent (50 percent per year)

STOCK GROWTH   ★ ★ ★

Past three years: 85 percent (23 percent per year)
Dollar growth: $10,000 over the past three years would have grown to $18,500.

CONSISTENCY   ★ ★ ★ ★

Increased earnings per share: four of the past four years
Increased revenue: four of the past four years

TECHNOLOGY SOLUTIONS AT A GLANCE

Fiscal year ended: May 31
Revenue and net income in $ millions

	1994	1995	1996	1997	1998	4-Year Growth Avg. Annual (%)	Total (%)
Revenue ($)	53.2	65.8	97.6	165.1	271.9	50	411
Net income ($)	0.035	3.4	4.6	15.1	21.0	395	59,900
Earnings/share ($)	—	0.11	0.15	0.43	0.54	70	391*
Avg. PE ratio	20	31	30	32	24	—	—

*Earnings per share returns are based on three-year performance.

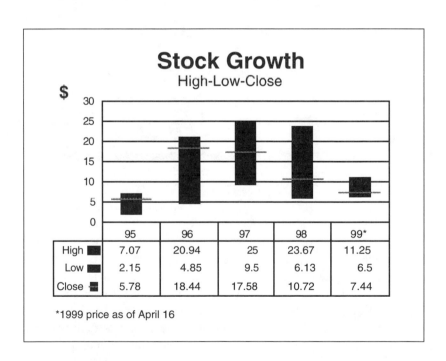

Stock Growth
High-Low-Close

	95	96	97	98	99*
High	7.07	20.94	25	23.67	11.25
Low	2.15	4.85	9.5	6.13	6.5
Close	5.78	18.44	17.58	10.72	7.44

*1999 price as of April 16

12
USANA, Inc.

3838 West Parkway Boulevard
Salt Lake City, UT 84120
801-954-7100
www.usana.com

Chairman, President, and CEO:
Dr. Myron Wentz

Earnings Growth	★ ★ ★ ★
Revenue Growth	★ ★ ★ ★
Stock Growth	★ ★ ★
Consistency	★ ★ ★ ★
Nasdaq: USNA	**15 points**

USANA is a multilevel marketing company that sells a wide selection of vitamins, minerals, nutritional supplements, and skin care products.

The Salt Lake City operation markets its products much like a number of its competitors in the vitamin business—through what the company terms "network marketing and direct selling channels," also known as multilevel or pyramid marketing. The system relies on word-of-mouth sales by the company's army of "distributors."

The distributors are individuals who buy the products at wholesale prices from USANA and resell them to their friends, family members, and other acquaintances. The distributors also encourage others to become distributors working under them to market the products. Distributors make their money based on their own sales and the sales of those distributors they've recruited to work under them.

In all, the company has about 85,000 distributors throughout the United States and Canada. USANA recently began operations in Australia and New Zealand. The company also has 9,000 "preferred customers," who buy the nutritional products for their own use and do not do any reselling.

USANA does most of its own manufacturing at its 98,000-square-foot facility in Salt Lake City. The plant produces more than 30 million tablets a month and fills more than 300,000 bottles a month. Its skin care products are also packaged at the plant, although they are manufactured by outside producers.

Among USANA's leading products are antioxidants, minerals, vitamins, nutritional supplements, meal replacement drinks, fiber drinks, and an energy bar. Its skin care products include natural oils, emollients, antioxidants, and botanical extracts. It also sells a line of personal care products using pure, natural substances. Among the products are shampoos, conditioners, hand and body lotion, and shower gel.

USANA went public with its initial stock offering in 1995. The company has about 360 employees and a market capitalization of about $212 million.

EARNINGS PER SHARE GROWTH ★ ★ ★ ★

Past four years: 2,167 percent (113 percent per year)

REVENUE GROWTH ★ ★ ★ ★

Past four years: 1,561 percent (102 percent per year)

STOCK GROWTH ★ ★ ★

Past three years: 78 percent (21 percent per year)
Dollar growth: $10,000 over the past three years would have grown to about $18,000.

CONSISTENCY ★ ★ ★ ★

Increased earnings per share: four of the past four years
Increased revenue: four of the past four years

USANA AT A GLANCE

Fiscal year ended: Dec. 31
Revenue and net income in $ millions

	1994	1995	1996	1997	1998	4-Year Growth Avg. Annual (%)	4-Year Growth Total (%)
Revenue ($)	7.32	24.5	56.7	85.2	121.6	102	1,561
Net income ($)	0.325	2.31	5.04	6.58	9.50	133	2,823
Earnings/share ($)	0.03	0.20	0.40	0.52	0.68	113	2,167
Avg. PE ratio	—	—	25	15	24	—	—

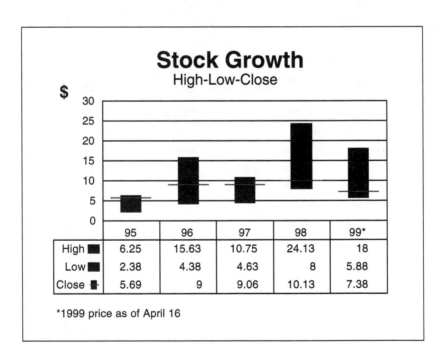

Stock Growth
High-Low-Close

$

	95	96	97	98	99*
High	6.25	15.63	10.75	24.13	18
Low	2.38	4.38	4.63	8	5.88
Close	5.69	9	9.06	10.13	7.38

*1999 price as of April 16

13
Mail-Well, Inc.

23 Inverness Way East
Englewood, CO 80112
303-790-8023
www.mail-well.com

Chairman and CEO:
Gerald F. Mahoney
President:
Paul V. Reilly

Earnings Growth	★ ★ ★ ★
Revenue Growth	★ ★ ★ ★
Stock Growth	★ ★ ★ ★
Consistency	★ ★ ★
NYSE: MWL	**15 points**

After a quick series of acquisitions over the past five years, Mail-Well has become the nation's largest printer and manufacturer of envelopes. It is also the leading commercial high-impact color printer. The Englewood, Colorado company operates about 100 envelope and commercial printing facilities throughout North America.

Mail-Well has a strong presence in the consumer direct segment of the envelope market in which envelopes are designed, printed, and manufactured to customer specifications. The company does a lot of specialty envelopes with color graphics or action devices.

Color printing makes up about 20 percent of the company's total revenue. U.S. envelope sales account for about 68 percent of revenue, and

Canadian envelope sales account for the other 12 percent. In addition to its envelope and high-impact color printing, the company does a lot of business communications printing and prints a lot of labels for foods, beverages, and spirits.

Mail-Well, in its present form, began operations in 1994 with the acquisition of the envelope business of Georgia-Pacific and Pavey Envelope & Tag Corp. It continued to buy up companies at an increasing pace through 1999, adding printing and envelope plants throughout the United States and Canada.

The printing and envelope industry is highly fragmented, with about 200 independent envelope companies and 500 high-impact color commercial printing companies in the United States. Mail-Well's long-term strategy is to continue to swallow up the independent operations and take advantage of the operating efficiencies of consolidation to increase profits.

Mail-Well markets its services through its broad network of sales representatives. The sales reps generally work with customers on their projects from the initial product design stage all the way through to delivery.

Mail-Well went public with its initial stock offering in 1995. The company has about 8,000 employees and a market capitalization of about $620 million.

EARNINGS PER SHARE GROWTH ★ ★ ★ ★

Past four years: 1,075 percent (83 percent per year)

REVENUE GROWTH ★ ★ ★ ★

Past four years: 474 percent (49 percent per year)

STOCK GROWTH ★ ★ ★ ★

Past three years: 180 percent (41 percent per year)
Dollar growth: $10,000 over the past three years would have grown to $28,000.

CONSISTENCY ★ ★ ★

Increased earnings per share: three of the past four years
Increased revenue: four of the past four years

MAIL-WELL AT A GLANCE

Fiscal year ended: Dec. 31
Revenue and net income in $ millions

	1994	1995	1996	1997	1998	4-Year Growth Avg. Annual (%)	4-Year Growth Total (%)
Revenue ($)	262.2	596.8	778.5	897.6	1,504.7	49	474
Net income ($)	1.45	10.4	16.9	28.3	47.6	140	3,183
Earnings/share ($)	0.08	0.47	0.47	0.79	0.94	83	1,075
Avg. PE ratio	—	9	9	17	17	—	—

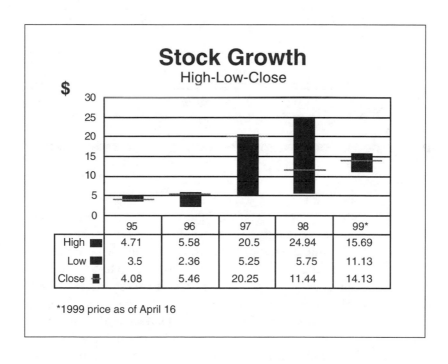

Stock Growth
High-Low-Close

$

	95	96	97	98	99*
High	4.71	5.58	20.5	24.94	15.69
Low	3.5	2.36	5.25	5.75	11.13
Close	4.08	5.46	20.25	11.44	14.13

*1999 price as of April 16

14

Integral Systems, Inc.

5000 Philadelphia Way
Suite A
Lanham, MD 20706
301-731-4233
www.integ.com

Chairman and CEO:
Steven R. Chamberlain
President:
Thomas L. Gough

Earnings Growth	★ ★ ★ ★
Revenue Growth	★ ★ ★
Stock Growth	★ ★ ★ ★
Consistency	★ ★ ★
Nasdaq: ISYS	**14 points**

Integral Systems offers the world's only off-the-shelf satellite command and control software capable of controlling any satellite from any manufacturer.

Traditionally, satellite operators had to develop their own ground control systems, a process that could take many years and up to $100 million to accomplish. Controllers with several satellites had to set up and use several different computer control programs to keep their satellites on course. In fact, Integral Systems was originally in the business of building some of those custom ground control systems. But with the universal acceptance of the personal computer, Integral began to develop software for PCs that could control any satellite.

Its software systems are not only practical because of their ability to control a whole fleet of different satellites from the same PC, they are also considerably cheaper than the old custom controllers and much faster to install. The company's Epoch 2000 software takes just six months to implement and reduces ground control costs by more than 90 percent.

The Lanham, Maryland operation markets its software to U.S. government organizations, such as NASA (9 percent of total revenue), the National Oceanic and Atmospheric Administration (41 percent), and the U.S. Air Force (7 percent), and to commercial satellite operators both in the United States and abroad (43 percent).

Integral has provided the software for nearly 100 different satellite missions. Its software controllers are used on missions for scientific research, remote sensing, meteorology, and communications applications. The firm also offers ground control system software for real-time environmental monitoring by satellite.

The firm operates one wholly owned subsidiary, Integral Marketing, which specializes in the sale of electronic test instrumentation and related products.

The company was first incorporated in 1982. Integral has about 125 employees and a market capitalization of about $115 million.

EARNINGS PER SHARE GROWTH ★ ★ ★ ★

Past four years: 1,550 percent (103 percent per year)

REVENUE GROWTH ★ ★ ★

Past four years: 215 percent (32 percent per year)

STOCK GROWTH ★ ★ ★ ★

Past three years: 339 percent (64 percent per year)
Dollar growth: $10,000 over the past three years would have grown to about $44,000.

CONSISTENCY ★ ★ ★

Increased earnings per share: three of the past four years
Increased revenue: four of the past four years

INTEGRAL SYSTEMS AT A GLANCE

Fiscal year ended: Sept. 30
Revenue and net income in $ millions

	1994	1995	1996	1997	1998	4-Year Growth Avg. Annual (%)	Total (%)
Revenue ($)	8.9	10.8	11.2	20.1	28	32	215
Net income ($)	0.129	0.380	0.324	0.628	1.91	96	1,381
Earnings/share ($)	0.02	0.07	0.06	0.11	0.33	103	1,550
Avg. PE ratio	146	61	74	49	56	—	—

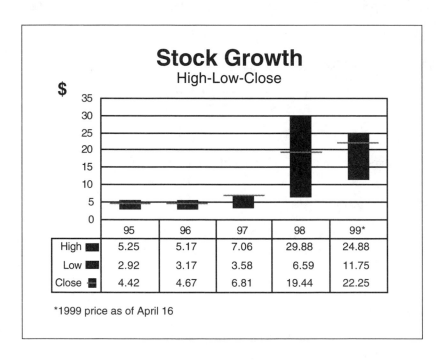

Stock Growth
High-Low-Close

$

	95	96	97	98	99*
High	5.25	5.17	7.06	29.88	24.88
Low	2.92	3.17	3.58	6.59	11.75
Close	4.42	4.67	6.81	19.44	22.25

*1999 price as of April 16

15
RWD Technologies, Inc.

10480 Little Patuxent Parkway
Suite 1200
Columbia, MD 21044
410-730-4377
www.rwd.com

Chairman and CEO:
Dr. Robert W. Deutsch
President:
John H. Beakes

Earnings Growth	★ ★ ★ ★
Revenue Growth	★ ★ ★ ★
Stock Growth	★ ★
Consistency	★ ★ ★ ★
Nasdaq: RWDT	**14 points**

A consortium of major oil companies and a foreign government that were trying to manage the operation of a large offshore oil platform project found themselves wading through more than just water and oil. The procedures manual to construct and operate the platform covered more than 150,000 pages of technical documents.

Consultants from RWD Technologies designed a computerized electronic document management system that enabled users to retrieve the documents they needed in just seconds—and print them out in less than a minute—rather than the eight- to ten-minute time frame needed to track down files under the old paper system.

The motto of the Columbia, Maryland operation is: "We bring people and technology together." The primary focus of the company's legion of information technology consultants is to help its client companies get the most effective use of their manufacturing systems and technologies.

RWD helps companies design and build a wide range of computerized document managment systems, electronic performance support systems, sales force automation systems, Internet/intranet applications, and related programs.

The company also produces specialized training manuals for complex technologies, serves as plant floor consultants to help integrate new equipment, and offers classroom and plant floor training. All of its programs are geared to helping clients improve their product quality, worker productivity, and competitiveness.

RWD serves about 100 corporate clients spread across about 20 industries. Many are large Fortune 500 companies, such as Bristol-Myers Squibb, Chevron, Chrysler, Ford, Dow Chemical, Procter & Gamble, and Merck.

RWD was founded in 1988 by Dr. Robert W. Deutsch and John H. Beakes, formerly the CEO and COO, respectively, of General Physics. Deutsch continues to serve as chairman and CEO of RWD, while Beakes is president and COO. The company went public with its initial stock offering in 1997. RWD has about 800 employees and a market capitalization of about $325 million.

EARNINGS PER SHARE GROWTH ★ ★ ★ ★

Past four years: 261 percent (37 percent per year)

REVENUE GROWTH ★ ★ ★ ★

Past four years: 290 percent (42 percent per year)

STOCK GROWTH ★ ★

Past one year: 20 percent
Dollar growth: $10,000 over the past year would have grown to $12,000.

CONSISTENCY ★ ★ ★ ★

Increased earnings per share: four of the past four years
Increased revenue: four of the past four years

RWD TECHNOLOGIES AT A GLANCE

Fiscal year ended: Dec. 31
Revenue and net income in $ millions

	1994	1995	1996	1997	1998	4-Year Growth Avg. Annual (%)	Total (%)
Revenue ($)	29.4	47.1	65.0	85.7	114.7	42	290
Net income ($)	2.39	3.92	5.17	9	13.1	53	448
Earnings/share ($)	0.23	0.32	0.41	0.62	0.83	37	261
Avg. PE ratio	—	—	—	32	25	—	—

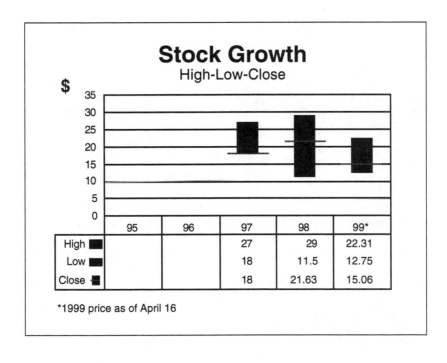

Stock Growth
High-Low-Close

$	95	96	97	98	99*
High			27	29	22.31
Low			18	11.5	12.75
Close			18	21.63	15.06

*1999 price as of April 16

16
Timberline Software Corporation

15195 N.W. Greenbrier Parkway
Beaverton, OR 97006
503-690-6775
www.timberline.com

Chairman:
James Meyer
President:
Curtis L. Peltz

Earnings Growth	★ ★ ★ ★
Revenue Growth	★ ★
Stock Growth	★ ★ ★ ★
Consistency	★ ★ ★ ★
Nasdaq: TMBS	**14 points**

Timberline Software Corporation makes software designed to help construction companies and real estate property management companies run their operations more effectively.

Timberline's construction accounting software helps companies handle job cost and equipment cost estimating and contract and payroll functions. Its more specialized cost-estimating software helps firms calculate their electrical, plumbing, lumber, masonry, site-preparation, and material costs right down to the final nut, bolt, or screw.

The Beaverton, Oregon operation offers software products for both large and small construction companies. Its Gold Collection–Extended

Edition is designed for medium to large construction companies with advanced management and accounting requirements. Its Gold Standard software package is for small to medium-size companies. The programs work with Microsoft Windows.

Timberline's estimating software allows an estimator to compile a bid on construction projects based on certain parameters, such as the architectural design, building materials required, and material and labor costs. The software is designed to allow the estimator to make fast, accurate estimates. The firm also sells databases and other software (including some developed by other companies) that allow estimators to be more productive and to develop more comprehensive estimates.

Timberline also has a line of property management accounting software designed for managers of residential and commercial properties. The software provides information regarding revenues and expenses of various properties and generates financial reports about the properties.

In addition to its software products, Timberline generates revenue through its maintenance and support services.

More than 90 percent of the company's sales are in the United States, but it also has sales in Canada, Australia, New Zealand, and other foreign countries. Timberline was founded in 1979. The company has about 312 employees and a market capitalization of about $150 million.

EARNINGS PER SHARE GROWTH ★ ★ ★ ★

Past four years: 429 percent (52 percent per year)

REVENUE GROWTH ★ ★

Past four years: 105 percent (20 percent per year)

STOCK GROWTH ★ ★ ★ ★

Past three years: 287 percent (57 percent per year)
Dollar growth: $10,000 over the past three years would have grown to about $39,000.

CONSISTENCY ★ ★ ★ ★

Increased earnings per share: four of the past four years
Increased revenue: four of the past four years

TIMBERLINE SOFTWARE AT A GLANCE

Fiscal year ended: Dec. 31
Revenue and net income in $ millions

	1994	1995	1996	1997	1998	4-Year Growth Avg. Annual (%)	Total (%)
Revenue ($)	21.6	24.8	28.7	35.2	44.3	20	105
Net income ($)	1.19	1.91	2.18	4.54	7.19	58	504
Earnings/share ($)	0.14	0.22	0.25	0.49	0.74	52	429
Avg. PE ratio	18	17	21	20	20	—	—

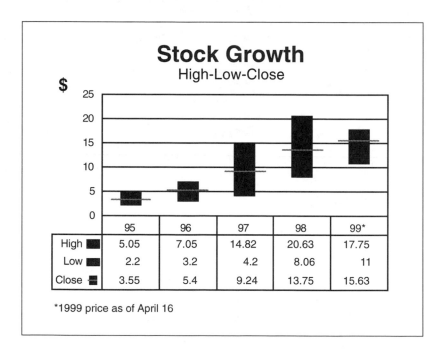

Stock Growth
High-Low-Close

$	95	96	97	98	99*
High	5.05	7.05	14.82	20.63	17.75
Low	2.2	3.2	4.2	8.06	11
Close	3.55	5.4	9.24	13.75	15.63

*1999 price as of April 16

Pure World, Inc.

376 Main Street
Bedminster, NJ 07921
908-234-9220

Chairman:
Paul O. Koether
President:
Natalie I. Koether

Earnings Growth	★ ★ ★
Revenue Growth	★ ★ ★
Stock Growth	★ ★ ★ ★
Consistency	★ ★ ★ ★
Nasdaq: PURW	**14 points**

In the real world, Pure World has discovered pure profits by serving the growing market for *nutraceuticals*—a term used in the new age world to describe a wide range of natural products, such as vitamins, minerals, antioxidants, and herbs.

Pure World extracts and develops natural ingredients derived primarily from plant materials. The extracts are marketed to other manufacturers that use them for vitamins, food and flavoring products, pharmaceuticals, and dietary supplements. In all, the company has produced more than a thousand botanical extracts.

Pure World produces its extracts and related products through its key subsidiary, Madis Botanicals. The Madis facility is the largest botanical extraction facility in North America. The plant, a 120,000-square-foot facility situated on four and one-half acres, has annual capacity to process more than eight million pounds of plants.

Among the products processed at the facility are casanthranol (derived from the bark of the cascara tree), coal tar (used for dandruff control shampoos), and benzoin (used as an antiseptic and skin protectant).

Pure World not only sells its extracts to other manufacturers, it also produces its own line of nutritional supplements, which it markets through health and nutrition retailers.

The company's biggest success recently has been its KavaPure fluid extract and gelatin capsules, which are purported to reduce stress and anxiety. The product is derived from the roots of the kava plant, which the company buys from South Pacific tribes.

In all, the company offers more than 20 standardized products.

The Bedminster, New Jersey operation has about 70 employees and a market capitalization of about $60 million. The company has no reported sales outside of North America.

EARNINGS PER SHARE GROWTH   ★ ★ ★

Past three years: 6,200 percent (300 percent per year)
Early 1999 returns were down dramatically.

REVENUE GROWTH   ★ ★ ★

Past four years: 1,233 percent (91 percent per year)
Early 1999 revenue was down substantially.

STOCK GROWTH   ★ ★ ★ ★

Past three years: 257 percent (53 percent per year)
Dollar growth: $10,000 over the past three years would have grown to about $36,000.

CONSISTENCY   ★ ★ ★ ★

Increased earnings per share: four of the past four years
Increased revenue: four of the past four years

PURE WORLD AT A GLANCE

Fiscal year ended: Dec. 31
Revenue and net income in $ millions

	1994	1995	1996	1997	1998	4-Year Growth Avg. Annual (%)	Total (%)
Revenue ($)	1.8	7.45	8.5	12.7	24	91	1,233
Net income ($)	0.026	0.041	0.229	2.33	5.69	285	21,780
Earnings/share ($)	—	0.01	0.03	0.31	0.63	300*	6,200*
Avg. PE ratio	500	490	90	17	17	—	—

*Earnings per share returns are based on three-year performance.

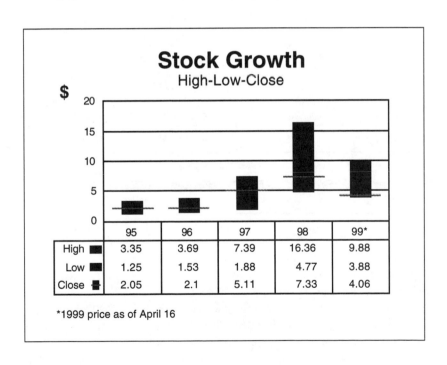

Stock Growth
High-Low-Close

	95	96	97	98	99*
High ■	3.35	3.69	7.39	16.36	9.88
Low ■	1.25	1.53	1.88	4.77	3.88
Close ▪	2.05	2.1	5.11	7.33	4.06

*1999 price as of April 16

18
Intelligroup, Inc.

499 Thornall Street
Edison, NJ 08837
732-750-1600
www.intelligroup.com

Co-Chairman:
Ashok Pandey
Co-Chairman:
Rajkumar Koneru
Co-Chairman:
Nagarjun Valluripalli
President and CEO:
Steven A. Carns

Earnings Growth	★ ★ ★ ★
Revenue Growth	★ ★ ★ ★
Stock Growth	★ ★ ★
Consistency	★ ★ ★
Nasdaq: ITIG	**14 points**

Intelligroup helps corporations set up their computer systems, software, networking, and Internet functions.

The Edison, New Jersey operation works with about 200 major corporations in the United States and abroad to help them get up to speed in the computer revolution. Intelligroup's army of consultants works with their corporate clients to install Internet applications; provides enterprisewide business computing assistance using SAP, Oracle, Peoplesoft, and Baan software applications; and provides systems integration and custom software development solutions in a wide variety of computing environments.

The firm offers assistance in the areas of client/server architectures, object-oriented technologies, distributed database management systems, computer networks, and telecommunications technologies.

Intelligroup tries to focus on the individual objectives of its customers, providing business process re-engineering, information systems strategic planning, technology implementation, comprehensive training, and organizational change management services.

Its leading product is the 4Sight Development Manager, which is used to monitor corporate computing projects, providing real-time information in such areas as the current stage of development of each program; the number of man-hours spent at each stage of development; programs developed by each programmer; and analysis of time spent on the developement of the project. It also provides technical information, such as source code, documentation, and tables used in the system.

Intelligroup markets its services around the world. It has 25 people in its U.S. sales and marketing department, 6 who cover the United Kingdom and Denmark and 2 in Australia and New Zealand. Asian marketing is done through the firm's subsidiary, Intelligroup Asia.

Intelligroup was founded in 1987 under the name Intellicorp. It changed to its current name in 1992. Intelligroup went public with its initial stock offering in 1996. The firm has about 800 employees and a market capitalization of about $240 million.

EARNINGS PER SHARE GROWTH   ★ ★ ★ ★

Past two years: 220 percent (73 percent per year)

REVENUE GROWTH   ★ ★ ★ ★

Past four years: 1,872 percent (155 percent per year)

STOCK GROWTH   ★ ★ ★

Past two years: 62 percent (27 percent per year)
Dollar growth: $10,000 over the past two years would have grown to about $16,000.

CONSISTENCY   ★ ★ ★

Increased earnings per share: three of the past four years
Increased revenue: four of the past four years

INTELLIGROUP AT A GLANCE

Fiscal year ended: Dec. 31
Revenue and net income in $ millions

	1994	1995	1996	1997	1998	4-Year Growth Avg. Annual (%)	Total (%)
Revenue ($)	6.80	24.6	47.2	80.2	134.1	155	1,872
Net income ($)	−0.437	−1.06	1.94	4.47	8.25	104*	325*
Earnings/share ($)	−0.03	−0.08	0.20	0.39	0.64	73*	220*
Avg. PE ratio	—	—	75	44	28	—	—

*Net income and earnings per share returns are based on two-year performance.

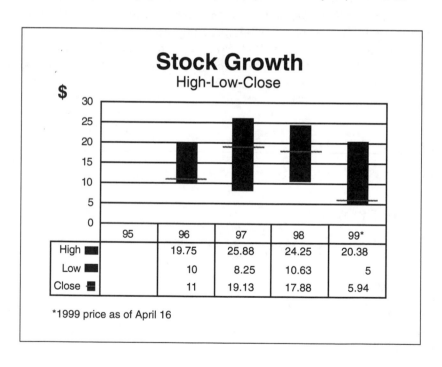

*1999 price as of April 16

Summa Industries

21250 Hawthorne Boulevard
Suite 500
Torrance, CA 90503
310-792-7024
www.summaindustries.com

Chairman, President, and CEO:
James R. Swartwout

Earnings Growth	★ ★ ★ ★
Revenue Growth	★ ★ ★ ★
Stock Growth	★ ★ ★
Consistency	★ ★ ★
Nasdaq: SUMX	**14 points**

Summa Industries may have the look and feel of a plastics manufacturer, but that's really just a sideline. Summa is actually in the acquisitions business.

The Torrance, California manufacturer has been pursuing a strategy of growth through acquisitions of profitable companies in the plastics manufacturing business with proprietary products or protected market niches. Typically, Summa holds onto the management of the companies it acquires, letting them continue to run the operations while Summa takes care of the financing, purchasing, employee benefits, marketing, and business development.

Summa recently acquired manufacturers Canyon Mold, GST Industries, Falcon Belting, and Calnetics Corp.

Summa manufactures products in three broad categories, including:

1. *Optical components.* Summa makes injection molded plastic prismatic lenses, refractors, and reflectors for commercial and industrial lighting fixtures, such as streetlights and traffic signals.

2. *Irrigation components.* The firm makes engineered fittings, valves, filters, and accessories for irrigation systems.
3. *Conveyor components.* The company makes engineered plastic components for conveyer belts and chains in the food processing industry. Its components are lightweight and require no lubrication, such as oil or grease, which helps keep the equipment free of contaminants that could taint the food.

Most of Summa's products are sold to manufacturers for use as components in their products. Most sales are made by the company's sales staff, although some sales are made through independent manufacturers representatives. Summa has thousands of active customers, many of which are Fortune 1,000 companies and large privately held businesses.

The company does most of its own manufacturing, although some products are produced by thrid party manufacturers.

Summa was founded in 1942 and went public with its initial stock offering in 1993. The company has about 700 employees and a market capitalization of about $40 million.

EARNINGS PER SHARE GROWTH ★ ★ ★ ★

Past four years: 627 percent (64 percent per year)

REVENUE GROWTH ★ ★ ★ ★

Past four years: 1,580 percent (101 percent per year)

STOCK GROWTH ★ ★ ★

Past three years: 101 percent (26 percent per year)
Dollar growth: $10,000 over the past three years would have grown to about $20,000.

CONSISTENCY ★ ★ ★

Increased earnings per share: three of the past four years
Increased revenue: four of the past four years

SUMMA INDUSTRIES AT A GLANCE

Fiscal year ended: Aug. 31
Revenue and net income in $ millions

	1994	1995	1996	1997	1998	4-Year Growth Avg. Annual (%)	Total (%)
Revenue ($)	5.1	6.6	8.1	39.1	85.7	101	1,580
Net income ($)	0.233	0.389	0.373	1.6	4.6	111	1,874
Earnings/share ($)	0.15	0.25	0.24	0.47	1.09	64	627
Avg. PE ratio	34	19	22	18	10	—	—

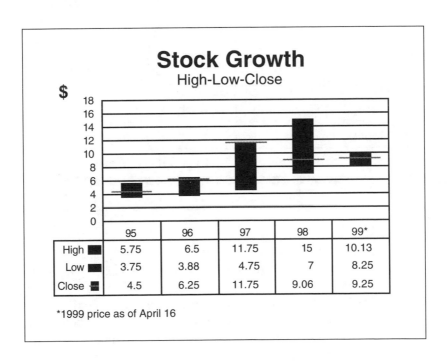

Stock Growth
High-Low-Close

$

	95	96	97	98	99*
High	5.75	6.5	11.75	15	10.13
Low	3.75	3.88	4.75	7	8.25
Close	4.5	6.25	11.75	9.06	9.25

*1999 price as of April 16

20

Chart Industries, Inc.

5885 Landerbrook Drive #150
Mayfield Heights, OH 44124
440-753-1490

Chairman and CEO:
Arthur Holmes
President:
James Sadowski

Earnings Growth	★ ★ ★ ★
Revenue Growth	★ ★ ★
Stock Growth	★ ★ ★
Consistency	★ ★ ★ ★
NYSE: CTI	**14 points**

Chart Industries has its own cold war brewing. The company specializes in "cryogenic" (low temperature) equipment. Its systems and equipment can operate at temperatures approaching absolute zero: −459° F or −273° C.

Most of Chart's products are used in the processing, liquefaction, storage, and transportation of low temperature gases and hydrocarbons. The firm makes heat exchangers, cold boxes, cryogenic tanks, and other cryogenic components. The firm also supplies products for special applications, including high vacuum systems and specialty stainless steel tubing.

The Ohio-based manufacturer operates globally, with about 25 percent of its business coming from outside the United States.

Chart's largest market is the industrial gas segment, which accounts for about 46 percent of its approximately $200 million in annual revenue.

Chart serves many of the world's leading industrial gas producers. Industrial gases are liquified through low temperature processing and then stored and transported for use by companies involved in the petrochemical, electronics, glass, paper, metals, food, fertilizer, welding, enhanced oil recovery, and medical industries.

Industrial gas producers use heat exchangers and cold boxes to produce liquid gases, and cryogenic tanks and other components—such as pumps, valves, and piping—to store, transport, and distribute liquid gases to end users.

About 27 percent of the company's revenues come from the hydrocarbon processing market. Chart's equipment is used in the gas separation and purification process, as well as the subsequent storage and distribution of liquid gases.

Chart also serves several special market niches. Its two largest are vacuum systems and specialty stainless steel tubing. Vacuum equipment is supplied primarily to the satellite testing market and to observatories for telescope mirror coating. Its stainless steel tubing is normally sold to distributors who resell it to the industrial market.

Founded in 1992, Chart has about 1,300 employees and a market capitalization of about $200 million.

EARNINGS PER SHARE GROWTH   ★ ★ ★ ★

Past four years: 259 percent (51 percent per year)

REVENUE GROWTH   ★ ★ ★

Past four years: 172 percent (29 percent per year)

STOCK GROWTH   ★ ★ ★

Past three years: 125 percent (31 percent per year)
Dollar growth: $10,000 over the past three years would have grown to about $23,000.

CONSISTENCY   ★ ★ ★ ★

Increased earnings per share: four of the past four years
Increased revenue: four of the past four years

CHART INDUSTRIES AT A GLANCE

Fiscal year ended: Dec. 31
Revenue and net income in $ millions

	1994	1995	1996	1997	1998	4-Year Growth Avg. Annual (%)	Total (%)
Revenue ($)	84.3	112.5	148.4	192.2	229.4	29	172
Net income ($)	−1.46	7.06	15	22.6	28.2	56*	299*
Earnings/share ($)	−0.07	0.32	0.67	1.01	1.15	51*	259*
Avg. PE ratio	—	9	8	12	12	—	—

*Net income and earnings per share returns are based on three years' growth.

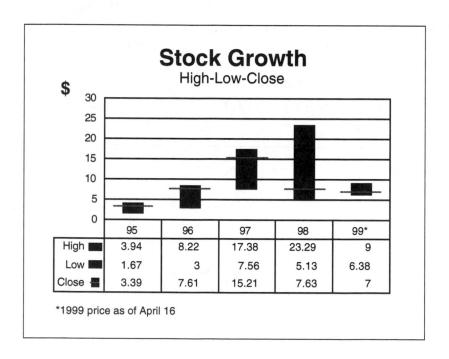

Stock Growth
High-Low-Close

	95	96	97	98	99*
High	3.94	8.22	17.38	23.29	9
Low	1.67	3	7.56	5.13	6.38
Close	3.39	7.61	15.21	7.63	7

*1999 price as of April 16

21
Brightpoint, Inc.

6402 Corporate Drive
Indianapolis, IN 46278
317-297-6100
www.brightpoint.com

Chairman and CEO:
Robert J. Laikin
President:
J. Mark Howell

Earnings Growth	★ ★ ★
Revenue Growth	★ ★ ★ ★
Stock Growth	★ ★ ★ ★
Consistency	★ ★ ★
Nasdaq: CELL	**14 points**

Brightpoint has carved out a profitable share of the rapidly growing cellular phone industry without developing a single new product. The Indianapolis-based operation is a distributor of wireless communications products produced by some of the world's leading manufacturers, including Ericsson, Motorola, Siemens, Philips, and Samsung.

Brightpoint markets its product line of cellular phones, pagers, and related products to network operators, agents, resellers, dealers, and retailers in the wireless communications market.

In addition to distribution, the company also does some light assembly and offers end-user support services for some customers. For instance, it provides integrated logistics and end-user fulfillment services for Sprint

PCS, and inventory management, fulfillment, and other logistics services for Omnipoint.

Brightpoint is worldwide in scope, with distribution offices in Argentina, Venezuela, Australia, Brazil, China, Ireland, the Philippines, South Africa, Sweden, England, and the United States. It boasts a customer base of more than 10,000 businesses in more than 75 countries on six continents.

The firm has continued to expand through a series of acquisitions. For instance, in 1998, the company acquired distributors in New Zealand, Taiwan, Poland, Mexico, France, and the Netherlands.

The wireless industry is one of the fastest-growing areas of the worldwide economy. There were fewer than 100 million cell phone subscribers in 1995, growing to well over 200 million in 1998. The subscriber base was projected to be more than 450 million in the year 2000. Unit demand is even higher, with about 90 million cell phones sold in 1997 and more than 100 million in 1998. Paging unit sales also have been a growing business, with about 20 million new subscribers each year. Brightpoint is well positioned to profit from the growth of both the cell phone and pager markets.

Brightpoint was founded in 1989 as Wholesale Cellular USA. It went public with its initial public offering in 1994. The company has about 700 employees and a market capitalization of about $800 million.

EARNINGS PER SHARE GROWTH   ★ ★ ★

Past four years: 118 percent (21 percent per year)

REVENUE GROWTH   ★ ★ ★ ★

Past four years: 428 percent (53 percent per year)

STOCK GROWTH   ★ ★ ★ ★

Past three years: 264 percent (54 percent per year)
Dollar growth: $10,000 over the past three years would have grown to about $36,000.

CONSISTENCY   ★ ★ ★

Increased earnings per share: three of the past four years
Increased revenue: four of the past four years

BRIGHTPOINT AT A GLANCE

Fiscal year ended: Dec. 31
Revenue and net income in $ millions

	1994	1995	1996	1997	1998	4-Year Growth Avg. Annual (%)	Total (%)
Revenue ($)	309.2	419.1	589.7	1,035.6	1,628.6	53	428
Net income ($)	4.56	7.31	14.4	25.9	20	44	339
Earnings/share ($)	0.17	0.22	0.31	0.55	0.37	21	118
Avg. PE ratio	15	19	26	30	36	—	—

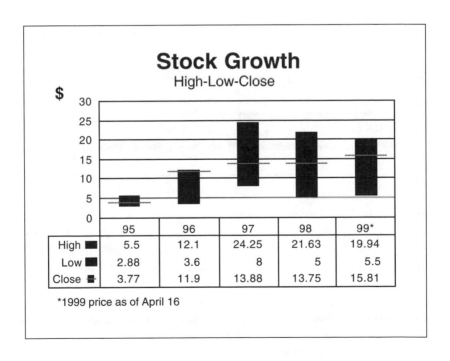

Stock Growth
High-Low-Close

$

	95	96	97	98	99*
High	5.5	12.1	24.25	21.63	19.94
Low	2.88	3.6	8	5	5.5
Close	3.77	11.9	13.88	13.75	15.81

*1999 price as of April 16

22

Ducommun Incorporated

DUCOMMUN INCORPORATED

111 West Ocean Boulevard
Suite 900
Long Beach, CA 90802
562-624-0800
www.ducommun.com

Chairman:
Norman A. Barkeley
President and CEO:
Joseph C. Berenato

Earnings Growth	★ ★ ★ ★
Revenue Growth	★ ★ ★
Stock Growth	★ ★ ★
Consistency	★ ★ ★ ★
NYSE: DCO	**14 points**

At 150 years old, Ducommun is the oldest company in California. But its current specialty—manufacturing parts for jets and spacecraft—was probably not the future Charles Louis Ducommun envisioned for the company when he opened his store in 1849 to sell picks and shovels to the gold miners during the great California gold rush.

A century later, at the close of World War II, the company had become the largest metal distributor west of the Mississippi. Its specialty was aluminum used for commercial and military aircraft.

The Long Beach operation currently provides a range of products and services to the aerospace industry through several subsidiaries. Its Aerochem subsidiary provides chemical milling on aluminum, titanium, steel, nickel-base, and super alloys for such aircraft parts as jet engine components, wing leading edges, and fuselage skins. The milling process enables Aerochem to produce lightweight, high-strength designs ideal for aircraft.

Ducommun's AHF-Ducommun division supplies aircraft and aerospace contractors with engineering, manufacturing, and testing of complex components using stretch forming of aluminum parts as large as 100 feet long.

The firm's Brice Manufacturing division makes plastic and metal aircraft seat parts, and in-flight entertainment equipment, primarily for the aftermarket.

Ducommun's Jay-El subsidiary makes illuminated switches, switch assemblies, and keyboard panels used in military aircraft, helicopters, commercial aircraft, and naval vessels.

About 59 percent of Ducommun's annual revenue comes from sales to the commercial aircraft and nonaerospace sectors. Defense-related sales account for about 31 percent of Ducommun's annual revenue, and space program sales account for about 10 percent of revenue.

About 40 percent of Ducommun's revenue comes from three large aerospace contractors—Boeing, Lockheed-Martin, and Northrop-Grumman.

Ducommun has about 1,300 employees and a market capitalization of about $160 million.

EARNINGS PER SHARE GROWTH   ★ ★ ★ ★

Past four years: 534 percent (58 percent per year)

REVENUE GROWTH   ★ ★ ★

Past four years: 177 percent (29 percent per year)

STOCK GROWTH   ★ ★ ★

Past three years: 109 percent (28 percent per year)
Dollar growth: $10,000 over the past three years would have grown to about $21,000.

CONSISTENCY   ★ ★ ★ ★

Increased earnings per share: four of the past four years
Increased revenue: four of the past four years

DUCOMMUN AT A GLANCE

Fiscal year ended: Dec. 31
Revenue and net income in $ millions

	1994	1995	1996	1997	1998	4-Year Growth Avg. Annual (%)	Total (%)
Revenue ($)	61.7	91.2	118.4	157.3	170.8	29	177
Net income ($)	2.20	5.05	10.3	14.3	23.7	81	977
Earnings/share ($)	0.32	0.75	1.04	1.30	2.03	58	534
Avg. PE ratio	9	7	11	16	9	—	—

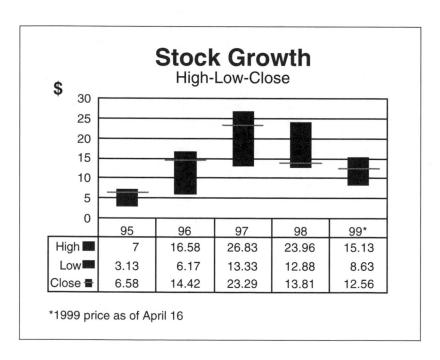

Stock Growth
High-Low-Close

$

	95	96	97	98	99*
High	7	16.58	26.83	23.96	15.13
Low	3.13	6.17	13.33	12.88	8.63
Close	6.58	14.42	23.29	13.81	12.56

*1999 price as of April 16

23
PC Connection, Inc.

730 Milford Road
Route 101A
Merrimack, NH 03054
603-423-2000
www.pcconnection.com

Chairman and CEO:
Patricia Gallup
President:
Wayne L. Wilson

Earnings Growth	★ ★ ★ ★
Revenue Growth	★ ★ ★ ★
Stock Growth	★
Consistency	★ ★ ★ ★
Nasdaq: PCCC	**13 points**

PC Connection is a mail order computer business that operates at cyber-speed.

With its "Everything Overnight" policy, if you order a computer from PC Connection by midnight—even if it's a custom-configured system to be built to your specifications—your computer will still be delivered to your door the next day, often by noon.

The Merrimack, New Hampshire company sells about 25,000 products from name brand manufacturers such as IBM, Compaq, Toshiba, Hewlett-Packard, Microsoft, and Apple. The company markets its products through catalogs, its online superstore, and its outbound corporate sales division.

In addition to its overnight delivery policy, PC Connection has several other customer service policies that set it apart from the competition. It offers one-minute mail order using caller ID, which enables customer account information to appear instantly on the salesperson's screen when the call connects. It offers Web site ordering and direct online interaction between the company's service technicians and customers to provide service solutions over the Internet. And it offers toll-free technical support for all of its products before, during, and after the sale.

That combination of services helped the company earn *PC World* magazine's "Best Mail Order Company" award seven out of the past eight years.

PC Connection's primary target customers are small and medium-size organizations with 20 to 1,000 employees. The company's mailing list includes about two million prospects, including about 500,000 who had made purchases from the company over the previous 12 months.

In addition to personal computers, the company sells a broad range of other computer related products, including printers, scanners, monitors, components, networking packages, digital cameras, software, keyboards, and other accessories. All of its products are competitively priced.

PC Connection was founded in 1982 and went public with its initial stock offering in 1998. The company has about 900 employees and a market capitalization of about $340 million.

EARNINGS PER SHARE GROWTH ★ ★ ★ ★

Past three years: 989 percent (121 percent per year)

REVENUE GROWTH ★ ★ ★ ★

Past four years: 272 percent (39 percent per year)

STOCK GROWTH ★

The company just issued its stock in 1998.

CONSISTENCY ★ ★ ★ ★

Increased earnings per share: four of the past four years
Increased revenue: four of the past four years

PC CONNECTION AT A GLANCE

Fiscal year ended: Dec. 31
Revenue and net income in $ millions

	1994	1995	1996	1997	1998	4-Year Growth Avg. Annual (%)	Total (%)
Revenue ($)	196.7	252.2	333.3	550.6	732.4	39	272
Net income ($)	−2.34	1.27	4.76	−1.12	12.9	111	916*
Earnings/share ($)	−0.17	0.09	0.34	0.79	0.98	121	989*
Avg. PE ratio	—	—	—	—	23	—	—

*Net income and earnings per share returns are based on three-year performance.

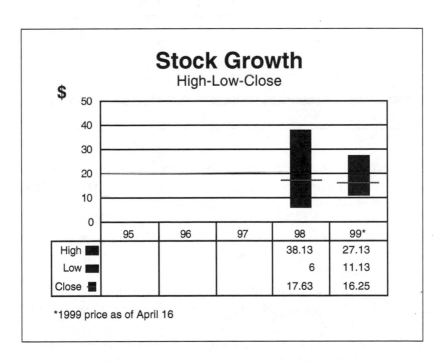

Stock Growth
High-Low-Close

	95	96	97	98	99*
High				38.13	27.13
Low				6	11.13
Close				17.63	16.25

*1999 price as of April 16

24

RCM Technologies, Inc.

2500 McClellan Avenue
Suite 350
Pennsauken, NJ 08109
609-486-1777
www.rcmt.com

Chairman, President, and CEO:
Leon Kopyt

Earnings Growth	★ ★ ★
Revenue Growth	★ ★ ★ ★
Stock Growth	★ ★ ★ ★
Consistency	★ ★
Nasdaq: RCMT	**13 points**

RCM Technologies is an outsourcing agency that provides information technology (IT) personnel, engineers, and a variety of other professionals and temporary workers for companies throughout the United States.

The company has more than 40 branch offices in nearly 20 states to serve its client base of about 1,300 companies, including such blue chip corporations as AT&T, Bell Atlantic, Chase Manhattan, MCI, Merck, Merrill Lynch, and 3M.

RCM's technology consultants help companies with enterprise software, network communications, database design and development, and client server migration.

The Pennsauken, New Jersey operation also provides professional engineering staffing and project management services for a variety of engineering disciplines, such as aeronautical, electromechanical, nuclear, and computer sciences.

RCM has made a radical change in its corporate strategy in the past few years. Prior to 1995, it was strictly a general support staffing service with no IT services. But since 1995, the company has acquired more than a dozen IT and engineering staffing service companies. Now about 60 percent of its revenue comes from the much more profitable IT and engineering services segment.

RCM uses a legion of about 1,000 IT consultants and 500 professional engineers. In all, it outsources about 11,000 full-time and part-time contract and temporary employees each year.

The company plans to continue its acquisition policy in an attempt to become one of the nation's leading providers of IT and other professional staffing services. The firm typically enters a new market by acquiring a profitable staffing operation in that region. It generally tries to keep the existing management in place to continue to handle regional operations. But RCM integrates the administrative functions of the acquired companies in order to cut costs, and it establishes financial controls and relieves local management of administrative functions so they can focus on growing sales.

Founded in 1971, RCM Technologies has about 370 employees and a market capitalization of about $215 million.

EARNINGS PER SHARE GROWTH ★ ★ ★

Past four years: 112 percent (21 percent per year)

REVENUE GROWTH ★ ★ ★ ★

Past four years: 590 percent (62 percent per year)

STOCK GROWTH ★ ★ ★ ★

Past three years: 746 percent (103 percent per year)
Dollar growth: $10,000 over the past three years would have grown to about $85,000.

CONSISTENCY ★ ★

Increased earnings per share: three of the past four years
Increased revenue: three of the past four years

RCM TECHNOLOGIES AT A GLANCE

Fiscal year ended: Oct. 31
Revenue and net income in $ millions

	1994	1995	1996	1997	1998	4-Year Growth Avg. Annual (%)	Total (%)
Revenue ($)	29.2	26.9	61	114	201.4	62	590
Net income ($)	1.42	0.849	2.37	4.84	9.78	62	589
Earnings/share ($)	0.49	0.28	0.55	0.76	1.04	21	112
Avg. PE ratio	9	12	17	16	19	—	—

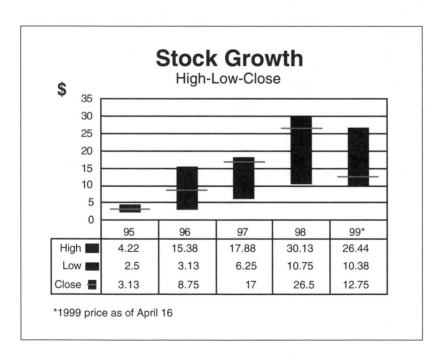

Stock Growth
High-Low-Close

$	95	96	97	98	99*
High	4.22	15.38	17.88	30.13	26.44
Low	2.5	3.13	6.25	10.75	10.38
Close	3.13	8.75	17	26.5	12.75

*1999 price as of April 16

Funco, Inc.

FuncoLand®
Bring Home The Fun®

10120 West 76th Street
Minneapolis, MN 55344
612-946-8883
www.funcoland.com

Chairman and CEO:
David R. Pomije
President:
Stanley A. Bodine

Earnings Growth	★ ★ ★ ★
Revenue Growth	★ ★ ★
Stock Growth	★ ★ ★ ★
Consistency	★ ★
Nasdaq: FNCO	**13 points**

Have fun. Make money. That's been the theme of video game retailer Funco-Land, which has become one of the fastest-growing retail chains in America, thanks to the proliferation of Nintendo, Sega, and Sony Playstation.

The Minneapolis-based retailer has more than 300 FuncoLand stores across the United States and is adding about 60 new stores each year.

Funco was founded in 1988 as a mail order seller of used Nintendo games. It opened its first retail store in 1990. The company continues to operate its mail order business, but it only accounts for about 4 percent of total sales. The company has added a Web site, the FuncoLand Superstore, that generates additional sales. Funco also publishes a video game magazine called the *Game Informer* that has about 200,000 subscribers.

The biggest difference between Funco and other retailers is that about half of Funco's sales are of used video games. In all, the stores carry about 4,000 new and used games, along with related hardware and accessories. Customers are allowed to try out games in the sampling area before they buy.

The home video business has gone through a period of rapid growth, and that growth should be sustained as the video game industry continues to release new games and more advanced equipment. The 8-bit Nintendo systems were first introduced in 1985, with upgrades coming every few years. By 1996, Nintendo and Sony had both released 64-bit game stations—and a whole new wave of games designed specifically for those stations. The next generation—128-bit game stations—are expected to be ready in the year 2000. The ongoing introduction of new equipment and new games should keep industry sales growing for years to come.

FuncoLand stores are generally located in "power strip centers" near major regional malls or in high-density retail areas. Its stores range in size from about 1,000 to 2,900 square feet and contain sections with both new and used merchandise and sampling areas.

Funco has about 800 employees and a market capitalization of about $100 million.

EARNINGS PER SHARE GROWTH ★ ★ ★ ★

Past four years: 800 percent (74 percent per year)

REVENUE GROWTH ★ ★ ★

Past four years: 223 percent (34 percent per year)

STOCK GROWTH ★ ★ ★ ★

Past three years: 507 percent (82 percent per year)
Dollar growth: $10,000 over the past three years would have grown to about $61,000.

CONSISTENCY ★ ★

Increased earnings per share: two of the past four years
Increased revenue: four of the past four years

FUNCO AT A GLANCE

Fiscal year ended: March 31
Revenue and net income in $ millions

	1994	1995	1996	1997	1998	4-Year Growth Avg. Annual (%)	Total (%)
Revenue ($)	50.5	80.4	81.4	120.6	163.3	34	223
Net Income ($)	0.88	−1.3	0.205	5.4	8.3	75	843
Earnings/share ($)	0.15	−0.22	0.04	0.90	1.35	74	800
Avg. PE ratio	—	156	7	12	10	—	—

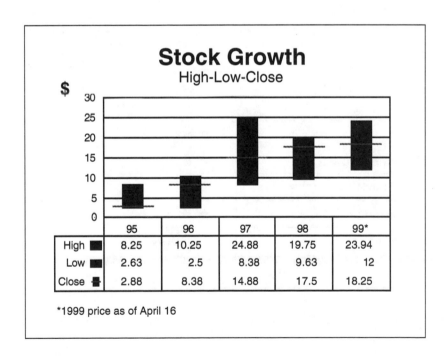

Stock Growth
High-Low-Close

	95	96	97	98	99*
High	8.25	10.25	24.88	19.75	23.94
Low	2.63	2.5	8.38	9.63	12
Close	2.88	8.38	14.88	17.5	18.25

*1999 price as of April 16

26

Capital Senior Living Corporation

CAPITAL SENIOR LIVING CORPORATION

14160 Dallas Parkway
Suite 300
Dallas, TX 75240
972-770-5600

Co-chairman and CEO:
J. L. Beck
Co-chairman:
J. A. Stroud
President:
K. N. Johannessen

Earnings Growth	★ ★ ★ ★
Revenue Growth	★ ★
Stock Growth	★ ★ ★
Consistency	★ ★ ★ ★
NYSE: CSU	**13 points**

With the aging of the baby boom generation, senior living quarters are becoming more and more in demand. Capital Senior Living is making a living capitalizing on that distinct demographic trend.

The company is one of the nation's largest providers of senior living services. It owns or operates 37 senior "communities" in 17 states. (Although the company refers to these establishments as "communities," they are not small towns, such as Sun City, Florida, but rather residential centers similar to an apartment complex.) Most have a capacity of under 200 residents.

Of its 33 communities, the Dallas-based operation owns 17 and manages 15 for third party owners. It also leases one community from a third party.

In all, the company's communities have a capacity of more than 6,000 residents. It is currently developing another 20 communities with an additional capacity of more than 4,000 residents.

Capital Senior Living also operates one home health care agency.

About 92 percent of its approximately $40 million in annual revenue comes from its managed communities.

Most of Capital Senior Living's communities are located in California, Florida, Arizona, Indiana, and Texas.

In addition to the living quarters offered to senior residents, the company also provides other services, such as transportation, personal maintenance, laundry, nonroutine care, and special care for residents with Alzheimer's and similar conditions.

The company offers skilled nursing facilites at its centers, with 24-hour nursing care, as needed. The firm also is working to expand its home health care services to additional senior living communities and to develop, acquire, or manage home health care service businesses at other similar communities.

Founded in 1993, the company went public with its initial stock offering in 1997. Capital Senior Living has about 900 employees and a market capitalization of about $275 million.

EARNINGS PER SHARE GROWTH   ★ ★ ★ ★

Past four years: 900 percent (79 percent per year)

REVENUE GROWTH   ★ ★

Past four years: 139 percent (24 percent per year)

STOCK GROWTH   ★ ★ ★

Past one year: 33 percent
Dollar growth: $10,000 over the past year would have grown to about $13,000.

CONSISTENCY   ★ ★ ★ ★

Increased earnings per share: four of the past four years
Increased revenue: four of the past four years

CAPITAL SENIOR LIVING AT A GLANCE

Fiscal year ended: Dec. 31
Revenue and net income in $ millions

	1994	1995	1996	1997	1998	4-Year Growth Avg. Annual (%)	Total (%)
Revenue ($)	17.9	18.1	19.9	30.7	42.8	24	139
Net income ($)	1.18	1.76	3.28	5.62	12.3	80	942
Earnings/share ($)	0.06	0.11	0.22	0.33	0.60	79	900
Avg. PE ratio	—	—	—	41	17	—	—

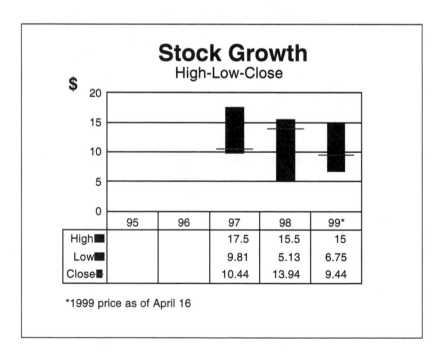

Stock Growth
High-Low-Close

$	95	96	97	98	99*
High			17.5	15.5	15
Low			9.81	5.13	6.75
Close			10.44	13.94	9.44

*1999 price as of April 16

Technisource, Inc.

⊽Technisource

1901 West Cypress Creek Road
Suite 202
Fort Lauderdale, FL 33309
954-493-8601
www.tsrc.net

President and CEO:
Joseph Collard

Earnings Growth	★ ★ ★ ★
Revenue Growth	★ ★ ★ ★
Stock Growth	★
Consistency	★ ★ ★ ★
Nasdaq: TSRC	**13 points**

Technisource is an outsourcing operation that provides information technology (IT) specialists to help corporations and organizations with their computer-related needs.

The Fort Lauderdale, Florida operation serves customers across the United States and Canada through more than 20 offices. The firm uses more than 1,000 trained IT consultants to handle a variety of computer-related projects for its customers.

Among the services offered by Technisource are database development, documentation and training, enterprise resource planning, package implementation, help desk/desktop support, Internet/intranet development, mainframe development, network engineering, real-time development, systems administration, and testing and quality assurance.

The company works with more than 200 corporate clients, including more than 400 divisions or businesses. Almost a third of its revenue has come from its two top customers, Motorola and Rockwell.

Recruiting and retaining IT consultants is one of the biggest challenges for outsourcing companies such as Technisource. Many of the Technisource specialists are independent consultants who also work with other companies.

Technisource has developed an internal growth system using what they term *development triangles* that are designed to systematically expand the business. Each development triangle is composed of an account manager, two recruiting professionals, and a group of IT consultants. Once that triangle has attracted enough business that it begins to outgrow its resources, a recruiting professional from that triangle is promoted to account manager and assigned to a new development triangle. The new triangle is financed with seed money and a few of the projects and consultants from the original triangle. Once that triangle has grown to a certain level, yet another triangle is formed. The company now has dozens of development triangles.

Technisource was founded in 1987. It went public with its initial stock offering in 1998. The company has about 1,100 employees and a market capitalization of about $100 million.

EARNINGS PER SHARE GROWTH ★ ★ ★ ★

Past four years: 500 percent (58 percent per year)

REVENUE GROWTH ★ ★ ★ ★

Past four years: 578 percent (62 percent per year)

STOCK GROWTH ★

The company just issued its stock in 1998.

CONSISTENCY ★ ★ ★ ★

Increased earnings per share: four of the past four years
Increased revenue: four of the past four years

TECHNISOURCE AT A GLANCE

Fiscal year ended: Dec. 31
Revenue and net income in $ millions

	1994	1995	1996	1997	1998	4-Year Growth	
						Avg. Annual (%)	Total (%)
Revenue ($)	15.6	29.1	40.4	67.3	105.7	62	578
Net income ($)	0.6	1.48	1.9	2.51	4.54	66	657
Earnings/share ($)	0.08	0.21	0.26	0.35	0.48	58	500
Avg. PE ratio	—	—	—	—	23	—	—

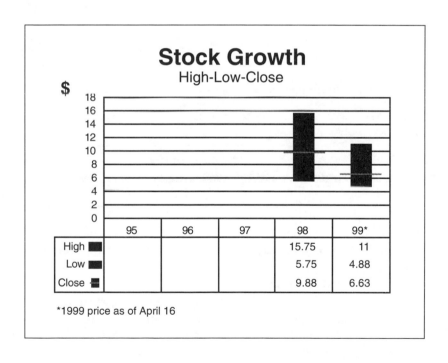

Stock Growth
High-Low-Close

$	95	96	97	98	99*
High				15.75	11
Low				5.75	4.88
Close				9.88	6.63

*1999 price as of April 16

Standard Pacific Corp.

 Standard Pacific

1565 W. MacArthur Blvd.
Costa Mesa, CA 92626
714-668-4300

Chairman and CEO:
Arthur E. Svendsen
President:
Stephen J. Scarborough

Earnings Growth	★ ★ ★ ★
Revenue Growth	★ ★ ★
Stock Growth	★ ★ ★ ★
Consistency	★ ★
NYSE: SPF	**13 points**

Standard Pacific has been building single-family homes in California for more than 30 years.

The Costa Mesa, California builder began in 1966 with a single tract of land in Orange County, California. Now it builds nearly 2,000 new homes each year. In all, the company has put up more than 35,000 homes, all in either California or Texas.

Most of Standard Pacific's homes are priced in the $150,000 to $400,000 range, with an average price of about $310,000. The company also builds some higher-end models that sell for as much as $800,000 in certain California markets.

About 80 percent of Standard Pacific's homes are built in California. Leading areas include Orange County, which accounts for about 25 percent of all new homes; San Francisco, which accounts for about 33 percent; San Diego, 7 percent; and Ventura County, 14 percent.

The other 20 percent are built in Texas, with 8 percent in Houston and 12 percent in the Dallas-Austin area.

Standard Pacific gears its marketing efforts to families who are move-up buyers—those who have owned a smaller home and are looking to move up to a larger, nicer home. Most of Standard Pacific homes are large, modern, high-quality dwellings ranging from about 1,500 to 5,000 square feet.

The company typically builds homes in groups, first acquiring unimproved or improved land zoned for residential use with enough space to build 50 to 500 homes. It generally begins a development with 10 to 30 homes, selling them almost as they build them, and then adds more homes over the years in additional increments of 10 to 30 units.

Standard Pacific recently formed its own mortgage lending agency, Family Lending Services, which is designed to help their homebuyers gain financing more conveniently.

Standard Pacific has about 430 employees and a market capitalization of about $400 million.

EARNINGS PER SHARE GROWTH ★ ★ ★ ★

Past four years: 732 percent (69 percent per year)

REVENUE GROWTH ★ ★ ★

Past four years: 82 percent (16 percent per year)

STOCK GROWTH ★ ★ ★ ★

Past three years: 121 percent (30 percent per year)
Dollar growth: $10,000 over the past three years would have grown to about $22,000.

CONSISTENCY ★ ★

Increased earnings per share: three of the past four years
Increased revenue: three of the past four years

STANDARD PACIFIC AT A GLANCE

Fiscal year ended: Dec. 31
Revenue and net income in $ millions

	1994	1995	1996	1997	1998	4-Year Growth Avg. Annual (%)	4-Year Growth Total (%)
Revenue ($)	417.9	346.3	399.9	584.6	759.6	16	82
Net income ($)	5.89	−22.4	7.75	24.0	47.4	68	705
Earnings/share ($)	0.19	−0.73	0.26	0.81	1.58	69	732
Avg. PE ratio	46	—	25	14	9	—	—

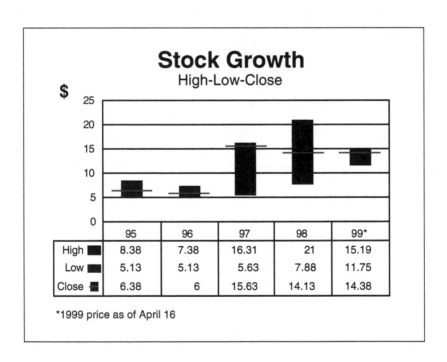

Stock Growth
High-Low-Close

	95	96	97	98	99*
High	8.38	7.38	16.31	21	15.19
Low	5.13	5.13	5.63	7.88	11.75
Close	6.38	6	15.63	14.13	14.38

*1999 price as of April 16

Stericycle, Inc.

28161 North Keith Drive
Lake Forest, IL 60045
847-945-6550
www.stericycle.com

Chairman:
Jack W. Schuler
President and CEO:
Mark C. Miller

Earnings Growth	★ ★ ★
Revenue Growth	★ ★ ★ ★
Stock Growth	★ ★
Consistency	★ ★ ★ ★
Nasdaq: SRCL	**13 points**

Stericycle specializes in medical waste. The company collects, transports, treats, and, when possible, recycles all types of medical wastes from hospitals, nursing homes, medical centers, schools, veterinary offices, fire and police departments, correctional facilities, funeral homes, dental offices, laboratories, dialysis centers, and other facilities.

The firm has treatment networks in nine geographic markets and serves nearly 40,000 customers in more than 30 states and the District of Columbia. The company operates a fleet of more than 150 vehicles to transport waste and uses well over 100 sales and market professionals who drum up new business.

Stericycle has grown through an aggressive series of acquisitions. After acquiring the medical waste business of Waste Management recently, Stericycle became the second largest medical waste service business in the United States.

Unlike most of its competitors who handle medical waste as part of a broader scope of waste services, Stericycle focuses exclusively on medical waste. The company's strategy is to continue to expand its customer base by acquiring smaller specialty medical waste companies throughout the country.

The Deerfield, Illinois operation uses its own proprietary waste treatment process called Electro-Thermal Deactivation (ETD). ETD uses an oscillating energy field of low-frequency radio waves to heat medical waste to temperatures that destroy pathogens without melting the plastic component of the waste.

The process kills potential human pathogens in the waste material and reduces the volume of medical waste by as much as 85 percent. It also provides for the recovery and recycling of usable plastics from the waste and allows the remaining medical waste to be safely landfilled or used as an alternative fuel in energy production.

Stericycle was founded in 1989. It went public with its initial stock offering in 1996. The company has about 400 employees and a market capitalization of about $200 million.

EARNINGS PER SHARE GROWTH ★ ★ ★

Past one year: 257 percent

REVENUE GROWTH ★ ★ ★ ★

Past four years: 314 percent (43 percent per year)

STOCK GROWTH ★ ★

Past two years: 40 percent (18 percent per year)
Dollar growth: $10,000 over the past two years would have grown to $14,000.

CONSISTENCY ★ ★ ★ ★

Increased earnings per share: four of the past four years
Increased revenue: four of the past four years

STERICYCLE AT A GLANCE

Fiscal year ended: Dec. 31
Revenue and net income in $ millions

	1994	1995	1996	1997	1998	4-Year Growth Avg. Annual (%)	4-Year Growth Total (%)
Revenue ($)	16.1	21.3	24.5	46.2	66.7	43	314
Net income ($)	−5.81	−4.54	−2.39	1.43	5.71	—	299*
Earnings/share ($)	−4.88	−0.81	−0.32	0.14	0.50	—	257*
Avg. PE ratio	—	—	—	83	33	—	—

*Net income and earnings per share returns are one-year performance measures.

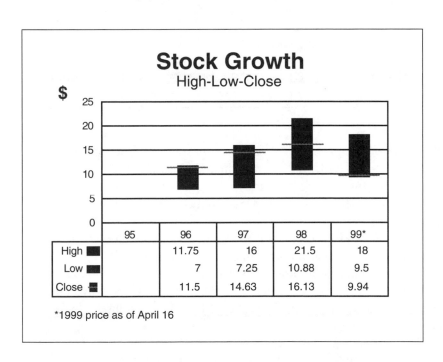

Stock Growth
High-Low-Close

$	95	96	97	98	99*
High		11.75	16	21.5	18
Low		7	7.25	10.88	9.5
Close		11.5	14.63	16.13	9.94

*1999 price as of April 16

30
FDP Corp.

2140 South Dixie Highway
Miami, FL 33133
305-858-8200
www.fdpcorp.com

Chairman, President, and CEO:
Michael C. Goldberg

Earnings Growth	★ ★ ★ ★
Revenue Growth	★ ★
Stock Growth	★ ★ ★
Consistency	★ ★ ★ ★
Nasdaq: FDPC	**13 points**

FDP's line of specialty software helps insurance agents and employee benefits managers build and operate their businesses.

The company's client base includes some of the nation's largest insurers, such as The Prudential, Metropolitan Life, New York Life, and John Hancock.

The Miami-based operation's Pension Partner software is used to promote sales of and assist in the administration of defined benefits, defined contributions, and cafeteria plans by providing clients with an analysis of tax benefits and funding assumptions. The software is used by actuaries, life insurance agents, employee benefit plan consultants, attorneys, bankers, and accountants.

FDP's Agency Partner software is used by life insurance agents to demonstrate to their clients interest-sensitive and other life insurance policies, and to market and manage their prospects and clients.

The firm also offers Home Office Systems software for use by life insurance company home offices and other financial institutions to handle administration and processing requirements of life insurance, pension, and annuity products.

FDP has been successful at penetrating its core market because it solves some problems that insurance agents and benefits managers have faced in the past. Traditionally, insurance companies have had to buy and integrate a variety of software packages to meet all of their needs. Each application had its own data storage and user interfacing, causing data to be entered and stored independently. That resulted in added expenses and duplication of training and resources.

With FDP's software, all systems share the same information, eliminating the need for repetitive data entry, reducing the risk of errors, and providing easy access to data.

FDP was founded in 1968 by Michael C. Goldberg, who still serves as chairman, president, and CEO, and owns about a 51 percent share of the stock. The company has about 400 employees and a market capitalization of about $65 million.

EARNINGS PER SHARE GROWTH ★ ★ ★ ★

Past four years: 377 percent (47 percent per year)

REVENUE GROWTH ★ ★

Past four years: 122 percent (22 percent per year)

STOCK GROWTH ★ ★ ★

Past three years: 97 percent (25 percent per year)
Dollar growth: $10,000 over the past three years would have grown to about $20,000.

CONSISTENCY ★ ★ ★ ★

Increased earnings per share: four of the past four years
Increased revenue: four of the past four years

FDP AT A GLANCE

Fiscal year ended: Nov. 30
Revenue and net income in $ millions

	1994	1995	1996	1997	1998	4-Year Growth Avg. Annual (%)	Total (%)
Revenue ($)	18.4	19.4	26.4	32.8	40.9	22	122
Net income ($)	0.652	1.46	2.23	2.98	3.83	56	487
Earnings/share ($)	0.13	0.27	0.39	0.50	0.62	47	377
Avg. PE ratio	29	18	21	17	19	—	—

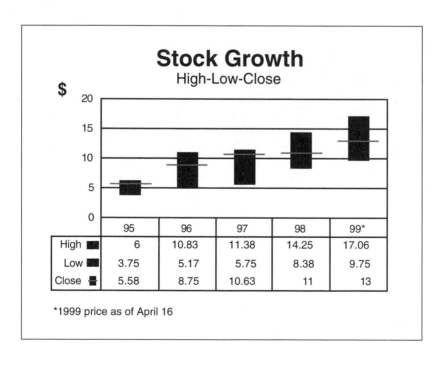

Stock Growth
High-Low-Close

	95	96	97	98	99*
High	6	10.83	11.38	14.25	17.06
Low	3.75	5.17	5.75	8.38	9.75
Close	5.58	8.75	10.63	11	13

*1999 price as of April 16

31
ATEC Group, Inc.

90 Adams Avenue
Hauppauge, NY 11788
516-231-2832
www.atecgroup.com

Chairman and CEO:
Surinder Rametra
President:
Balwinder Singh Batthla

Earnings Growth	★ ★ ★ ★
Revenue Growth	★ ★ ★ ★
Stock Growth	★ ★
Consistency	★ ★ ★
Nasdaq: ATEC	**13 points**

ATEC Group is a one-stop shop serving the computer needs of businesses, professionals, government agencies, and educational institutions.

Its arsenal of services includes Y2K solutions, computer hardware, software, connectivity devices, multimedia products, data communication via satellite, video conferencing, system integration networking, high-speed data transmission, graphic arts, Internet, and intranet.

ATEC also has begun outsourcing information technology professionals for the telecommunications industry and offshore software development. The firm has teamed up with Switch Now (a New York company) to provide a broad range of telecommunications services through low-cost switching platforms capable of managing voice, fax, Internet, messaging, and other forms of communications traffic. Its target market is small and medium-size businesses, departments of large corporations, and telecommunications carriers that want to extend their services to the premises of new customers.

ATEC's leading business continues to be delivering computer technology to corporate clients. It is an authorized dealer of microcomputers, client/servers, and peripherals manufactured by major companies such as IBM, Compaq, Gateway, Hewlett-Packard, Apple, Novell, Informix, 3Com, Toshiba, Oracle, Sybase, and others.

ATEC also operates a digital arts division that sells and installs graphics software and then helps train clients in the use of the software.

ATEC acquired Logix Solutions, Inc., in 1998 to expand its Year 2000 computer solutions services. The firm offers assessment, planning, conversion, testing, and implementaion of Y2K solutions for corporations.

The firm also provides technical support services for corporate clients, including assistance in such computer-related areas as local and wide area networks, gateways, bridges, system conversion planning, hardware and software specifications, database/server development and implementation, video conferencing, and high speed data transmission.

The Hauppauge, New York operation went public with its intial stock offering in 1994. It has about 110 employees and a market capitalization of about $70 million.

EARNINGS PER SHARE GROWTH ★ ★ ★ ★

Past two years: 181 percent (67 percent per year)

REVENUE GROWTH ★ ★ ★ ★

Past four years: 330 percent (44 percent per year)

STOCK GROWTH ★ ★

Past three years: 68 percent (19 percent per year)
Dollar growth: $10,000 over the past three years would have grown to about $17,000.

CONSISTENCY ★ ★ ★

Increased earnings per share: three of the past four years
Increased revenue: four of the past four years

ATEC GROUP AT A GLANCE

Fiscal year ended: June 30
Revenue and net income in $ millions

	1994	1995	1996	1997	1998	4-Year Growth Avg. Annual (%)	Total (%)
Revenue ($)	43.5	47.6	81.8	100.8	187.2	44	330
Net income ($)	−0.226	−2.25	0.837	1.67	2.74	81*	227*
Earnings/share ($)	−0.22	−1.25	0.16	0.28	0.45	67*	181*
Avg. PE ratio	—	—	32	21	15	—	—

*Net income and earnings per share returns are based on two-year performance.

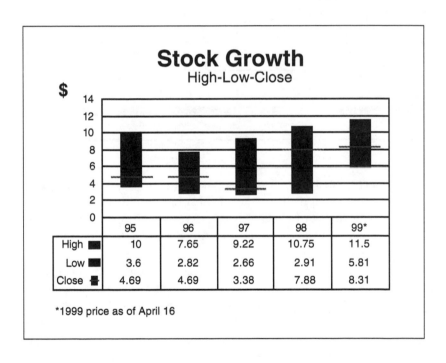

Stock Growth
High-Low-Close

	95	96	97	98	99*
High	10	7.65	9.22	10.75	11.5
Low	3.6	2.82	2.66	2.91	5.81
Close	4.69	4.69	3.38	7.88	8.31

*1999 price as of April 16

32
Essef Corporation

Essef

220 Park Drive
Chardon, OH 44024
440-286-2200
www.essef.com

Chairman:
Ralph T. King
President and CEO:
Thomas Waldin

Earnings Growth	★ ★ ★
Revenue Growth	★ ★ ★
Stock Growth	★ ★ ★ ★
Consistency	★ ★ ★
Nasdaq: ESSF	**13 points**

It's a wet business, but Essef has become a dominant player in the swimming pool and spa equipment market. It also has established a growing presence in the business of moving, treating, and storing water. It is the world's largest provider of composite components and subsystems for water and other liquids.

Essef makes water treatment systems and swimming pool and spa equipment for markets worldwide. Through its Anthony and Sylvan subsidiary, it is the leading designer and installer of in-ground concrete swimming pools in the United States.

The Chardon, Ohio operation's Pac-Fab division makes a broad range of swimming pool components, including high pressure pumps, sand filters, cartridge filters, heaters, valves, drains, fittings, underwater lights, skimmers, and accessories. Among its brands are WhisperFlo, Ultra-Flow, Challenger, Maxim, Pinnacle, and Triton.

Essef handles its other business lines through several divisions, including:

- *Structural pressure vessels.* The firm makes small composite and fiberglass pressure vessels used for filtration, ion exchange, hot water and liquid processing, and chemical storage.
- *Codeline pressure vessels.* The firm's high pressure housing for filtration and separations is used for reverse osmosis, ultrafiltration, and microfiltration of water and other liquid streams.
- *WellMate Water Systems.* The company makes composite hydropneumatic pressure vessels for water well and pressure boosting systems.
- *Enpac Corp.* The firm makes spill prevention and containment products for industrial and environmental applications.

Essef was founded in 1954 as a maker of fiberglass-reinforced plastic for aircraft and military components, but the corporate mission has changed radically since then. It eventually became the industry leader in the design and manufacture of water treatment pressure vessels. The company now has about 1,200 employees and a market capitalization of about $220 million.

EARNINGS PER SHARE GROWTH ★ ★ ★

Past four years: 144 percent (25 percent per year)

REVENUE GROWTH ★ ★ ★

Past four years: 225 percent (34 percent per year)

STOCK GROWTH ★ ★ ★ ★

Past three years: 195 percent (43 percent per year)
Dollar growth: $10,000 over the past three years would have grown to about $30,000.

CONSISTENCY ★ ★ ★

Increased earnings per share: three of the past four years
Increased revenue: four of the past four years

ESSEF AT A GLANCE

Fiscal year ended: Sept. 30
Revenue and net income in $ millions

	1994	1995	1996	1997	1998	4-Year Growth Avg. Annual (%)	Total (%)
Revenue ($)	134.0	149.3	193.8	306.1	436.0	34	225
Net income ($)	7.0	5.9	9.3	11.8	16.6	24	137
Earnings/share ($)	0.50	0.42	0.64	0.84	1.22	25	144
Avg. PE ratio	13	16	11	14	13	—	—

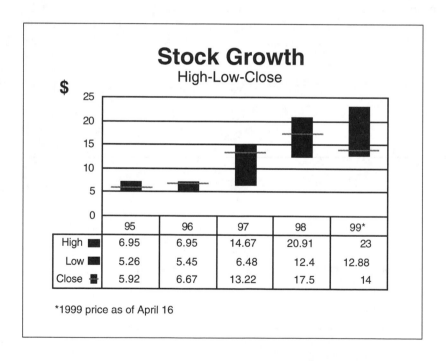

Stock Growth
High-Low-Close

	95	96	97	98	99*
High	6.95	6.95	14.67	20.91	23
Low	5.26	5.45	6.48	12.4	12.88
Close	5.92	6.67	13.22	17.5	14

*1999 price as of April 16

33

Del Global Technologies Corp.

One Commerce Park
Valhalla, NY 10595
914-686-3600

Chairman, President, and CEO:
Leonard A. Trugman

Earnings Growth	★ ★ ★ ★
Revenue Growth	★ ★ ★
Stock Growth	★ ★
Consistency	★ ★ ★ ★
Nasdaq: DGTC	**13 points**

Del Global Technologies specializes in the design and manufacturing of medical imaging and diagnostic equipment, including mammography systems, high frequency X-ray generators, and stationary and portable imaging systems. Their products and systems are sold worldwide to a broad range of manufacturers, distributors, hospitals, radiologists, and defense agencies.

The Valhalla, New York manufacturer operates through six divisions, including:

1. *Gendex-Del* manufactures mammography systems, stationary imaging systems, high frequency X-ray generators, X-ray examination tables, and a full line of associated imaging accessories. The equipment is used by hospitals, clinics, private practices, and foreign governments.
2. *Dynarad* makes mobile medical imaging systems, portable dental X-ray units, and advanced neonatal imaging systems used by hospitals, clinics, private practices, sports complexes, and defense forces.

3. The *power conversion division* sells high-voltage power supplies to medical, industrial, and defense customers. Applications include medical scanning, laser surgery, nuclear medicine, blood analysis, and cancer therapy, as well as airport security systems, ion implantation, electron beam welding, energy exploration, and radar systems.
4. *Bertan* manufactures high-voltage power supplies and high-voltage instrumentation for a variety of medical applications, including bone densitometry imaging equipment, scanning electron microscopes, X-ray instrumentation, and electron beam systems.
5. *RFI* makes electronic noise suppression filters, high-voltage capacitors, pulse transformers, pulse forming networks, and specialty magnetics. Applications include cellular and hard-wired telecommunications systems, data communication equipment, and computer systems.
6. *Del Medical Systems* markets medical diagnostic products worldwide.

The firm markets its medical imaging systems through a network of about 250 dealers. Most of its sales are in the United States. Its electronic subsystems are sold worldwide through exclusive agents in Europe, Asia, the Middle East, Australia, and India.

Del Global was founded in 1954. It has about 500 employees and a market capitalization of about $90 million.

EARNINGS PER SHARE GROWTH ★ ★ ★ ★

Past four years: 196 percent (32 percent per year)

REVENUE GROWTH ★ ★ ★

Past four years: 156 percent (26 percent per year)

STOCK GROWTH ★ ★

Past three years: 86 percent (17 percent per year)
Dollar growth: $10,000 over the past three years would have grown to about $19,000.

CONSISTENCY ★ ★ ★ ★

Increased earnings per share: four of the past four years
Increased revenue: four of the past four years

DEL GLOBAL TECHNOLOGIES AT A GLANCE

Fiscal year ended: July 31
Revenue and net income in $ millions

	1994	1995	1996	1997	1998	4-Year Growth Avg. Annual (%)	4-Year Growth Total (%)
Revenue ($)	24.3	32.6	43.7	54.7	62.3	26	156
Net income ($)	1.1	1.9	2.9	4.9	5.8	52	427
Earnings/share ($)	0.26	0.43	0.59	0.66	0.77	32	196
Avg. PE ratio	24	13	21	15	13	—	—

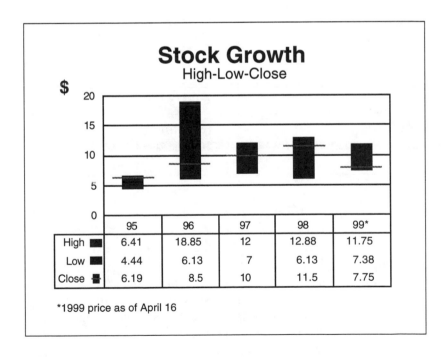

Stock Growth
High-Low-Close

	95	96	97	98	99*
High	6.41	18.85	12	12.88	11.75
Low	4.44	6.13	7	6.13	7.38
Close	6.19	8.5	10	11.5	7.75

*1999 price as of April 16

American Science & Engineering, Inc.

829 Middlesex Turnpike
Billerica, MA 01821
978-262-8700
www.as-e.com

Chairman:
Herman Feshbach
President and CEO:
Ralph S. Sheridan

Earnings Growth	★ ★ ★ ★
Revenue Growth	★ ★ ★
Stock Growth	★ ★
Consistency	★ ★ ★ ★
AMEX: ASE	**13 points**

Broad and all-inclusive as the name may sound, American Science & Engineering (ASE) actually operates in a very narrow realm of the scientific field. It makes X-ray machines designed to detect terrorist explosives, illegal drugs, and smuggled goods.

The firm's machines are used in border control, protection of high-risk government offices, mail and parcel screening, correctional facility security, military security, executive security, aviation security, and special event security (such as the Olympics and World Cup soccer).

ASE uses special transmission and backscatter X-ray detection to differentiate between bombs, drugs, and contraband in camouflaged environments.

The Massachusetts-based operation offers 12 models of X-ray machines within four model groups. Its Micro-Dose Model 101 Series includes six models—the Model 101Van, which is a vehicle-mounted inspection system used by U.S. Customs officials; the Model 101ZZ Trailer, which is a field-deployable system for extended on-site security details; and four move-able, conveyor-based systems that allow rapid inspection of high volumes of luggage and other packages.

Other models include the Model 66, which handles small packages; the CargoSearch family of machines used for X-ray scanning of trucks, cars, cargo containers, pallets, and air cargo; and the MobileSearch System, which is a self-contained unit inside a conventional truck that can be quickly deployed to remote areas. The MobileSearch Systems have become pop-ular with the U.S. government and some foreign governments.

Although the U.S. government had been by far the company's largest customer, ASE is expanding quickly into foreign markets. Foreign gov-ernments typically use ASE's equipment to protect against terrorist threats and trade fraud. U.S. government purchases once accounted for about 80 percent of the firm's revenue; now it accounts for about 50 percent of rev-enue, with foreign sales making up the other 50 percent.

ASE was founded in 1958. The company has about 200 employees and a market capitalization of about $55 million.

EARNINGS PER SHARE GROWTH ★ ★ ★ ★

Past two years: 456 percent (110 percent per year)

REVENUE GROWTH ★ ★ ★

Past four years: 195 percent (31 percent per year)

STOCK GROWTH ★ ★

Past three years: 50 percent (15 percent per year)
Dollar growth: $10,000 over the past three years would have grown to $15,000.

CONSISTENCY ★ ★ ★ ★

Increased earnings per share: four of the past four years
Increased revenue: four of the past four years

AMERICAN SCIENCE & ENGINEERING AT A GLANCE

Fiscal year ended: March 31
Revenue and net income in $ millions

	1994	1995	1996	1997	1998	4-Year Growth Avg. Annual (%)	Total (%)
Revenue ($)	11.1	13.0	17.8	28.5	32.7	31	195
Net income ($)	−3.3	−0.967	0.802	1.9	4.7	112*	486*
Earnings/share ($)	−0.83	−0.23	0.18	0.43	1.00	110*	456*
Avg. PE ratio	—	38	31	12	13	—	—

*Net income and earnings per share growth based on two-year performance.

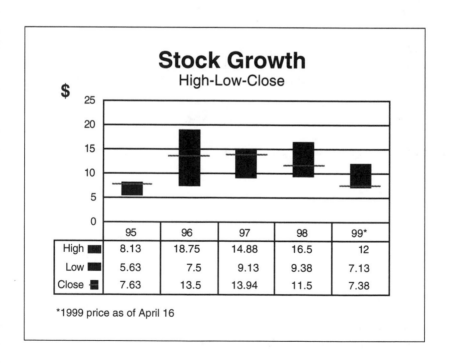

Stock Growth
High-Low-Close

	95	96	97	98	99*
High	8.13	18.75	14.88	16.5	12
Low	5.63	7.5	9.13	9.38	7.13
Close	7.63	13.5	13.94	11.5	7.38

*1999 price as of April 16

DBT Online, Inc.

DBT ONLINE

5550 W. Flamingo Road
Suite B-5
Las Vegas, NV 89103
702-257-1112

Chairman:
Frank Borman
President and CEO:
Charles A. Lieppe

Earnings Growth	★ ★ ★ ★
Revenue Growth	★ ★ ★ ★
Stock Growth	★ ★ ★
Consistency	★ ★
NYSE: DBT	**13 points**

DBT Online is in the information-gathering business. The company provides online information on millions of individuals and businesses for law enforcement agencies and other government services, law firms, insurance companies, and investigation companies.

Users of the service can access the wealth of information and print out full reports from their own desktop computers. In preparing the reports, the DBT system automatically accesses more than a thousand data sources containing billions of records as if they were all part of a single database.

The Las Vegas operation's leading product is AutoTrack Plus, which provides online access to billions of national, state, and county public records 24 hours a day, seven days a week. Users can search a particular database, then cross-reference other databases within AutoTrack Plus to expand the information available.

AutoTrack can help users find current and past addresses, telephone numbers, neighbors, and associates, as well as professional licenses, driving histories, business profile reports, real estate, vehicles, and other assets.

DBT also offers AutoTrack information packages on "Corporations of the Nation," "Properties of the Nation," "Vehicles of the Nation," "Drivers of the Nation," and "Liens/Judgments/Bankruptcies" (which contains information on business and consumer bankruptcies and related information in all 50 states).

The firm's customer base has grown rapidly, from about 1,000 users in 1994 to well over 10,000 currently.

DBT also operates a patent enforcement business called Patlex, which enforces the laser patent established by Gordon Gould in 1959. The firm identifies laser products and laser applications that infringe on Gould's laser patent and executes licensing agreements allowing manufacturers to use the laser technology.

DBT went public with its intial stock offering in 1996. The firm has about 225 employees and a market capitalization of about $315 million.

EARNINGS PER SHARE GROWTH   ★ ★ ★ ★

Past four years: 483 percent (56 percent per year)

REVENUE GROWTH   ★ ★ ★ ★

Past four years: 1,845 percent (106 percent per year)

STOCK GROWTH   ★ ★ ★

Past two years: 67 percent (29 percent per year)
Dollar growth: $10,000 over the past two years would have grown to about $17,000.

CONSISTENCY   ★ ★

Increased earnings per share: two of the past four years
Increased revenue: four of the past four years

DBT ONLINE AT A GLANCE

Fiscal year ended: Dec. 31
Revenue and net income in $ millions

	1994	1995	1996	1997	1998	4-Year Growth Avg. Annual (%)	4-Year Growth Total (%)
Revenue ($)	2.75	8.08	18.7	37.5	53.5	106	1,845
Net income ($)	0.43	−1.19	0.52	6.0	6.7	99	1,458
Earnings/share ($)	0.06	−0.13	0.04	0.35	0.35	56	483
Avg. PE ratio	—	—	410	71	65	—	—

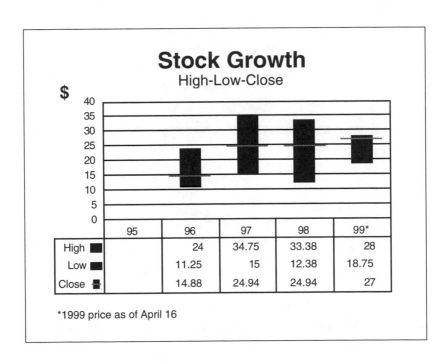

Stock Growth
High-Low-Close

	95	96	97	98	99*
High ■		24	34.75	33.38	28
Low ■		11.25	15	12.38	18.75
Close ▤		14.88	24.94	24.94	27

*1999 price as of April 16

Ingram Micro, Inc.

1600 East St. Andrew Place
Santa Ana, CA 92799
714-566-1000
www.ingrammicro.com

Chairman and CEO:
Jerre Stead
President:
Jeffrey Rodek

Earnings Growth	★ ★ ★
Revenue Growth	★ ★ ★ ★
Stock Growth	★ ★
Consistency	★ ★ ★ ★
NYSE: IM	**13 points**

Ingram Micro sells computers by the millions.

The Santa Ana, California operation is the leading worldwide wholesale distributor of computer-based technology products, including PCs and other microcomputer hardware, networking equipment, and software.

Ingram markets computer products from more than 1,400 manufacturers and suppliers. Its customer base includes major retailers and other resellers around the world. In all, Ingram has more than 100,000 reseller customers in 120 countries.

The company sells more than 150,000 products, including desktop and notebook PCs, servers and workstations, storage devices, CD-ROM drives, monitors, printers, scanners, modems, networking hubs, routers, switches, network interface cards, and a wide range of business and entertainment software.

Ingram handles products from nearly every major manufacturer, including Microsoft, IBM, Compaq, Apple, Corel, Epson, Hewlett-Packard, Intel, Novell, Sun Microsystems, 3Com, and Cisco Systems.

Its customer base includes a number of leading computer resellers, such as CompUSA, Office Max, PC Connection, Staples, Electronic Data Systems, and Connected Resources.

The firm markets its products through more than 2,000 telesales representatives around the world. Ingram also has more than 200 field agents around the world. The company has 33 distribution centers worldwide and attempts to maintain high order fill rates by maintaining an extensive inventory of supplies.

In addition to wholesale products, Ingram offers some value-added services, including technical support, order fulfillment, financing programs, contract warehousing, contract telesales, and contract inventory management. The company also assembles and configures computer systems for Acer, Compaq, Digital Equipment, IBM, and Hewlett-Packard.

Ingram was founded as Micro D, Inc., in 1979 and grew through a series of acquisitions and mergers. The company went public with its initial stock offering in 1996. Ingram has about 12,000 employees and a market capitalization of about $2.6 billion.

EARNINGS PER SHARE GROWTH ★ ★ ★

Past four years: 178 percent (29 percent per year)

REVENUE GROWTH ★ ★ ★ ★

Past four years: 277 percent (40 percent per year)

STOCK GROWTH ★ ★

Past two years: 53 percent (24 percent per year)
Dollar growth: $10,000 over the past two years would have grown to about $15,000.

CONSISTENCY ★ ★ ★ ★

Increased earnings per share: four of the past four years
Increased revenue: four of the past four years

INGRAM MICRO AT A GLANCE

Fiscal year ended: Dec. 31
Revenue and net income in $ millions

	1994	1995	1996	1997	1998	4-Year Growth Avg. Annual (%)	4-Year Growth Total (%)
Revenue ($)	5.83	8.62	12.02	16.6	22.0	40	277
Net income ($)	61.1	81.5	111.9	195.0	245.4	42	302
Earnings/share ($)	0.59	0.79	0.99	1.43	1.64	29	178
Avg. PE ratio	—	—	25	19	25	—	—

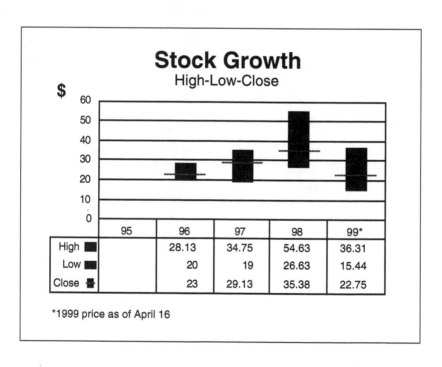

Stock Growth
High-Low-Close

	95	96	97	98	99*
High		28.13	34.75	54.63	36.31
Low		20	19	26.63	15.44
Close		23	29.13	35.38	22.75

*1999 price as of April 16

37

Astronics Corporation

ASTRONICS CORPORATION

1801 Elmwood Avenue
Buffalo, NY 14207
716-447-9013

President and CEO:
Kevin T. Keane

Earnings Growth	★ ★ ★ ★
Revenue Growth	★
Stock Growth	★ ★ ★ ★
Consistency	★ ★ ★ ★
Nasdaq: ATRO	**13 points**

Astronics helps brighten the night. The company designs and manufactures electroluminescent (EL) lamps, which use phosphors to emit light. Its EL lamps are efficient, durable, thin, and flexible. They are used for automobiles, home light fixtures, and consumer electronics.

The Buffalo-based operation also makes power conversion devices known as "inverters" that are used to power the EL lamps. Astronics also makes other types of lighting sources, including incandescent lights, light-emitting diodes, and cold cathode fluorescence lights.

Its lighting systems are used in a wide range of applications, including escape path lighting or exit signs for buildings, aircraft, and trains. It also makes aircraft cockpit lighting systems for commercial and military aricraft, as well as military aircraft formation lights found on most modern Western military aircraft.

EL lamps produce light by sandwiching phosphors between two electrodes that are exposed to alternating current. EL lights are bright yet cheap to operate.

Lighting systems account for about 50 percent of the company's $40 million in annual revenue. About 27 percent of its lighting business comes from outside the United States.

The company's other primary segment is specialty packaging, which accounts for the other 50 percent of revenue. Astronics designs and manufactures folding cartons and presentation products for about 10,000 corporate customers in ten countries. Astronics also produces wedding and party invitations, monogrammed napkins, and related party accessories. Its specialty printed products are marketed through stationery stores, printers, gift shops, and specialty boutiques in the United States.

The firm also makes ruggedized keyboards used primarily by the military. The keyboards range from simple mechanical devices to complex systems that utilize encoding topologies and communication protocols.

Astronics has been in business for more than 25 years. It has about 450 employees and a market capitalization of about $43 million.

EARNINGS PER SHARE GROWTH ★ ★ ★ ★

Past four years: 204 percent (31 percent per year)

REVENUE GROWTH ★

Past four years: 85 percent (17 percent per year)

STOCK GROWTH ★ ★ ★ ★

Past three years: 277 percent (56 percent per year)
Dollar growth: $10,000 over the past three years would have grown to about $38,000.

CONSISTENCY ★ ★ ★ ★

Increased earnings per share: four of the past four years
Increased revenue: four of the past four years

ASTRONICS AT A GLANCE

Fiscal year ended: Dec. 31
Revenue and net income in $ millions

	1994	1995	1996	1997	1998	4-Year Growth Avg. Annual (%)	4-Year Growth Total (%)
Revenue ($)	24.9	28.5	38.4	41.0	46.1	17	85
Net income ($)	1.31	1.76	2.66	3.55	4.30	34	228
Earnings/share ($)	0.24	0.37	0.51	0.65	0.73	31	204
Avg. PE ratio	8	6	8	12	14	—	—

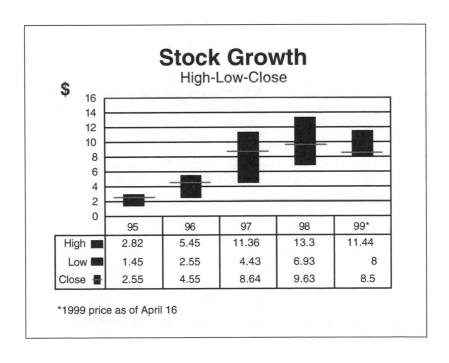

Stock Growth
High-Low-Close

	95	96	97	98	99*
High	2.82	5.45	11.36	13.3	11.44
Low	1.45	2.55	4.43	6.93	8
Close	2.55	4.55	8.64	9.63	8.5

*1999 price as of April 16

CryoLife, Inc.

CryoLife, Inc.

1655 Roberts Boulevard N.W.
Kennesaw, GA 30144
770-419-3355
www.cryolife.com

Chairman, President, and CEO:
Steven G. Anderson

Earnings Growth	★ ★ ★ ★
Revenue Growth	★ ★ ★
Stock Growth	★ ★
Consistency	★ ★ ★ ★
NYSE: CRY	**13 points**

If you can believe Hollywood's vision of the future, someday scientists may be able to freeze human beings alive and suspend them safely in time to be revived at some later date.

That futuristic fantasy is beginning to show very preliminary signs of reality, thanks to a new technology used by CryoLife. The Kennesaw, Georgia operation is the first biomedical company to develop a commercially viable ultra-low-temperature process for preserving human tissue for transplants.

The CryoLife process is used to preserve human heart valves and vascular and orthopedic connective tissue for use in transplant operations by cardiovascular, vascular, and orthopedic surgeons.

CryoLife provides about 80 percent of the cryopreserved human tissue implanted in the United States.

The company also makes stentless porcine heart valves for the European market and an extensive line of specialty cardiovascular and vascular medical instruments and devices. The firm's research scientists are also in the process of developing surgical bioadhesives (BioGlue surgical adhesive) and a variety of new tissue-engineered implantable living biological devices.

CryoLife's key business, however, continues to be its cryopreservation of human heart valves and conduits, human vascular tissue, and human connective tissue for the knee. Its cryopreservation business accounts for about 87 percent of total revenue.

Cryopreserved heart valves and conduits have certain advantages over mechanical, synthetic, and animal-derived alternatives, including more natural functionality, elimination of a chronic need for anticoagulation drug therapy, reduced incidence of reoperation, and reduced risk of catastrophic failure, stroke, or calcification.

The firm supplies the medical market through its relationship with more than 250 tissue banks and organ procurement agencies nationwide.

The company was founded in 1987 and went public with its initial stock offering in 1993. It has 330 employees and a market capitalization of about $160 million.

EARNINGS PER SHARE GROWTH ★ ★ ★ ★

Past four years: 271 percent (39 percent per year)

REVENUE GROWTH ★ ★ ★

Past four years: 155 percent (26 percent per year)

STOCK GROWTH ★ ★

Past three years: 53 percent (15 percent per year)
Dollar growth: $10,000 over the past three years would have grown to about $15,000.

CONSISTENCY ★ ★ ★ ★

Increased earnings per share: four of the past four years
Increased revenue: four of the past four years

CRYOLIFE AT A GLANCE

Fiscal year ended: Dec. 31
Revenue and net income in $ millions

	1994	1995	1996	1997	1998	4-Year Growth Avg. Annual (%)	Total (%)
Revenue ($)	23.8	29.2	37.2	50.9	60.7	26	155
Net income ($)	1.27	2.20	3.93	4.73	6.44	51	407
Earnings/share ($)	0.14	0.23	0.41	0.49	0.52	39	271
Avg. PE ratio	26	26	34	28	27	—	—

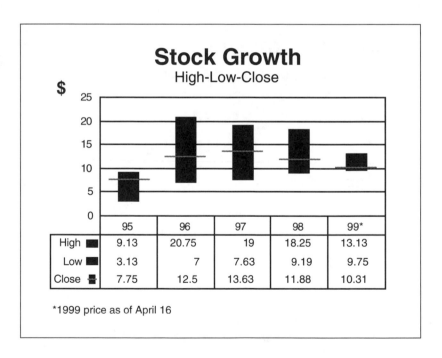

Stock Growth
High-Low-Close

	95	96	97	98	99*
High	9.13	20.75	19	18.25	13.13
Low	3.13	7	7.63	9.19	9.75
Close	7.75	12.5	13.63	11.88	10.31

*1999 price as of April 16

Litchfield Financial Corporation

430 Main Road
Williamstown, MA 01267
413-458-1000
lfc@ltchfld.com (E-mail)

President and CEO:
Richard A. Stratton

Earnings Growth	★ ★
Revenue Growth	★ ★ ★ ★
Stock Growth	★ ★ ★
Consistency	★ ★ ★ ★
Nasdaq: LTCH	**13 points**

Litchfield Financial is a specialty finance company that offers loans primarily for time-share operations.

The Williamstown, Massachusetts operation provides financing for the purchase of rural and vacation properties and vacation ownership interests—known as time-share interests—and provides financing to rural land dealers, time-share resort developers, and others for the development of rural land and time-share resorts. The loans are secured by consumer receivables.

The company has made land loans secured by property located in 34 states, primarily in the southern United States. Its VOI loans are used to finance the purchase of ownership interests in fully furnished vacation properties and are secured by the property. The company has outstanding loans for property in California, Florida, Pennsylvania, and about 15 other states.

Litchfield also makes acquisition and development loans to rural land dealers with whom it has ongoing relationships for the acquisition and subdivision of rural land, and to resort developers for the acquisition and development of time-share resorts. Its loans typically have a loan-to-value ratio of 60 to 80 percent and a variable interest rate based on the prime plus 2 to 4 percent.

The company also purchases other loans, such as consumer home equity loans, builder construction loans, and consumer construction loans.

It also provides financing to other businesses secured by receivables or other assets.

Litchfield's largest segment is its purchased loans from land dealers and resort developers. The dealers and developers typically make loans to consumers using Litchfield's standard forms and urderwriting criteria. Litchfield then purchases the loans, if they meet specific credit guidelines.

Litchfield's principal sources of revenue are interest and fees on loans, gain from the sale of loans, and servicing and other fee income.

The company was founded in November 1988. It went public with its initial stock offering in 1992. Litchfield has about 100 employees and a market capitalization of about $145 million.

EARNINGS PER SHARE GROWTH ★ ★

Past four years: 102 percent (19 percent per year)

REVENUE GROWTH ★ ★ ★ ★

Past four years: 253 percent (37 percent per year)

STOCK GROWTH ★ ★ ★

Past three years: 53 percent (15 percent per year)
Dollar growth: $10,000 over the past three years would have grown to about $15,000.

CONSISTENCY ★ ★ ★ ★

Increased earnings per share: four of the past four years
Increased revenue: four of the past four years

LITCHFIELD FINANCIAL AT A GLANCE

Fiscal year ended: Dec. 31
Revenue and net income in $ millions

						4-Year Growth	
						Avg. Annual (%)	Total (%)
	1994	**1995**	**1996**	**1997**	**1998**		
Revenue ($)	11.0	17.5	23.7	29.7	38.8	37	253
Net income ($)	2.7	3.45	5.27	6.58	8.83	33	227
Earnings/share ($)	0.66	0.80	0.95	1.18	1.33	19	102
Avg. PE ratio	17	16	13	15	13	—	—

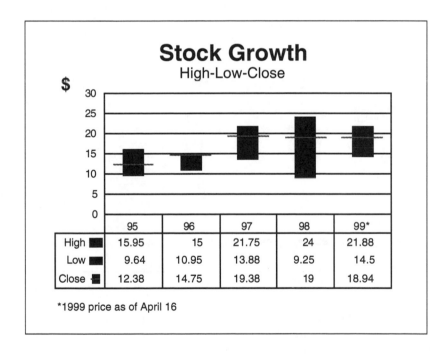

Stock Growth
High-Low-Close

$

	95	96	97	98	99*
High	15.95	15	21.75	24	21.88
Low	9.64	10.95	13.88	9.25	14.5
Close	12.38	14.75	19.38	19	18.94

*1999 price as of April 16

40

Global Payment Technologies, Inc.

GLOBAL PAYMENT TECHNOLOGIES

20 East Sunrise Highway
Suite 201
Valley Stream, NY 11581
516-256-1000
www.gpt.thomasregister.com

Chairman and CEO:
Stephen Katz
President:
William H. Wood

Earnings Growth	★ ★
Revenue Growth	★ ★ ★ ★
Stock Growth	★ ★ ★ ★
Consistency	★ ★
Nasdaq: GPTX	**12 points**

Next time you feed a dollar bill into a vending machine or a casino slot machine, you may be feeding the coffers of Global Payment Technologies (GPT). The Valley Stream, New York operation is a leading manufacturer of automated currency acceptance and validation systems used in vending and gaming machines.

GPT sells its products worldwide. Sales to the casino industry account for about 79 percent of the firm's revenues, while sales to the beverage and vending industry make up the other 21 percent. GPT recently created a new division to concentrate specifically on pumping up sales in the beverage and vending sectors.

The company custom-manufactures its currency acceptance systems to fit the requirements of vending and gaming machine manufacturers.

GPT is constantly working on new technologies to keep its products up-to-date. Although its validators are not 100 percent counterfeit-currency-proof, they do offer significant protection against tampering and counterfeit currencies.

The firm has been developing validators with multiple-country currency-reading capability. It also has been developing coupon and bar code scanning systems for retailers. Another concept in the product pipeline is a bill validator for cash registers that includes a computer chip that tracks all transactions, including the number of bills inserted as well as their denomination and total amount of money enclosed in the cash register box before being delivered to the bank.

Marketing of the machines both in the United States and internationally is handled by GPT's in-house sales force.

GPT was formed in 1988 under the name Coin Bill Validator, Inc. The company changed to its current name in 1997. GPT went public with its initial stock offering in 1995. The firm has about 250 employees and a market capitalization of about $40 million.

EARNINGS PER SHARE GROWTH ★ ★

Past four years: 97 percent (18 percent per year)

REVENUE GROWTH ★ ★ ★ ★

Past four years: 306 percent (43 percent per year)

STOCK GROWTH ★ ★ ★ ★

Past three years: 150 percent (35 percent per year)
Dollar growth: $10,000 over the past three years would have grown to $25,000.

CONSISTENCY ★ ★

Increased earnings per share: two of the past four years
Increased revenue: four of the past four years

GLOBAL PAYMENT TECHNOLOGIES AT A GLANCE

Fiscal year ended: Sept. 30
Revenue and net income in $ millions

	1994	1995	1996	1997	1998	4-Year Growth Avg. Annual (%)	4-Year Growth Total (%)
Revenue ($)	9.7	14.1	16.7	23.9	39.4	43	306
Net income ($)	1.4	1.2	0.28	1.5	3.4	9	43
Earnings/share ($)	0.31	0.22	0.05	0.275	0.61	18	97
Avg. PE ratio	—	18	97	31	16	—	—

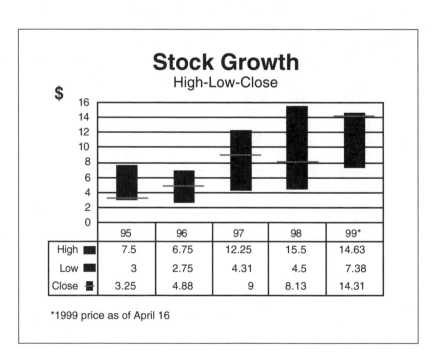

Stock Growth
High-Low-Close

	95	96	97	98	99*
High	7.5	6.75	12.25	15.5	14.63
Low	3	2.75	4.31	4.5	7.38
Close	3.25	4.88	9	8.13	14.31

*1999 price as of April 16

41

Compass International Services Corporation

One Penn Plaza
Suite 4430
New York, NY 10119
212-967-7770
www.compassisc.com

Chairman and CEO:
Michael J. Cunningham
President:
Mahmud U. Haq

Earnings Growth	★ ★ ★ ★
Revenue Growth	★ ★ ★ ★
Stock Growth	★
Consistency	★ ★ ★
Nasdaq: CMPS	**12 points**

Compass International Services helps its clients find their way through a broad range of operations. Compass is an outsourcing operation that specializes in accounts receivable, mailing services, and teleservices for a variety of industries, including telecommunications, financial services, insurance, health care, education, government, and utilities.

The firm also offers an accelerated payment systems service with a telephone check drafting service that allows clients to accept payments through checks authorized by phone.

The New York–based business operates five separate subsidiaries, including:

1. *The Mail Box, Inc.* Founded in 1971, Mail Box provides direct mailing services, billing, mail presorting, freight and drop shipping, data

processing, laser printing, mailing list rental, and related services to companies located in the southwest United States.

2. *National Credit Management Corp.* Founded in 1984, the firm provides accounts receivable management services and telephonic check drafting services.

3. *BRMC.* Founded in 1984, the company provides accounts receivable management services for clients in the telecommunications, insurance, financial services, and health care industries.

4. *Mid-Continent Agencies.* Founded in 1932, Mid-Continent offers accounts receivable management services to companies in the manufacturing, insurance, wholesale distribution, and commercial sectors.

5. *Impact Telemarketing Group.* Founded in 1984, Impact provides outbound telemarketing services to national and regional companies in the insurance, financial services, telecommunications, and utilities industries.

Compass has expanded its business through a series of acquisitions and through internal growth strategies involving cross-selling of its core business services to existing clients.

The company went public with its initial stock offering in 1998. Compass has about 1,000 employees and a market capitalization of about $150 million.

EARNINGS PER SHARE GROWTH ★ ★ ★ ★

Past four years: 1,433 percent (95 percent per year)

REVENUE GROWTH ★ ★ ★ ★

Past four years: 725 percent (70 percent per year)

STOCK GROWTH ★

The company just issued stock in 1998.

CONSISTENCY ★ ★ ★

Increased earnings per share: three of the past four years
Increased revenue: four of the past four years

COMPASS INTERNATIONAL SERVICES AT A GLANCE

Fiscal year ended: Dec. 31
Revenue and net income in $ millions

	1994	1995	1996	1997	1998	4-Year Growth Avg. Annual (%)	4-Year Growth Total (%)
Revenue ($)	15.4	17.4	26.2	32.6	127.1	70	725
Net income ($)	0.326	0.162	1.28	1.88	6.01	107	1,744
Earnings/share ($)	0.03	0.02	0.12	0.18	0.46	95	1,433
Avg. PE ratio	—	—	—	—	26	—	—

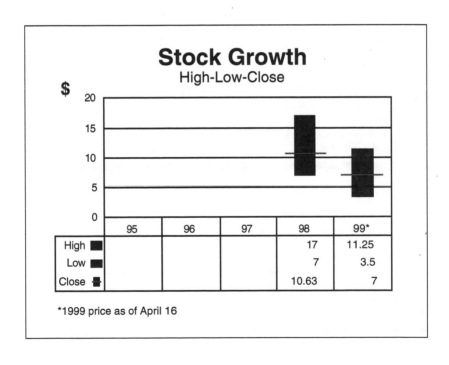

Stock Growth
High-Low-Close

	95	96	97	98	99*
High				17	11.25
Low				7	3.5
Close				10.63	7

*1999 price as of April 16

Chase Corporation

26 Summer Street
Braintree, MA 02324
508-279-1789
www.chasecorp.com

President and CEO:
Peter R. Chase

Earnings Growth	★ ★ ★ ★
Revenue Growth	
Stock Growth	★ ★ ★ ★
Consistency	★ ★ ★ ★
AMEX: CCF	**12 points**

Chase Corporation is a broadly diversified holding company, with market positions in several specialties, including wire and cable, specialty chemicals, bridge construction, advanced converting, and electronics.

The Braintree, Massachusetts business operates several subsidiaries, including the following:

- *Chase & Sons* produces insulating and semiconducting tapes and water blocking compounds for power and telecommunications companies.
- *Chase Canada* sells tapes for electronic, telecommunications, and fiber-optic cables, as well as specialty tapes and laminates for packaging and industrial applications.
- *Humiseal* produces insulating conformal coatings, potting compounds, and ancillary products for electronics applications.

- *Royston Laboratories* makes insulating and protective mastics, coatings, and tapes for pipelines, highways, and bridges, as well as waterproofing membranes for commercial and residential construction.
- *Fluid Polymers* makes solventless sealants, adhesives, coatings, and dielectric materials for fluid purification, construction, and wire and cable industries.
- *DC Scientific* provides full contract manufacturing services to the electronics industry, including circuit board design, prototyping, assembly, and packaging.

Chase also has an export operation based in Barbados, West Indies. Foreign sales outside North America account for about 10 percent of total sales. Canadian sales account for about 7 percent of the company's total revenue.

Chase was founded in 1946 and went public with its initial stock offering in 1995. It has about 220 employees and a market capitalization of about $50 million.

EARNINGS PER SHARE GROWTH   ★ ★ ★ ★

Past four years: 339 percent (45 percent per year)

REVENUE GROWTH

Past four years: 62 percent (13 percent per year)

STOCK GROWTH   ★ ★ ★ ★

Past three years: 176 percent (40 percent per year)
Dollar growth: $10,000 over the past three years would have grown to about $28,000.

CONSISTENCY   ★ ★ ★ ★

Increased earnings per share: four of the past four years
Increased revenue: four of the past four years

CHASE AT A GLANCE

Fiscal year ended: Aug. 31
Revenue and net income in $ millions

| | 1994 | 1995 | 1996 | 1997 | 1998 | 4-Year Growth | |
						Avg. Annual (%)	Total (%)
Revenue ($)	28.7	32.7	34.4	41.0	46.6	13	62
Net income ($)	1.61	1.91	2.19	2.81	4.10	26	155
Earnings/share ($)	0.36	0.44	0.61	0.84	1.58	45	339
Avg. PE ratio	—	12	11	13	9	—	—

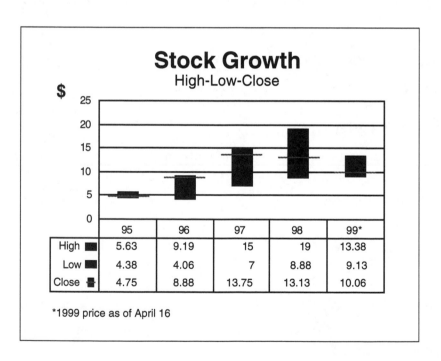

Stock Growth
High-Low-Close

	95	96	97	98	99*
High	5.63	9.19	15	19	13.38
Low	4.38	4.06	7	8.88	9.13
Close	4.75	8.88	13.75	13.13	10.06

*1999 price as of April 16

43

Mity-Lite, Inc.

1301 West 400 North
Orem, UT 84057
801-224-0589
www.mitylite.com

Chairman, President, and CEO:
Gregory Wilson

Earnings Growth	★ ★
Revenue Growth	★ ★ ★
Stock Growth	★ ★ ★
Consistency	★ ★ ★ ★
Nasdaq: MITY	**12 points**

Mity-Lite makes a broad range of lightweight folding tables designed to last longer and look better than the traditional style folding tables.

Most folding tables were made with particle board or plywood, which tends to wear out fairly quickly. Mity-Lite engineers totally redesigned the folding table, with durable-yet-lightweight plastic materials and a reengineered folding leg assemble designed to last longer and work more easily.

In all, the company has 48 different plastic table sizes in a variety of colors. It also offers its Elite line of wood veneer tables for offices, conference rooms, and training rooms, and an aluminum table for outdoor use.

Mity-Lite tables cost two to three times as much as its competitors, but they tend to look better and last longer. And, Mity-Lite offers a five-year warranty.

The Orem, Utah firm also manufactures five lines of stacking chairs—all with warranties of seven to ten years—as well as a line of accessory products, such as chair carts, tablecloths, skirting, and skirt clips.

Mity-Lite sells its products to educational, recreational, hotel and hospitality, government, office, health care, religious, and other public assembly operations throughout the United States and in some foreign countries. About 8 percent of its sales are outside the United States, including Canada, Mexico, South America, Europe, and Asia.

The company markets its products directly to end users through the company's 40-person sales staff.

Mity-Lite plans to pursue market growth by continuing to increase market share, introducing new lines of tables and chairs, expanding to new markets, and improving and economizing its manufacturing process.

Mity-Lite was founded in 1987 by Gregory Wilson, who still serves as chairman, president, and CEO. The company went public with its initial stock offering in 1994. It has about 160 employees and a market capitalization of about $50 million.

EARNINGS PER SHARE GROWTH   ★ ★

Past four years: 104 percent (19 percent per year)

REVENUE GROWTH   ★ ★ ★

Past four years: 155 percent (26 percent per year)

STOCK GROWTH   ★ ★ ★

Past three years: 93 percent (25 percent per year)
Dollar growth: $10,000 over the past three years would have grown to about $19,000.

CONSISTENCY   ★ ★ ★ ★

Increased earnings per share: four of the past four years
Increased revenue: four of the past four years

MITY-LITE AT A GLANCE

Fiscal year ended: March 31
Revenue and net income in $ millions

	1994	1995	1996	1997	1998	4-Year Growth Avg. Annual (%)	Total (%)
Revenue ($)	9.9	13.0	15.4	18.7	25.3	26	155
Net income ($)	1.1	1.7	1.9	2.5	3.2	31	189
Earnings/share ($)	0.46	0.55	0.60	0.76	0.94	19	104
Avg. PE ratio	14	15	13	17	16	—	—

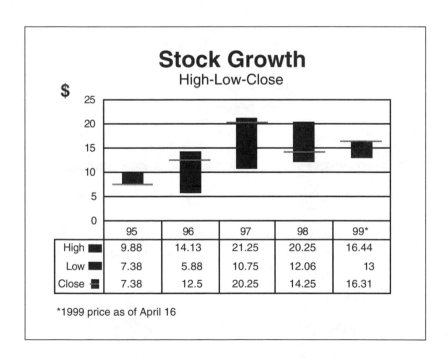

Stock Growth
High-Low-Close

	95	96	97	98	99*
High	9.88	14.13	21.25	20.25	16.44
Low	7.38	5.88	10.75	12.06	13
Close	7.38	12.5	20.25	14.25	16.31

*1999 price as of April 16

44

Applied Signal Technology, Inc.

Applied Signal Technology, Inc.

400 West California Avenue
Sunnyvale, CA 94086
408-749-1888
www.appsig.com

Chairman, President, and CEO:
Gary L. Yancey

Earnings Growth	★ ★ ★ ★
Revenue Growth	★
Stock Growth	★ ★ ★ ★
Consistency	★ ★ ★
Nasdaq: APSG	**12 points**

In the simplest terms, Applied Signal Technology (AST) is in the spy business. The company makes signal processing equipment used by the U.S. government and its allies to listen in on radio and cellular phone conversations outside the United States.

AST deals in two stages of the information gathering technology—collection and signal processing. Its collection equipment consists of sophisticated receivers that scan the radio frequency spectrum—including cellular telephones, microwave, ship-to-shore, and military transmissions—to collect certain signals. Its signal processing equipment uses sophisticated software and hardware to evaluate the characteristics of the collected signals and selects signals that are likely to contain relevant information.

The Sunnyvale, California operation has specialized primarily in the signal processing end of the spying business, although it also provides specialized collection equipment, as well as complete "signal reconnaissance systems."

Its product line includes:

- Voice grade channel processors, which can scan thousands of signals in less than one second and use sophisticated processing technology to detect and record relevant data for the U.S. government. Prices range from $40,000 to $200,000 for the processors.
- Wideband processors, which "clean" telecommunication signals for further processing by voice grade channel processors by adjusting for signal distortions that commonly occur during transmission.
- Processing systems, which process the data collected through scanning equipment.
- Collection products, which collect very complex signaling formats. The price of its units range from about $20,000 to $60,000.

Nearly 100 percent of the company's revenue is generated through sales to the U.S. government, although it also has subcontracts under which it supplies products to prime contractors doing projects for the government.

AST went public with its initial stock offering in 1993. The company has about 600 employees and a market capitalization of about $100 million.

EARNINGS PER SHARE GROWTH

Past four years: 186 percent (30 percent per year)

REVENUE GROWTH   ★

Past four years: 71 percent (15 percent per year)

STOCK GROWTH

Past three years: 196 percent (44 percent per year)
Dollar growth: $10,000 over the past three years would have grown to about $30,000.

CONSISTENCY

Increased earnings per share: three of the past four years
Increased revenue: four of the past four years

APPLIED SIGNAL TECHNOLOGY AT A GLANCE

Fiscal year ended: Oct. 31
Revenue and net income in $ millions

	1994	1995	1996	1997	1998	4-Year Growth Avg. Annual (%)	Total (%)
Revenue ($)	64.3	67.7	77.4	96.3	110.1	15	71
Net income ($)	3.14	0.90	1.82	7.67	10.1	34	221
Earnings/share ($)	0.42	0.12	0.23	0.94	1.20	30	186
Avg. PE ratio	13	41	24	11	12	—	—

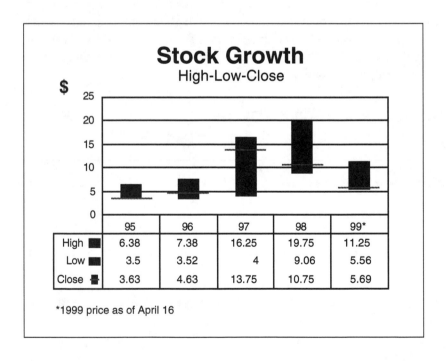

Stock Growth
High-Low-Close

$	95	96	97	98	99*
High	6.38	7.38	16.25	19.75	11.25
Low	3.5	3.52	4	9.06	5.56
Close	3.63	4.63	13.75	10.75	5.69

*1999 price as of April 16

45

Southwest Water Company

225 North Barranca Avenue
Suite 200
West Covina, CA 91791
626-915-1551
www.southwestwater.com

Chairman and President:
Anton C. Garnier

Earnings Growth	★ ★ ★ ★
Revenue Growth	
Stock Growth	★ ★ ★ ★
Consistency	★ ★ ★ ★
Nasdaq: SWWC	**12 points**

Southwest Water Company supplies water and treats wastewater for communities in California, New Mexico, Texas, and Mississippi.

The West Covina, California company owns the water supply systems and wastewater treatment systems in several communities and operates other systems owned by cities, utility districts, and private companies. In all, the company serves about 750,000 customers throughout its four-state area.

The company conducts business through two subsidiaries: Suburban Water Systems and ECO Resources.

Suburban is a regulated water utility that produces and supplies water for residents, businesses, and industrial and public authority use in Los Angeles and Orange County, California. The firm owns 15 wells and operates one other that pumps water from the Central Basin and the Main San Gabriel Basin in Southern California.

The Suburban customer base is growing slowly, limited to extensions into new subdivisions along the periphery of the service area. There is little business or industrial growth in its service area.

The company acquired New Mexico Utilities in 1987 and has seen its customer base grow from about 800 customers to 6,000 since then. The firm offers both water and sewage collection services.

Southwest's ECO subsidiary focuses on operating water supply and wastewater systems owned by others. It takes over the maintenance operations of private and publicly owned municipal utility districts. ECO has about 140 contracts with municipal utilities, primarily in the Houston and Austin, Texas, suburban areas.

The company also has 18 operations and maintenance contracts for water systems in other parts of Texas, as well as Mississippi, New Mexico, and California.

Southwest Water was founded in 1954. The company has about 525 employees and a market capitalization of about $62 million.

EARNINGS PER SHARE GROWTH   ★ ★ ★ ★

Past four years: 196 percent (31 percent per year)

REVENUE GROWTH

Past four years: 42 percent (9 percent per year)

STOCK GROWTH   ★ ★ ★ ★

Past three years: 155 percent (37 percent per year)
Dollar growth: $10,000 over the past three years would have grown to about $26,000.

CONSISTENCY   ★ ★ ★ ★

Increased earnings per share: four of the past four years
Increased revenue: four of the past four years

SOUTHWEST WATER AT A GLANCE

Fiscal year ended: Dec. 31
Revenue and net income in $ millions

	1994	1995	1996	1997	1998	4-Year Growth Avg. Annual (%)	Total (%)
Revenue ($)	50.9	56.8	66.1	71.0	72.1	9	42
Net income ($)	1.06	1.44	1.92	2.60	3.35	33	216
Earnings/share ($)	0.26	0.35	0.46	0.62	0.77	31	196
Avg. PE ratio	24	16	19	19	18	—	—

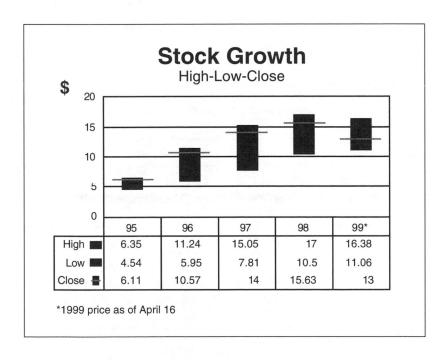

Stock Growth
High-Low-Close

	95	96	97	98	99*
High	6.35	11.24	15.05	17	16.38
Low	4.54	5.95	7.81	10.5	11.06
Close	6.11	10.57	14	15.63	13

*1999 price as of April 16

46
Embrex, Inc.

1035 Swabia Court
Durham, NC 27703
919-941-5185
www.embrex.com

Chairman:
Charles E. Austin
President and CEO:
Randall L. Marcuson

Earnings Growth	★ ★ ★ ★
Revenue Growth	★ ★ ★ ★
Stock Growth	
Consistency	★ ★ ★ ★
Nasdaq: EMBX	**12 points**

Embrex is in the chicken health care business. The Durham, North Carolina operation develops biological delivery technology and biological products to increase the productivity and profitability of the global poultry industry.

Embrex's leading product is the Inovoject system, an automated in-the-egg injection system that can inoculate 20,000 to 50,000 eggs per hour and eliminate the need for manual, posthatch injection of certain vaccines. Inovoject is now used to vaccinate more than 80 percent of the poultry raised in North America. The firm has more than 300 Inovoject systems installed in the United States and Canada.

The Inovoject system is designed to inject vaccines and other compounds in precisely calibrated volumes into targeted compartments within the egg. Embrex markets the system to commercial poultry producers, charging a fee for each egg injected.

The Inovoject systems are now being marketed (or tested) in Europe, the Middle East, Asia, Australia, and Africa.

In addition to the Inovoject system, Embrex has developed a Viral Neutralizing Factor antibody, which permits single-dose immunization of the avian embryo effective for the life of the bird. Embrex also makes Bursaplex, a vaccine for protection against avian bursal disease, a condition that weakens the bird's immune system.

Embrex is actively researching and developing other related pharmaceutical and biological products to improve bird health, reduce production costs, and provide other economic benefits to poultry producers. Products in the pipeline include vaccines, immune enhancers, performance modifiers, and genetic materials designed to increase poultry productivity.

Embrex was first incorporated in 1985. It went public with its initial stock offering in 1991. The stock has been stagnant for most of this decade, but the firm is beginning to show growing earnings after many years of losses. Embrex has 115 employees and a market capitalization of about $45 million.

EARNINGS PER SHARE GROWTH   ★ ★ ★ ★

Past two years: 600 percent (165 percent per year)

REVENUE GROWTH   ★ ★ ★ ★

Past four years: 315 percent (42 percent per year)

STOCK GROWTH

Past three years: −17 percent
Dollar growth: $10,000 over the past three years would have declined to $8,300.

CONSISTENCY   ★ ★ ★ ★

Increased earnings per share: four of the past four years
Increased revenue: four of the past four years

EMBREX AT A GLANCE

Fiscal year ended: Dec. 31
Revenue and net income in $ millions

	1994	1995	1996	1997	1998	4-Year Growth Avg. Annual (%)	Total (%)
Revenue ($)	6.89	13.7	20.6	24.8	28.6	42	315
Net income ($)	−6.71	−4.51	0.341	1.76	2.86	190	739*
Earnings/share ($)	−1.12	−0.73	0.05	0.22	0.35	165	600*
Avg. PE ratio	—	—	146	30	16	—	—

*Net income and earnings per share returns are based on two-year performance.

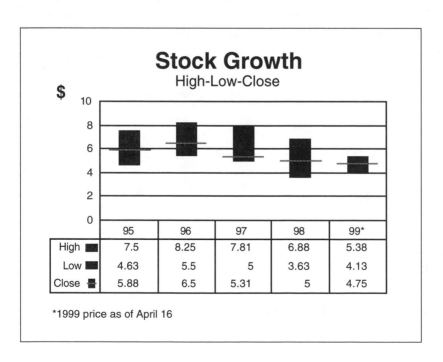

Stock Growth
High-Low-Close

$	95	96	97	98	99*
High	7.5	8.25	7.81	6.88	5.38
Low	4.63	5.5	5	3.63	4.13
Close	5.88	6.5	5.31	5	4.75

*1999 price as of April 16

Seaway Food Town, Inc.

SEAWAY
FOOD TOWN INC.

1020 Ford Street
Maumee, OH 43537
419-893-9401

Chairman:
Wallace D. Iott
President and CEO:
Richard B. Iott

Earnings Growth	★ ★ ★ ★
Revenue Growth	
Stock Growth	★ ★ ★ ★
Consistency	★ ★ ★ ★
Nasdaq: SEWY	**12 points**

Seaway Food Town is a regional supermarket and discount chain that serves an area in northern Ohio and southern Michigan within about 150 miles of its home office in Maumee, Ohio.

The company has about 70 stores in all, including 45 supermarkets and 25 Pharm drugstores.

Seaway operates supermarkets in three different formats. Its conventional Food Town supermarkets offer the traditional line grocery items, such as canned goods, fresh meats and produce, bakery goods, and related products.

Its more upscale Food Town Plus combination stores offer a wider selection of merchandise, as well as some extras, such as prepared foods,

ATMs, video rentals, dry cleaning, event ticketing, pharmacies, food court, full-service delicatessen, in-store bank, and parcel mailing services.

Its new Kash N Karry discount stores are smaller, limited-assortment discount convenience stores.

The Pharm drugstores are large discount outlets with pharmacy services, a large selection of discounted health and beauty aids and other standard drugstore products. They also have a convenience-store food section with refrigerated and frozen foods, snacks, and a limited range of fresh foods.

Seaway also has been working to expand its home delivery and Internet grocery shopping services.

Seaway management plans to continue adding new stores within its regional area but are in no hurry to spread stores across the country. "We know this geographic region well, and we believe it holds excellent promise for future growth," says Seaway chairman Wallace D. Iott. "Expansion beyond the 150-mile perimeter, although not an immediate priority, is a possibility if the right opportunity were to present itself."

The company traces its founding to 1948, although the first Food Town store was opened in 1945, and Seaway Food Town was incorporated in 1957. Seaway has about 2,400 employees and a market capitalization of about $105 million.

EARNINGS PER SHARE GROWTH   ★ ★ ★ ★

Past four years: 200 percent (31 percent per year)

REVENUE GROWTH

Past four years: 14 percent (3 percent per year)

STOCK GROWTH   ★ ★ ★ ★

Past three years: 200 percent (44 percent per year)
Dollar growth: $10,000 over the past three years would have grown to $30,000.

CONSISTENCY   ★ ★ ★ ★

Increased earnings per share: four of the past four years
Increased revenue: four of the past four years

SEAWAY FOOD TOWN AT A GLANCE

Fiscal year ended: Aug. 31
Revenue and net income in $ millions

	1994	1995	1996	1997	1998	4-Year Growth Avg. Annual (%)	4-Year Growth Total (%)
Revenue ($)	546.2	559.2	597.5	608.4	625.2	3	14
Net income ($)	2.1	4.5	5.5	6.4	7.0	32	233
Earnings/share ($)	0.35	0.68	0.84	0.97	1.05	31	200
Avg. PE ratio	11	7	9	13	16	—	—

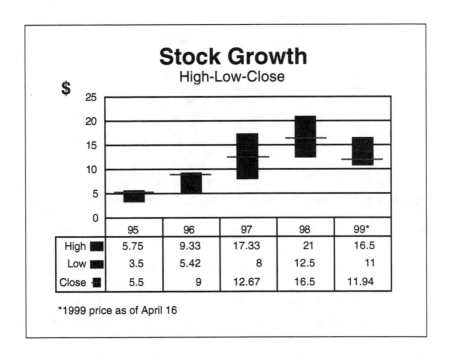

Stock Growth
High-Low-Close

$	95	96	97	98	99*
High	5.75	9.33	17.33	21	16.5
Low	3.5	5.42	8	12.5	11
Close	5.5	9	12.67	16.5	11.94

*1999 price as of April 16

Hot Topic, Inc.

HOT TOPIC, INC.

3410 Pomona Boulevard
Pomona, CA 91768
909-869-6373
www.hottopic.com

Chairman:
Robert M. Jaffe
President and CEO:
Orval D. Madden

Earnings Growth	★ ★ ★ ★
Revenue Growth	★ ★ ★ ★
Stock Growth	
Consistency	★ ★ ★ ★
Nasdaq: HOTT	**12 points**

If it's hot, Hot Topic wants to have it in stock. Hot Topic is a retail specialty chain geared to the MTV generation—young men and women between the ages of 12 and 22. It sells music-licensed and "music-influenced" apparel, accessories, and gift items.

The Pomona, California retailer locates its stores in malls across America. It has about 160 stores in 38 states and adds about 40 new stores a year.

The music-licensed apparel industry began in the 1960s with bootleggers selling T-shirts at music concerts. Over the next two decades, the industry became mainstream as musical artists began to realize the huge commercial potential of licensing their likenesses and logos to T-shirt makers and other companies who produced assorted gifts and merchandise.

With millions of kids watching MTV on a regular basis, pop-rock merchandise has become very popular.

Hot Topic has taken advantage of that market by packing its stores with merchandise that caters to the MTV generation. In all, Hot Topic sells about 12,000 different products.

Its music-licensed merchandise includes T-shirts, caps, posters, stickers, patches, postcards, books, and other items. Its music-influenced merchandise includes woven and knit tops, dresses, jeans, shorts, jackets, shoes, costume jewelry, body jewelry, sunglasses, cosmetics, and gift items. The stores carry more than 100 different band T-shirts, from alternative artists such as Nine Inch Nails, Korn, Blink 182, and Nirvana to the classic rock favorites such as the Grateful Dead, the Doors, the Beatles, Led Zeppelin, and Jimi Hendrix.

Apparel sales account for about 47 percent of total revenue. Gifts make up about 20 percent, accessories account for 25 percent, and hosiery, shoes, and outerwear combine for about 8 percent of revenue.

Hot Topic has five lines of private label merchandise to complement its current offerings for other suppliers.

The Pomona, California operation opened its first store in 1989. It went public with its initial stock offering in 1996. The firm has about 400 employees and a market capitalization of about $65 million.

EARNINGS PER SHARE GROWTH ★ ★ ★ ★

Past four years: 1,000 percent (81 percent per year)

REVENUE GROWTH ★ ★ ★ ★

Past four years: 639 percent (64 percent per year)

STOCK GROWTH

Past three years: −34 percent
Dollar growth: $10,000 over the past three years would have declined to $6,600.

CONSISTENCY ★ ★ ★ ★

Increased earnings per share: four of the past four years
Increased revenue: four of the past four years

HOT TOPIC AT A GLANCE

Fiscal year ended: Jan. 31
Revenue and net income in $ millions

	1995	1996	1997	1998	1999	4-Year Growth Avg. Annual (%)	Total (%)
Revenue ($)	14.0	23.6	43.6	70.5	103.4	64	639
Net income ($)	0.292	0.437	2.6	4.5	6.0	109	1,955
Earnings/share ($)	0.11	0.14	0.71	0.97	1.21	81	1,000
Avg. PE ratio	—	32	24	17	22	—	—

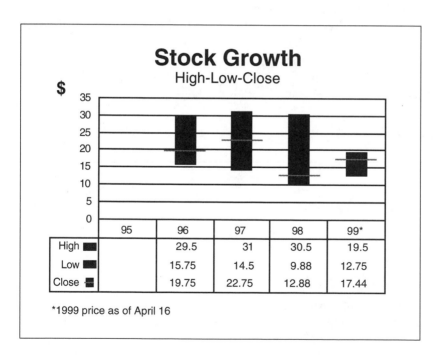

Stock Growth
High-Low-Close

	95	96	97	98	99*
High		29.5	31	30.5	19.5
Low		15.75	14.5	9.88	12.75
Close		19.75	22.75	12.88	17.44

*1999 price as of April 16

49
ViaSat, Inc.

2290 Cosmos Court
Carlsbad, CA 92009
760-438-8099
www.viasat.com

Chairman, President, and CEO:
Mark D. Dankberg

Earnings Growth	★ ★ ★ ★
Revenue Growth	★ ★ ★ ★
Stock Growth	
Consistency	★ ★ ★ ★
Nasdaq: VSAT	**12 points**

ViaSat makes digital satellite telecommunications and wireless signal processing equipment.

The firm is a leading provider of Demand Assigned Multiple Access (DAMA) technology, which allows large numbers of satellite subscribers to share common satellite transponders for high-performance voice, fax, or data communications.

ViaSat's DAMA products include satellite modems, networking processors, and network control systems for managing large numbers of network subscribers. The company's DAMA technology consists of proprietary software designed to run on industry-standard digital signal processors. Its technology operates on satellites in the military UHF and SHF frequency bands, and commercial C and K bands.

The Carlsbad, California operation also provides network information security products, communications simulation and test equipment, and spread spectrum digital radios for satellite and terrestrial data networks.

Traditionally, the majority of ViaSat revenue has come from military related projects, but recently the company has made significant investments in commercial satellite networking operations. For instance, its new StarWire system is used to enable telephone, fax, data, video-conferencing, and Internet access over satellites in geosynchronous orbits. The StarWire system consists of two major elements: a network control system and a subscriber terminal. The network control system sends and receives messages over the satellite, while the subscriber terminal switches all user voice and data ports individually, connecting them call by call to an available satellite modem.

ViaSat continues to rely on the military for the bulk of its revenue. It recently installed a DAMA satellite network control system for the Department of Defense that allows deployment of satellite terminals by ground, air, and sea forces. It also began producing UHF satellite antenna processing systems for installation on U.S. Navy P3 aircraft.

Founded in 1986, ViaSat went public with its initial stock offering in 1996. The company has about 350 employees and a market capitalization of about $85 million.

EARNINGS PER SHARE GROWTH   ★ ★ ★ ★

Past four years: 325 percent (43 percent per year)

REVENUE GROWTH   ★ ★ ★ ★

Past four years: 453 percent (53 percent per year)

STOCK GROWTH

Past two years: 11 percent (5 percent per year)
Dollar growth: $10,000 over the past two years would have grown to about $11,000.

CONSISTENCY   ★ ★ ★ ★

Increased earnings per share: four of the past four years
Increased revenue: four of the past four years

VIASAT AT A GLANCE

Fiscal year ended: March 31
Revenue and net income in $ millions

	1994	1995	1996	1997	1998	4-Year Growth Avg. Annual (%)	Total (%)
Revenue ($)	11.6	22.3	29	47.7	64.2	53	453
Net income ($)	0.485	1.3	1.6	3.1	5.3	81	993
Earnings/share ($)	0.16	0.42	0.50	0.66	0.68	43	325
Avg. PE ratio	—	—	14	25	16	—	—

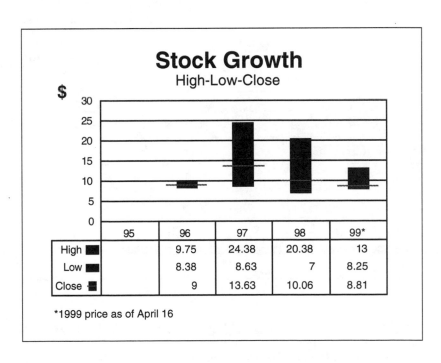

Stock Growth
High-Low-Close

$	95	96	97	98	99*
High		9.75	24.38	20.38	13
Low		8.38	8.63	7	8.25
Close		9	13.63	10.06	8.81

*1999 price as of April 16

American Oncology Resources, Inc.

AOR

American Oncology Resources

16825 Northchase Drive
Suite 1300
Houston, TX 77060
281-873-2674
www.aori.com

Chairman and CEO:
R. Dale Ross
President:
Lloyd K. Everson

Earnings Growth	★ ★ ★ ★
Revenue Growth	★ ★ ★ ★
Stock Growth	
Consistency	★ ★ ★ ★
Nasdaq: AORI	**12 points**

American Oncology Resources (AOR) is a specialty physician practice management company that focuses almost entirely on outpatient care for cancer patients. The Houston-based operation has 44 oncology centers in 24 states, with more than 700 physicians treating about 13 percent of all new cancer cases in the United States.

Oncologists specialize in the treatment of cancer, using such techniques as chemotherapy, radiation therapy, surgery, and immunotherapy. There are about 6,000 oncologists in the United States, most of whom operate in small practices of two to five physicians. AOR acquires these small operations (and some larger ones) to form a larger, more cost-efficient network of oncology centers.

For the physicians, the arrangement frees them of the administrative headaches of managing their offices and gives them more time to focus on treating their patients.

AOR provides a comprehensive range of services for its physicians, including strategic planning, billing, collection, reimbursement, tax filing, and accounting. The firm also provides administrative services such as patient recordkeeping and purchasing of drugs, supplies, equipment, insurance, and other needs.

AOR also hires and manages all nonmedical personnel at the centers and handles employee benefits and salary issues. The company also helps market the services of its oncologists and coordinates clinical research into both improving the treatment of cancer and cutting the costs of cancer treatment.

The firm plans to continue its aggressive expansion by recruiting new physicians to its existing centers, acquiring new centers around the country, adding new related services at their centers, and negotiating new cancer care relationships for their centers.

AOR went public with its initial stock offering in 1995. It has about 1,200 employees and a market capitalization of about $480 million.

EARNINGS PER SHARE GROWTH ★ ★ ★ ★

Past four years: 757 percent (71 percent per year)

REVENUE GROWTH ★ ★ ★ ★

Past four years: 2,135 percent (115 percent per year)

STOCK GROWTH

Past three years: −40 percent
Dollar growth: $10,000 over the past three years would have declined to $6,000.

CONSISTENCY ★ ★ ★ ★

Increased earnings per share: four of the past four years
Increased revenue: four of the past four years

AMERICAN ONCOLOGY RESOURCES AT A GLANCE

Fiscal year ended: Dec. 31
Revenue and net income in $ millions

	1994	1995	1996	1997	1998	4-Year Growth Avg. Annual (%)	Total (%)
Revenue ($)	20.4	99.2	205.5	321.8	455.9	115	2,135
Net income ($)	1.24	11.6	17.7	22.9	30.2	118	2,335
Earnings/share	0.07	0.33	0.37	0.50	0.60	71	757
Avg. PE ratio	—	57	41	26	21	—	—

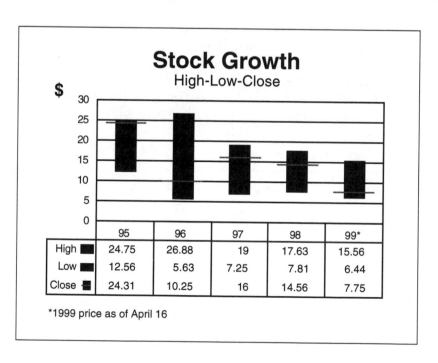

Stock Growth
High-Low-Close

	95	96	97	98	99*
High	24.75	26.88	19	17.63	15.56
Low	12.56	5.63	7.25	7.81	6.44
Close	24.31	10.25	16	14.56	7.75

*1999 price as of April 16

Hall, Kinion & Associates, Inc.

19925 Stevens Creek Boulevard
Suite 180
Cupertino, CA 95014
408-863-5720
www.hallkinion.com

Chairman and CEO:
Brenda C. Hall
President:
Paul H. Bartlett

Earnings Growth	★ ★ ★ ★
Revenue Growth	★ ★ ★ ★
Stock Growth	
Consistency	★ ★ ★ ★
Nasdaq: HAKI	**12 points**

The field of information technology has become increasingly specialized in recent years, creating staffing headaches for many leading high-tech companies. Consider Hall, Kinion & Associates the aspirin for that headache. The company specializes in providing information technology professionals on a contract or permanent basis for high-tech companies in need.

The Cupertino, California operation has more than 20 offices in 13 major technology centers throughout the United States and in London.

Hall, Kinion provides its services primarily to the product development, engineering, and research departments of high-tech companies, such as software developers and computer systems manufacturers. The firm also offers information technology services for information systems departments of corporate clients and international recruiting.

The company is organized into two divisions—contract services, which accounts for about 87 percent of the company's approximately $100 million in annual revenue, and permanent placement, which accounts for the other 13 percent. Its contract services division provides technology specialists on a temporary basis for corporate research and development departments and information systems departments. Its placement division places professionals in permanent positions with high-tech companies and other corporate clients.

Hall, Kinion's clients include an extensive group of global high-tech companies, such as IBM, Cisco Systems, Microsoft, Motorola, and Oracle.

The firm is banking on the continued rapid growth of the high-tech industry. Because of the competition in the high-tech area—as well as the rapid pace of product turnover—high-tech companies have been forced to shorten product life cycles and time-to-market for their new products. To accelerate the time-to-market for new products, they have been turning increasingly to outside agencies such as Hall, Kinion to find qualified information technology professionals to augment their internal staff.

Hall, Kinion was founded in 1991 and went public with its initial stock offering in 1997. The company has about 1,000 employees and a market capitalization of about $75 million.

EARNINGS PER SHARE GROWTH   ★ ★ ★ ★

Past four years: 4,200 percent (156 percent per year)

REVENUE GROWTH   ★ ★ ★ ★

Past four years: 676 percent (68 percent per year)

STOCK GROWTH

Past one year: −68 percent
Dollar growth: $10,000 over the past year would have declined to $3,200.

CONSISTENCY   ★ ★ ★ ★

Increased earnings per share: four of the past four years
Increased revenue: four of the past four years

HALL, KINION & ASSOCIATES AT A GLANCE

Fiscal year ended: Dec. 31
Revenue and net income in $ millions

	1994	1995	1996	1997	1998	4-Year Growth Avg. Annual (%)	Total (%)
Revenue ($)	16.0	29.4	50.6	92.8	124.1	68	676
Net income ($)	0.033	0.682	1.36	2.51	4.41	250	13,264
Earnings/share ($)	0.01	0.11	0.22	0.34	0.43	156	4,200
Avg. PE ratio	—	—	—	53	31	—	—

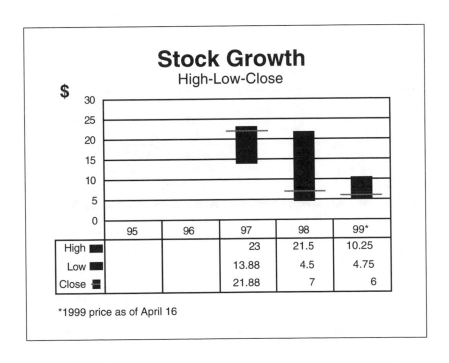

Stock Growth
High-Low-Close

$

	95	96	97	98	99*
High			23	21.5	10.25
Low			13.88	4.5	4.75
Close			21.88	7	6

*1999 price as of April 16

Trex Medical Corporation

TREX Medical Corporation

37 Apple Ridge Road
Danbury, CT 06810
781-622-1000
www.thermo.com/subsid/txm.html

Chairman:
Gary S. Weinstein
President and CEO:
Hal Kirshner

Earnings Growth	★ ★ ★ ★
Revenue Growth	★ ★ ★ ★
Stock Growth	
Consistency	★ ★ ★ ★
AMEX: TXM	**12 points**

Trex Medical makes X-ray machines, mammography equipment, and other types of medical imaging systems.

The Danbury, Connecticut operation has several core product groups, including:

- *Breast cancer detection products.* The company makes mammography systems, which are a form of X-ray machine used to examine the breast. Mammography exams are used to detect breast cancer. Trex is working to develop a digital mammography system that would replace the traditional film with a solid state detector capable of directly recording the X-ray image in an electronic format. The firm also makes a variety of minimally invasive digital breast-biopsy systems.

- *General-purpose radiography equipment.* Through its Bennett and Continental subsidiaries, the firm makes basic X-ray systems used in medical outpatient facilities, such as doctors' offices and surgicare centers. The company also makes imaging systems designed specifically for chiropractors and veterinarians.
- *Cardiac catheterization, angiography, and electrophysiology.* The Trex imaging equipment is used in catheterization labs where angiography (the examination of blood vessels) is performed by a cardiologist. Its systems are designed to provide real-time images of peripheral blood vessels and of the heart and coronary arteries for physicians performing diagnostic and interventional procedures such as balloon angioplasty.

Trex also makes radiographic and fluoroscopic imaging systems and other imaging systems. The firm also manufactures lasers used for hair removal. It is also the world's largest manufacturer of digital dental X-ray equipment.

The company sells its products through a worldwide network of more than 100 independent dealers, who are supervised by the company's own regional sales managers.

About 79 percent of the company's stock is held by ThermoTrex, a publicly traded subsidiary of Thermo Electron Corp.

Trex went public with its initial stock offering in 1996. The company has about 340 employees and a market capitalization of about $275 million.

EARNINGS PER SHARE GROWTH   ★ ★ ★ ★

Past four years: 833 percent (75 percent per year)

REVENUE GROWTH   ★ ★ ★ ★

Past four years: 391 percent (49 percent per year)

STOCK GROWTH

Past two years: −34 percent
Dollar growth: $10,000 over the past two years would have declined to $6,600.

CONSISTENCY   ★ ★ ★ ★

Increased earnings per share: four of the past four years
Increased revenue: four of the past four years

TREX MEDICAL AT A GLANCE

Fiscal year ended: Sept. 30
Revenue and net income in $ millions

	1994	1995	1996	1997	1998	4-Year Growth Avg. Annual (%)	Total (%)
Revenue ($)	54.4	55.3	150.2	229.3	267	49	391
Net income ($)	1.2	3.5	9.3	14.7	18.2	97	1,417
Earnings/share ($)	0.06	0.17	0.40	0.51	0.56	75	833
Avg. PE ratio	—	—	48	28	19	—	—

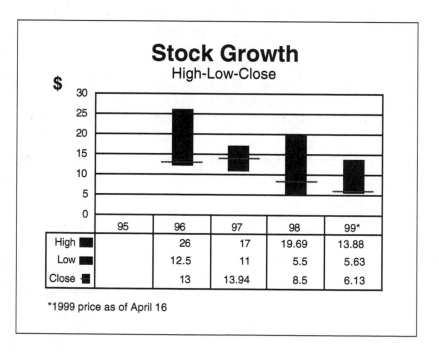

Stock Growth
High-Low-Close

$		95	96	97	98	99*
High			26	17	19.69	13.88
Low			12.5	11	5.5	5.63
Close			13	13.94	8.5	6.13

*1999 price as of April 16

53

Gehl Company

143 Walter Street
West Bend, WI 53095
414-334-9461
www.gehl.com

Chairman, President, and CEO:
William D. Gehl

Earnings Growth	★ ★ ★ ★
Revenue Growth	★
Stock Growth	★ ★ ★
Consistency	★ ★ ★ ★
Nasdaq: GEHL	**12 points**

Gehl's light construction and farm equipment has been used around the world for nearly half a century. The firm's agricultural division has been making agricultural implements for 140 years (although the company did not sell outside North America until about 1950).

Gehl makes a wide range of equipment used primarily in the dairy and livestock industries, including haymaking, forage harvesting, materials handling, manure handling, and feedmarking equipment. The West Bend, Wisconsin operation's construction division makes skid steer loaders, rough-terrain telescopic forklifts, and asphalt pavers used by contractors, owner-operators, and municipalities.

Construction equipment accounts for about 52 percent of Gehl's annual revenue, while farm equipment makes up the other 48 percent. Gehl construction equipment is manufactured at plants in Minnesota and South Dakota, while its Gehl agricultural equipment is manufactured in Wisconsin, South Dakota, and Pennsylvania.

Gehl offers a full line of related products along with its main staples. For instance, its haymaking line includes disc mowers, pull-type disc mower conditioners, hay rakes, and variable chamber round balers. Its forage harvesting line includes harvesters, wagons, and blowers. Its feedmaking line includes grinder mixers, mixer feeders, and feeder wagons for mixing and delivery to livestock feeders.

The firm maintains separate marketing divisions for its farm and construction equipment divisions. The firm has more than 300 independent dealers in North America for its construction equipment and 64 distributors worldwide. The farm equipment is marketed through 500 dealers in North America and 31 distributors outside the United States. The company sells both farm and construction equipment in Europe, the Middle East, Australia, the Pacific Rim, and Latin America.

The Company was founded in 1859. Gehl has about 1,200 employees and a market capitalization of about $95 million.

EARNINGS PER SHARE GROWTH   ★ ★ ★ ★

Past four years: 183 percent (30 percent per year)

REVENUE GROWTH   ★

Past four years: 79 percent (15 percent per year)

STOCK GROWTH   ★ ★ ★

Past three years: 115 percent (29 percent per year)
Dollar growth: $10,000 over the past three years would have grown to about $22,000.

CONSISTENCY   ★ ★ ★ ★

Increased earnings per share: four of the past four years
Increased revenue: four of the past four years

GEHL AT A GLANCE

Fiscal year ended: Dec. 31
Revenue and net income in $ millions

	1994	1995	1996	1997	1998	4-Year Growth Avg. Annual (%)	Total (%)
Revenue ($)	146.6	153.4	159.7	197.1	262.2	15	79
Net income ($)	5.04	9.01	9.57	12.8	15.3	32	204
Earnings/share ($)	0.81	1.44	1.56	2.06	2.29	30	183
Avg. PE ratio	9	6	6	9	8	—	—

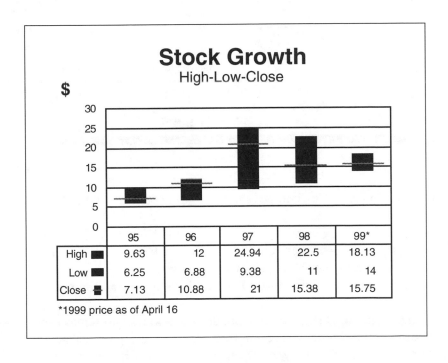

Stock Growth

High-Low-Close

$

	95	96	97	98	99*
High ■	9.63	12	24.94	22.5	18.13
Low ■	6.25	6.88	9.38	11	14
Close ▦	7.13	10.88	21	15.38	15.75

*1999 price as of April 16

TECHNE CORPORATION

614 McKinley Place N.E.
Minneapolis, MN 55413
612-379-8854

Chairman, President, and CEO:
Thomas Oland

Earnings Growth	★ ★ ★ ★
Revenue Growth	
Stock Growth	★ ★ ★
Consistency	★ ★ ★ ★
Nasdaq: TECH	**11 points**

Techne is a biotechnology company at the leading edge of two advanced technologies.

Techne is a holding company for Research and Diagnostic Systems, a Minneapolis-based operation that manufactures blood-analysis-related equipment and highly specialized biotech products.

The firm introduces about 400 new products a year and now has a product list of about 2,000 products.

Techne is the world's leading supplier of cytokines and related antibodies to the biotechnology research community. These proteins exist in minute amounts in different types of cells and can be extracted from these cells or made through recombinant DNA technology.

There is a growing interest in cytokines in the medical research field because of the profound effect a tiny amount of a cytokine can have on the cells and tissues of the body. Cytokines are intercellular messengers. They act as signals by interacting with specific receptors on the affected cells.

They carry vital signals to the cell's genetic machinery that can trigger events and lead to significant changes in a cell. For instance, cytokines can stimulate cells surrounding a wound to grow and divide and to attract migratory cells to the injury site.

Techne also makes hematology controls and calibrators, which are made up of the various cellular components of blood. Accurate diagnosis of many illnesses requires a thorough and accurate analysis of the patient's blood cells, which is usually done with automatic or semiautomatic hematology instruments. Techne's controls and calibrators ensure that these instruments are performing accurately and reliably.

The company has more than 8,000 customers worldwide. In addition to its U.S. operations, Techne operates a subsidiary in England, Research and Diagnostic Systems Europe, which distributes its products overseas.

Techne recently acquired the research products business of Genzyme Corp., which has been one of the leaders in the cytokines market.

Techne was founded in 1976. The company has about 300 employees and a market capitalization of about $420 million.

EARNINGS PER SHARE GROWTH   ★ ★ ★ ★

Past four years: 196 percent (31 percent per year)

REVENUE GROWTH

Past four years: 67 percent (14 percent per year)

STOCK GROWTH   ★ ★ ★

Past three years: 110 percent (28 percent per year)
Dollar growth: $10,000 over the past three years would have grown to $21,000.

CONSISTENCY

Increased earnings per share: four of the past four years
Increased revenue: four of the past four years

TECHNE AT A GLANCE

Fiscal year ended: June 30
Revenue and net income in $ millions

	1994	1995	1996	1997	1998	4-Year Growth Avg. Annual (%)	Total (%)
Revenue ($)	40.3	47.7	54.6	60.9	67.3	14	67
Net income ($)	5.1	6.7	8.6	10.9	15.2	31	198
Earnings/share ($)	0.27	0.35	0.46	0.58	0.80	31	196
Avg. PE ratio	20	24	28	27	21	—	—

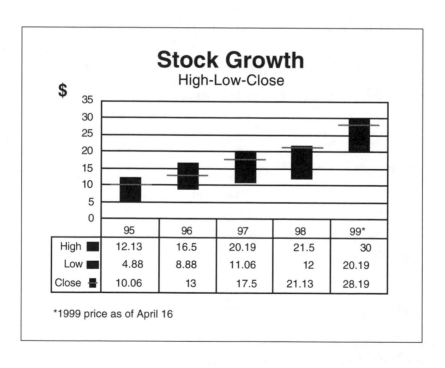

Stock Growth
High-Low-Close

$		95	96	97	98	99*
High		12.13	16.5	20.19	21.5	30
Low		4.88	8.88	11.06	12	20.19
Close		10.06	13	17.5	21.13	28.19

*1999 price as of April 16

Xylan Corporation

26707 West Agoura Road
Calabasas, CA 91302
818-880-3500
www.xylan.com

Chairman, President, and CEO:
Steve Y. Kim

Earnings Growth	★ ★ ★ ★
Revenue Growth	★ ★ ★ ★
Stock Growth	
Consistency	★ ★ ★
Nasdaq: XYLN	**11 points**

Xylan makes switching systems used for telecommunications and computer networks.

The Calabasas, California operation offers three lines of switching systems, including:

1. *OmniSwitch.* This modular chassis-based switch provides local area network (LAN) computer switching and routing. OmniSwitch eliminates the traditional central switching engine, enabling data to move more quickly through its switching modules. It supports a variety of LAN types, interconnecting Ethernet, Fast Ethernet, token ring, frame relay, and other functions. Cost of the systems ranges from $10,000 to $100,000. A network might require one OmniSwitch or hundreds, depending on the size and type of the network.
2. *OmniStack.* Similar to the OmniSwitch, OmniStack is suitable for smaller networks. Cost ranges from $3,350 to $37,000.
3. *PizzaSwitch.* Similar to the other two switches, PizzaSwitch is for applications that require a small access switch with Fiber Distributed Data Interface uplinks.

Xylan also makes a line of OmniVision software that provides a graphical network management capability designed to work with the user's network environment.

The company has strategic partnerships with leading communications and networking companies, including Alcatel and IBM, who use Xylan switches in their products. The company also sells its products through more than 100 system integrators worldwide. System integrators are generally responsible for system installation, technical support, and follow-up services. System integrator sales account for about 38 percent of the company's revenue.

Xylan's products are used for a variety of organizations, including telecommunications, manufacturing, medical, computer services, media, financial and insurance companies, educational institutions, and the federal government. The company has sales worldwide. Its international operations account for about 53 percent of total revenue.

Xylan was founded in 1993 and went public with its initial stock offering in 1996. The company has about 730 employees and a market capitalization of about $705 million.

EARNINGS PER SHARE GROWTH   ★ ★ ★ ★

Past two years: 93 percent (39 percent per year)

REVENUE GROWTH   ★ ★ ★ ★

Past four years: 78,365 percent (430 percent per year)

STOCK GROWTH

Past three years: −36 percent
Dollar growth: $10,000 over the past three years would have declined to $6,400.

CONSISTENCY   ★ ★ ★

Increased earnings per share: three of the past four years
Increased revenue: four of the past four years

XYLAN AT A GLANCE

Fiscal year ended: Dec. 31
Revenue and net income in $ millions

	1994	1995	1996	1997	1998	4-Year Growth Avg. Annual (%)	Total (%)
Revenue ($)	0.443	29.7	128.4	210.8	347.6	430	78,365
Net income ($)	−4.1	−9.4	15.2	24.1	39.4	60*	158*
Earnings/share ($)	−0.19	−0.45	0.43	0.57	0.83	39*	93*
Avg. PE ratio	—	—	117	44	25	—	—

*Net income and earnings per share returns are based on two-year performance.

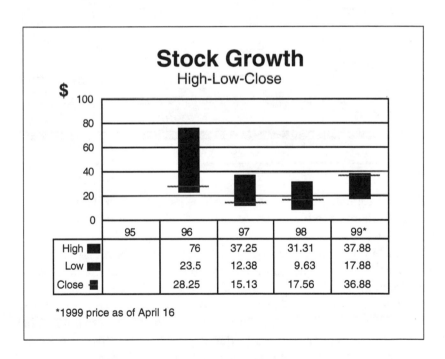

Stock Growth
High-Low-Close

	95	96	97	98	99*
High		76	37.25	31.31	37.88
Low		23.5	12.38	9.63	17.88
Close		28.25	15.13	17.56	36.88

*1999 price as of April 16

56

Catellus Development Corporation

201 Mission Street
San Francisco, CA 94105
415-974-4500
www.catellus.com

Chairman:
J. R. Seiger
President and CEO:
Nelson C. Rising

Earnings Growth	★ ★ ★ ★
Revenue Growth	
Stock Growth	★ ★ ★ ★
Consistency	★ ★ ★
NYSE: CDX	**11 points**

Catellus Development is a diversified real estate operation with a strong portfolio of income-producing properties and substantial holdings of undeveloped land.

The San Francisco–based operation is involved in a broad range of development projects, including industrial, residential, and major mixed-use developments.

Catellus was originally formed to conduct the nonrailroad real estate activities of the Santa Fe Pacific Corp. It was spun off to stockholders in 1990. Its railroad background led to the acquisition of a diverse base of developable properties located near transportation corridors of major urban areas.

The firm has successfully developed many of those areas as industrial parks, retail centers, offices, and residential areas, but other large tracts of the company's land remain undeveloped. One of the company's key strategies is to develop the remaning lands as profitable properties.

In all, the company has about 50 million square feet of undeveloped land that could be converted to commercial properties, as well as additional property that could facilitate construction of about 21,000 residential units. It also owns 782,000 acres of desert land in the western United States.

Most of the company's property is located in California, although it also has properties in Texas, Colorado, Illinois, Arizona, Oklahoma, Oregon, and Kansas. In all, the company has about 60 industrial properties, 13 office sites, 12 retail centers, 4 land developments, and 55 land leases.

Catellus pursues an aggressive program of acquiring promising new properties. It recently acquired a 3,500-acre residential land development project in San Clemente, California; a 300-acre site adjacent to Stapleton Airport in Denver for use as a warehouse, distribution, and light industrial center; a 27-acre industrial site in Northern California; and a 62-acre industrial site in Southern California.

Catellus has about 360 employees and a market capitalization of about $1.53 billion.

EARNINGS PER SHARE GROWTH ★ ★ ★ ★

Past two years: 1,700 percent (106 percent per year)

REVENUE GROWTH

Past four years: 51 percent (11 percent per year)

STOCK GROWTH ★ ★ ★ ★

Past three years: 143 percent (35 percent per year)
Dollar growth: $10,000 over the past three years would have grown to about $24,000.

CONSISTENCY ★ ★ ★

Increased earnings per share: three of the past four years
Increased revenue: four of the past four years

CATELLUS DEVELOPMENT AT A GLANCE

Fiscal year ended: Dec. 31
Revenue and net income in $ millions

	1994	1995	1996	1997	1998	4-Year Growth Avg. Annual (%)	4-Year Growth Total (%)
Revenue ($)	99.2	102.8	115.9	129.0	149.4	11	51
Net income ($)	−2.44	−33.0	25.4	25.2	59.9	54*	136*
Earnings/share ($)	−0.36	−0.78	0.03	0.25	0.54	106*	1,700*
Avg. PE ratio	—	—	347	68	28	—	—

*Net income and earnings per share returns are based on two-year performance.

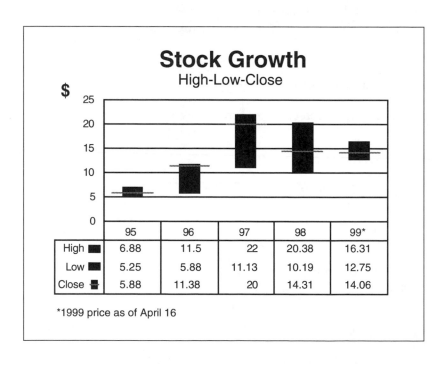

Stock Growth
High-Low-Close

$

	95	96	97	98	99*
High	6.88	11.5	22	20.38	16.31
Low	5.25	5.88	11.13	10.19	12.75
Close	5.88	11.38	20	14.31	14.06

*1999 price as of April 16

Equinox Systems, Inc.

EQUINOX

One Equinox Way
Sunrise, FL 33351
954-746-9000
www.equinox.com

Chairman, President, and CEO:
William A. Dambrackas

Earnings Growth	★ ★ ★
Revenue Growth	★
Stock Growth	★ ★ ★ ★
Consistency	★ ★ ★
Nasdaq: EQNX	**11 points**

Equinox Systems makes add-on products for computer networks that enable the networks to expand the scope and speed of their applications. The company's "server-based" communications products are used for such applications as remote access, commercial point-of-sale, and industrial automation.

The firm's products allow computers such as laptops and notebooks to dial into local area networks (LANs). Its products also are used for multi-user personal computers—typically at retail outlets—to connect to cash registers and bar code scanners.

Equinox makes both "bus-attached" and "LAN-attached" products. The bus-attached products plug directly into the bus expansion slots of the computer motherboard, while the LAN-attached products connect to the computer server through an Ethernet LAN.

The company's leading product line is its SuperSerial products, which can add up to 128 high-performance serial ports to the server.

The firm's bus-attached products account for 78 percent of its approximately $30 million in annual sales. LAN-attached products account for the other 22 percent.

The Sunrise, Florida operation sells its products through a worldwide distribution network, including Ingram Micro, Tech Data, and Merisel, who resell the products to system integrators and value-added resellers. These companies typically incorporate the Equinox products into servers along with other hardware and software for resale to end users.

Equinox also sells its products directly to original equipment manufacturers, such as IBM, Hewlett-Packard, AT&T, and Unisys, who incorporate the products into their own systems.

The firm uses about 25 national and regional distributors in the United States. Internationally, it sells its products through about 50 independent distributors in more than 40 countries. The international distributors also provide technical support and follow-up service.

Equinox Systems went public with its initial stock offering in 1993. The company has 100 employees and a market capitalization of about $60 million.

EARNINGS PER SHARE GROWTH   ★ ★ ★

Past four years: 141 percent (25 percent per year)

REVENUE GROWTH   ★

Past four years: 57 percent (12 percent per year)

STOCK GROWTH   ★ ★ ★ ★

Past three years: 136 percent (33 percent per year)
Dollar growth: $10,000 over the past three years would have grown to about $24,000.

CONSISTENCY   ★ ★ ★

Increased earnings per share: three of the past four years
Increased revenue: four of the past four years

EQUINOX SYSTEMS AT A GLANCE

Fiscal year ended: Dec. 31
Revenue and net income in $ millions

	1994	1995	1996	1997	1998	4-Year Growth Avg. Annual (%)	Total (%)
Revenue ($)	20	20.2	24.8	28.4	31.3	12	57
Net income ($)	2.08	1.62	2.76	3.91	4.56	21	119
Earnings/share ($)	0.34	0.27	0.48	0.77	0.82	25	141
Avg. PE ratio	11	23	16	12	15	—	—

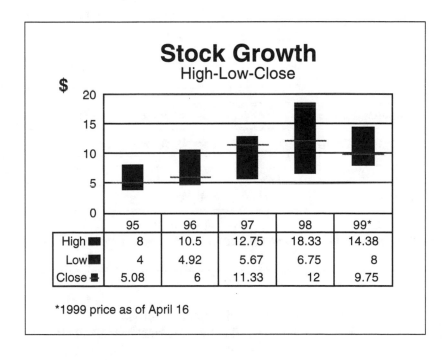

Stock Growth
High-Low-Close

	95	96	97	98	99*
High	8	10.5	12.75	18.33	14.38
Low	4	4.92	5.67	6.75	8
Close	5.08	6	11.33	12	9.75

*1999 price as of April 16

58
Cable Design Technologies Corp.

Foster Plaza 7
661 Anderson Drive
Pittsburgh, PA 15220
412-937-2300
www.cdtc.com

Chairman:
Bryan Cressey
President and CEO:
Paul Olson

Earnings Growth	★ ★ ★ ★
Revenue Growth	★ ★ ★ ★
Stock Growth	
Consistency	★ ★ ★
NYSE: CDT	**11 points**

Cable Design Technologies (CDT) manufactures a broad line of specialty electronic data transmission cables and network wiring systems. Its leading products include electronic copper cable, fiber-optic cable, and network structured wiring components.

CDT sells to leading manufacturers of communications products, regional Bell phone companies, and independent distributors.

The firm has grown quickly through a series of acquisitions, buying well over a dozen smaller companies during the past decade.

The Pittsburgh-based operation breaks its product offerings into several groups, including network products (42 percent of total sales), communications products (19 percent of sales), automation and process control (22 percent), and specialty wire and cable products (16 percent). The firm also makes precision tire molds and sheet metal products, but they account for less than 2 percent of revenue.

Network products include connectors, wiring racks and panels, outlets, and interconnecting hardware for local area networks (LANs) and wide area networks (WANs). Communications products include switchboard and equipment cable.

Automation and process control products include climate control, premise video distribution, and sophisticated security and signal systems involving motion detection, electronic card, and video surveillance technologies. It also makes remote signaling and electronic monitoring systems, and voice activation, evacuation, and similiar systems.

Specialty products include highly engineeered wire and cable products for specialized applications such as commercial aviation and marine, automotive electronics, broadcast, wireless component assemblies, medical electronics, robotics, home entertainment, and appliances.

CDT was founded in 1985 and incorporated in 1988. It went public with its initial stock offering in 1993. The company has 3,200 employees and a market capitalization of about $550 million.

EARNINGS PER SHARE GROWTH ★ ★ ★ ★

Past four years: 338 percent (44 percent per year)

REVENUE GROWTH ★ ★ ★ ★

Past four years: 348 percent (45 percent per year)

STOCK GROWTH

Past three years: −5 percent
Dollar growth: $10,000 over the past three years would have declined to $9,500.

CONSISTENCY ★ ★ ★

Increased earnings per share: three of the past four years
Increased revenue: four of the past four years

CABLE DESIGN TECHNOLOGIES AT A GLANCE

Fiscal year ended: July 31
Revenue and net income in $ millions

	1994	1995	1996	1997	1998	4-Year Growth Avg. Annual (%)	4-Year Growth Total (%)
Revenue ($)	145.4	188.9	357.4	517	651.7	45	348
Net income ($)	10.1	14.7	15.9	36	40.5	42	301
Earnings/share ($)	0.32	0.67	0.64	1.31	1.40	44	338
Avg. PE ratio	13	21	37	15	15	—	—

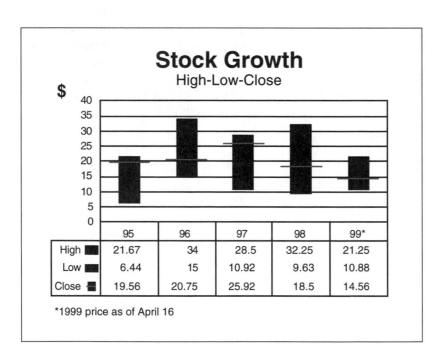

Stock Growth
High-Low-Close

	95	96	97	98	99*
High	21.67	34	28.5	32.25	21.25
Low	6.44	15	10.92	9.63	10.88
Close	19.56	20.75	25.92	18.5	14.56

*1999 price as of April 16

59

Goody's Family Clothing, Inc.

400 Goody's Lane
Knoxville, TN 37922
423-966-2000

Chairman and CEO:
Robert M. Goodfriend
President:
Harry M. Call

Earnings Growth	★ ★ ★	
Revenue Growth	★	
Stock Growth	★ ★ ★ ★	
Consistency	★ ★ ★	
Nasdaq: GDYS	**11 points**	

Goody's is a clothing retailer that has been cutting its own swath across mid-America in midsize markets from Tuscaloosa, Alabama, to Carbondale, Illinois.

Nearly all 250 Goody's stores are located within an 800-mile radius of its corporate headquarters in Knoxville, Tennessee. The stores sell a wide array of men's, women's, and children's apparel at prices of 10 to 30 percent lower than traditional department stores.

Goody's sells both name brand merchandise and private label brands that offer a similar look and quality of name brand apparel at discounted prices. Among the leading brand names Goody's carries are Adidas, Bugle Boy, Dockers, Lee, Leslie Fay, Nike, Reebok, Sag Harbor, and Levi's.

The company's stores, which are generally located in strip shopping centers, are very spacious, covering between 20,000 and 35,000 square feet. Unlike many apparel specialty stores that appeal to a select segment, Goody's offers clothing, shoes, and accessories for the whole family.

Women's clothing is the largest segment, accounting for about 42 percent of Goody's total revenue; denim products account for 23 percent; men's apparel makes up about 20 percent; children's contributes 7 percent; and shoes and accessories account for about 8 percent.

Goody's opens about 30 new stores each year. Most of its stores are located in small to midsize markets and suburban growth areas where the retailer can take advantage of lower rent and occupancy costs and fewer competitors.

The company takes an aggressive advertising approach, running ads in local newspapers at least once a week, 52 weeks a year, and television and radio ads about 39 weeks a year. All ads are produced by the company's corporate office. The Knoxville headquarters also handles all purchasing, pricing, marketing, distribution, finance, and information systems.

Goody's was founded in 1954. The company has about 9,000 employees and a market capitalization of about $360 million.

EARNINGS PER SHARE GROWTH ★ ★ ★

Past four years: 137 percent (24 percent per year)

REVENUE GROWTH ★

Past four years: 92 percent (18 percent per year)

STOCK GROWTH ★ ★ ★ ★

Past three years: 128 percent (32 percent per year)
Dollar growth: $10,000 over the past three years would have grown to about $23,000.

CONSISTENCY ★ ★ ★

Increased earnings per share: three of the past four years
Increased revenue: four of the past four years

GOODY'S FAMILY CLOTHING AT A GLANCE

Fiscal year ended: Jan. 31
Revenue and net income in $ millions

| | | | | | | 4-Year Growth | |
| | | | | | | Avg. Annual (%) | Total (%) |
	1994	1995	1996	1997	1998		
Revenue ($)	505	613.7	696.9	819.1	971.9	18	92
Net income ($)	13.8	6.94	10.5	17.2	33.3	24	141
Earnings/share ($)	0.43	0.21	0.33	0.53	1.02	24	137
Avg. PE ratio	33	18	12	14	10	—	—

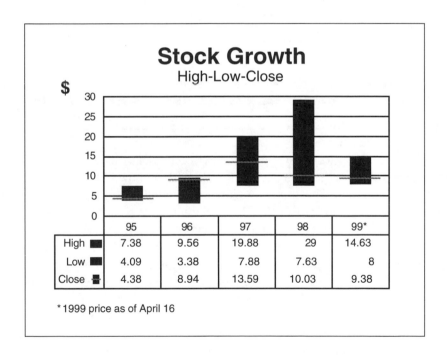

Stock Growth
High-Low-Close

	95	96	97	98	99*
High	7.38	9.56	19.88	29	14.63
Low	4.09	3.38	7.88	7.63	8
Close	4.38	8.94	13.59	10.03	9.38

*1999 price as of April 16

60
CBT Group, PLC

900 Chesapeake Drive
Redwood City, CA 94063
650-817-5900

Chairman:
William G. McCabe
President and CEO:
Gregory M. Priest

Earnings Growth	★ ★ ★ ★
Revenue Growth	★ ★ ★ ★
Stock Growth	
Consistency	★ ★ ★
Nasdaq: CBTSY	**11 points**

If you've ever tried to wrestle with a new computer software program without benefit of a tutor, you can readily understand how CBT Group attracts new customers. The company works with hundreds of corporations and institutions around the world to develop interactive computer software designed specifically to help people run their computers.

For instance, CBT has been working recently with the U.S. Air Force to provide interactive educational software for all of its personnel worldwide.

CBT has developed an extensive library of training packages, including about 500 titles in all. The interactive training software is designed to help businesspeople work with computer software programs developed by such companies as Microsoft, Oracle, Netscape, Cisco, Lotus, Novell, and Powersoft. CBT's training software is used by more than 1,000 major corporations around the world.

One of its more popular packages, the CBT JavaScript Object Model courseware, helps computer program developers and programmers who are new to scripting languages learn the basics of designing Internet applications. Founded in Dublin, Ireland, CBT's stock trades in the United

States on the Nasdaq exchange. About 75 percent of the firm's revenue is generated in the United States.

There are several advantages to interactive training software. Users can run through the training programs on their own schedule at their own computer—no travel and no special schedules to meet. And users learn at their own pace.

CBT derives its revenues primarily from agreements under which customers license its software for periods of one, two, or three years. The multiyear agreements generally allow customers to exchange training titles for other titles in the CBT library on an annual basis.

The company also generates revenue by forming development and marketing alliances with some of the leading software companies (such as Informix Software) to develop training software for their newer products.

CBT went public with its initial public offering in 1995. The company has about 1,200 employees and a market capitalization of about $650 million.

EARNINGS PER SHARE GROWTH   ★ ★ ★ ★

Past four years: 640 percent (65 percent per year)

REVENUE GROWTH   ★ ★ ★ ★

Past four years: 579 percent (61 percent per year)

STOCK GROWTH

Past three years: 12 percent (3 percent per year)
Dollar growth: $10,000 over the past three years would have grown to about $11,000.

CONSISTENCY   ★ ★ ★

Increased earnings per share: three of the past four years
Increased revenue: four of the past four years

CBT GROUP AT A GLANCE

Fiscal year ended: Dec. 31
Revenue and net income in $ millions

	1994	1995	1996	1997	1998	4-Year Growth Avg. Annual (%)	4-Year Growth Total (%)
Revenue ($)	23.9	49.3	73.6	118.6	162.2	61	579
Net income ($)	1.58	6.03	11.8	22.2	16.5	79	944
Earnings/share ($)	0.05	0.20	0.34	0.58	0.37	65	640
Avg. PE ratio	—	48	62	52	40	—	—

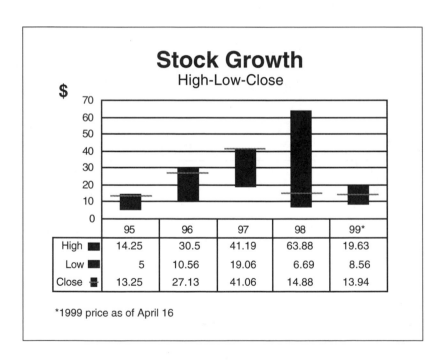

Stock Growth
High-Low-Close

$

	95	96	97	98	99*
High	14.25	30.5	41.19	63.88	19.63
Low	5	10.56	19.06	6.69	8.56
Close	13.25	27.13	41.06	14.88	13.94

*1999 price as of April 16

K&G Men's Center, Inc.

1225 Chattahoochee Avenue N.W.
Atlanta, GA 30318
404-351-7987

Chairman, President, and CEO:
Stephen H. Greenspan

Earnings Growth	★ ★ ★ ★
Revenue Growth	★ ★ ★
Stock Growth	
Consistency	★ ★ ★ ★
Nasdaq: MENS	**11 points**

K&G Men's Center is a growing men's apparel superstore chain that sells its clothing at 30 to 70 percent below prices typically charged by traditional department stores.

The Atlanta-based retailer has about 30 stores in 16 states, spread broadly across all U.S. regions. There are three K&G Men's Centers in its hometown of Atlanta, plus stores in Baltimore, Boston, Charlotte, Cincinnati, Cleveland, Dallas, Denver, Houston, Indianapolis, Long Island, Los Angeles, Minneapolis, Philadelphia, Seattle, Washington, D.C., Kansas City Kansas, and several other locations.

But you probably won't find a K&G at your local mall. Most of the firm's outlets are destination stores located in low-cost warehouses and secondary strip malls that are easily accessible from major highways and thoroughfares.

The stores, which are vast, stark, brightly lit warehouse rooms with long rows of clothing racks and display tables, are open only on Fridays, Saturdays, and Sundays—a total of about 24 hours a week. The barebones operation is designed to keep overhead to a minimum, while still accommodating the shopping habits of working men.

The company also stresses high inventory turnover through low cost pricing. It sells suits, blazers, dress pants, ties, dress shirts, and other business attire, as well as casual apparel such as slacks, shorts, polo shirts, sweaters, coats, jackets, socks, shoes, and sportswear.

The firm sells both brand name and private label merchandise in a wide range of sizes and styles.

K&G plans to open more than 70 new stores over the next five to six years. Most will be located in the top 50 metropolitan markets. Stores will be clustered in market areas to take advantage of advertising and operating efficiencies.

K&G was founded in 1989. It went public with its initial stock offering in 1996. The firm has about 175 employees and a market capitalization of about $85 million.

EARNINGS PER SHARE GROWTH ★ ★ ★ ★

Past four years: 250 percent (52 percent per year)

REVENUE GROWTH ★ ★ ★

Past four years: 204 percent (33 percent per year)

STOCK GROWTH

Past two years: −48 percent
Dollar growth: $10,000 over the past two years would have declined to about $5,000.

CONSISTENCY ★ ★ ★ ★

Increased earnings per share: four of the past four years
Increased revenue: four of the past four years

K&G MEN'S CENTER AT A GLANCE

Fiscal year ended: Jan. 30
Revenue and net income in $ millions

	1994	1995	1996	1997	1998	4-Year Growth Avg. Annual (%)	Total (%)
Revenue ($)	37.1	49.8	60.0	88.1	112.8	33	204
Net income ($)	1.4	2.3	3.2	4.7	6.6	67	371
Earnings/share ($)	0.18	0.32	0.38	0.47	0.63	52	250
Avg. PE ratio	—	—	26	30	14	—	—

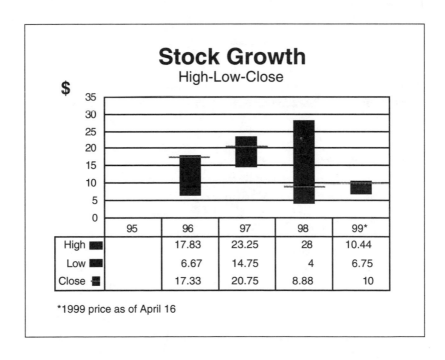

Stock Growth
High-Low-Close

$	95	96	97	98	99*
High		17.83	23.25	28	10.44
Low		6.67	14.75	4	6.75
Close		17.33	20.75	8.88	10

*1999 price as of April 16

Lawrence Savings Bank

30 Massachusetts Avenue
North Andover, MA 01845
978-725-7500

Chairman:
Salvatore F. Cataudella
President:
Paul A. Miller

Earnings Growth	★ ★ ★ ★
Revenue Growth	
Stock Growth	★ ★ ★ ★
Consistency	★ ★ ★
Nasdaq: LSBX	**11 points**

Lawrence Savings Bank is a small regional institution that serves consumers and businesses in the Merrimack Valley of Massachusetts and southern New Hampshire. The North Andover, Massachusetts operation has just five branch offices. They are located in North Andover, Andover, Lawrence, and Methuen (two).

Although the company traces its roots to 1868, its real growth has come in the past few years, with earnings growing more than ten-fold in the past five years.

The bank offers a wide range of services for both consumers and businesses. In the commercial real estate market, the bank originates loans secured by commercial real estate, including retail, manufacturing office, and office condominiums and small businesses.

It also offers loans securied by non–real estate business assets. The loans are based on the creditworthiness of the company, security offered, and future cash flow of the borrower.

Lawrence makes a number of construction loans for land development, construction of residential homes built on speculation, construction of homes for homeowners with permanent financing, and commercial facilities.

The bank caters to individuals with fixed- and adjustable-rate residential mortgage loans, home equity loans, and second mortgages. Consumers also can receive overdraft lines of credit, collateral loans, and secured and unsecured personal loans.

The bank's principal source of funding includes deposits, loan payments and prepayments, investment securities payments and maturities, advances from the Federal Home Loan Bank, and other federal funds.

The company has about 100 employees and a market capitalization of about $50 million. It has annual deposits of about $260 million and total assets of about $360 million. Its gross loans total about $170 million.

EARNINGS PER SHARE GROWTH   ★ ★ ★ ★

Past four years: 1,357 percent (95 percent per year)

REVENUE GROWTH

Past four years: 34 percent (8 percent per year)

STOCK GROWTH   ★ ★ ★ ★

Past three years: 176 percent (40 percent per year)
Dollar growth: $10,000 over the past three years would have grown to about $28,000.

CONSISTENCY   ★ ★ ★

Increased earnings per share: four of the past four years
Increased revenue: three of the past four years

LAWRENCE SAVINGS BANK AT A GLANCE

Fiscal year ended: Dec. 31
Revenue and net income in $ millions

	1994	1995	1996	1997	1998	4-Year Growth Avg. Annual (%)	4-Year Growth Total (%)
Revenue ($)	18.8	19.8	22.9	25.4	25.1	8	34
Net income ($)	0.588	2.92	5.23	8.11	8.81	14	70
Earnings/share ($)	0.14	0.69	1.23	1.90	2.04	95	1,357
Avg. PE ratio	31	6	6	7	8	—	—

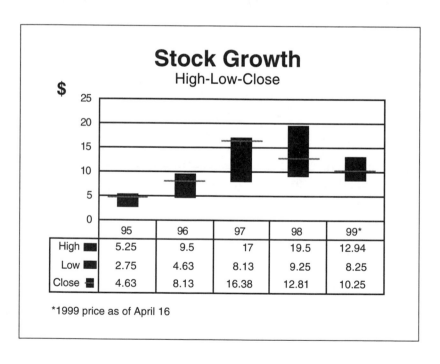

Stock Growth
High-Low-Close

	95	96	97	98	99*
High	5.25	9.5	17	19.5	12.94
Low	2.75	4.63	8.13	9.25	8.25
Close	4.63	8.13	16.38	12.81	10.25

*1999 price as of April 16

63
UBICS, Inc.

UBICS

333 Technology Drive
Suite 210
Canonsburg, PA 15317
724-746-6001
www.ubics.com

Chairman:
Vijay Mallya
President:
Manohar B. Hira

Earnings Growth	★ ★ ★ ★	
Revenue Growth	★ ★ ★ ★	
Stock Growth		
Consistency	★ ★ ★	
Nasdaq: UBIX	**11 points**	

UBICS provides information technology services for large and midsize corporations and organizations, including every aspect of the life cycle of the computer system, from strategy and design to development and implementation to maintenance and support. The company specializes in database management and systems administration.

The Pittsburgh-based operation offers its services on a time-and-materials basis, with UBICS professionals working within the client company's project team.

UBICS has more than 130 client companies in a wide range of industries. Among its leading clients are Caterpillar, Fruit of the Loom, Ralston

Purina, and The Hartford. The company has placed more than 200 information technology professionals with its corporate clients.

To maintain its growing pool of professionals, UBICS recruits information technology professionals from India and other countries worldwide. It has a recruiting and training center in India.

The company's consultants help clients solve data processing and computing problems in several key areas, including client/server design and development. UBICS consultants help companies design and set up their corporate computer systems and link up to the Internet.

Other areas of expertise include enterprise resource planning (including implementation of packaged software, customization, database administration, and end-user training); application maintenance programming (including Y2K conversion services, system design, data conversion, and user interface conversion); and database and system administration.

The company markets its services through a direct sales force of about 20 professionals located throughout the United States. The firm is in the midst of plans to open offices in South Africa, the United Kingdom, Singapore, and the Middle East.

Founded in 1994, the company went public with its initial stock offering in 1997. UBICS has about 200 corporate employees and a market capitalization of about $36 million.

EARNINGS PER SHARE GROWTH ★ ★ ★ ★

Past two years: 700 percent (285 percent per year)

REVENUE GROWTH ★ ★ ★ ★

Past four years: 9,867 percent (217 percent per year)

STOCK GROWTH

Past one year: −64 percent
Dollar growth: $10,000 over the past year would have declined to $3,600.

CONSISTENCY ★ ★ ★

Increased earnings per share: two of the past three years
Increased revenue: four of the past four years

UBICS AT A GLANCE

Fiscal year ended: Dec. 31
Revenue and net income in $ millions

	1994	1995	1996	1997	1998	4-Year Growth Avg. Annual (%)	Total (%)
Revenue ($)	0.303	1.45	9.07	20.5	30.2	217	9,867
Net income ($)	0.003	0.004	0.218	1.88	2.1	498	69,990
Earnings/share ($)	—	—	0.04	0.36	0.32	285*	700*
Avg. PE ratio	—	—	—	39	43	—	—

*Earnings per share returns are based on two-year performance.

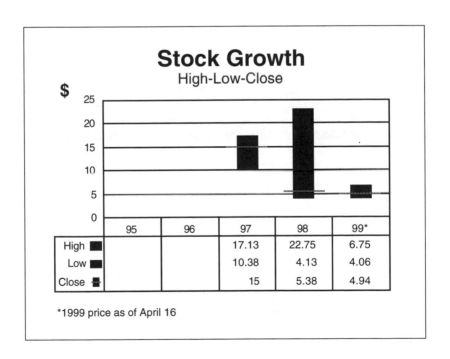

Stock Growth
High-Low-Close

$	95	96	97	98	99*
High ■			17.13	22.75	6.75
Low ■			10.38	4.13	4.06
Close ■			15	5.38	4.94

*1999 price as of April 16

AmeriPath, Inc.

7289 Garden Road
Suite 200
Riviera Beach, FL 33404
561-845-1850
www.ameripath.com

Chairman:
Thomas S. Roberts
President and CEO:
James C. New

Earnings Growth	★ ★ ★ ★
Revenue Growth	★ ★ ★ ★
Stock Growth	
Consistency	★ ★ ★
Nasdaq: PATH	**11 points**

AmeriPath is a physician practice management firm operating within a very specific niche of the medical field. The company acquires and operates anatomic pathology practices. Pathologists analyze lab samples to help doctors diagnose diseases.

The Riviera Beach, Florida operation has practices in ten states, with more than 220 pathologists who provide medical services through outpatient pathology laboratories, hospital inpatient laboratories, and outpatient surgery centers. Most of its practices are in the South and Midwest. The firm has been focusing particularly on building its base in Florida and Texas.

The practice of pathology includes the diagnosis of diseases through examination of tissues and cells. It is a very lucrative part of the medical business.

AmeriPath manages and controls all of the nonmedical functions of its practices, including recruiting, training, and management of the technical and support staff of the practices; developing, equipping, and staffing laboratory facilities; negotiating and maintaining contracts with hospitals, clinical laboratories, and managed care organizations; providing financial reporting and administration, clerical, purchasing, payroll, billing, and collection; and handling payrolls, benefits, purchasing, information systems, sales and marketing, and accounting.

AmeriPath also provides slide preparation and other technical services.

AmeriPath's rapid growth has come primarily through acquisitions. The company picked up five new practices, including 45 pathologists, in 1997, and added about a dozen new practices in 1998. It is the only company that focuses specifically on anatomic pathology.

In addition to the administrative functions it offers, AmeriPath also helps drum up business for its member pathologists through increased marketing and additional contracts with hospitals. The increased business, along with the administrative cost savings brought about by the consolidation of its practices, has helped bolster the company's profit margins.

The company went public with its initial stock offering in 1997. AmeriPath has about 1,000 employees and a market capitalization of about $210 million.

EARNINGS PER SHARE GROWTH   ★ ★ ★ ★

Past four years: 642 percent (65 percent per year)

REVENUE GROWTH   ★ ★ ★ ★

Past four years: 1,123 percent (85 percent per year)

STOCK GROWTH

Past one year: −47 percent
Dollar growth: $10,000 over the past one-year period would have declined to $5,300.

CONSISTENCY   ★ ★ ★

Increased earnings per share: three of the past four years
Increased revenue: four of the past four years

AMERIPATH AT A GLANCE

Fiscal year ended: Dec. 31
Revenue and net income in $ millions

	1994	1995	1996	1997	1998	4-Year Growth Avg. Annual (%)	4-Year Growth Total (%)
Revenue ($)	14.5	16	42.6	108.4	177.3	85	1,123
Net income ($)	1.15	0.902	2.03	7.32	18.6	100	1,517
Earnings/share ($)	0.12	0.10	0.22	0.83	0.89	65	642
Avg. PE ratio	—	—	—	21	13	—	—

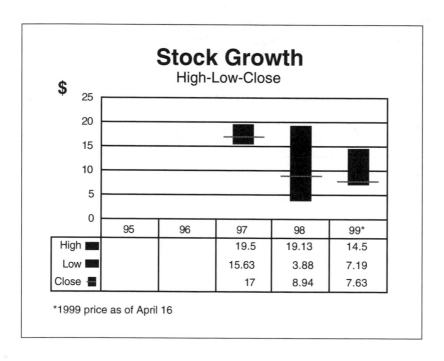

Stock Growth
High-Low-Close

$	95	96	97	98	99*
High			19.5	19.13	14.5
Low			15.63	3.88	7.19
Close			17	8.94	7.63

*1999 price as of April 16

65
ICU Medical, Inc.

951 Calle Amanecer
San Clemente, CA 92763
949-366-2183
www.icumed.com

Chairman, President, and CEO:
George A. Lopez, M.D.

Earnings Growth	★ ★ ★
Revenue Growth	★ ★ ★
Stock Growth	
Consistency	★ ★ ★ ★
Nasdaq: ICUI	**10 points**

ICU Medical makes needleless, disposable intravenous (IV) connection systems designed to prevent accidental disconnection of IV lines and to protect health care workers and their patients from the spread of infectious diseases.

The company's rapid growth has come amid heightened awareness of the risk of infection from needlesticks and the substantial expense in complying with stringent regulations regarding needlesticks. ICU's protective IV connectors are a safer, better option for IV patients.

ICU's first products were the Click Lock and Piggy Lock IVs, which use protected needles designed to prevent accidental needle contact and locking mechanisms to prevent accidental disconnections.

Its more advanced needleless IV connection systems were developed in 1993 to avoid the risks of needle handling and disposal. The ICU Clave

IV connection system allows protected, secure, and sterile IV connections without needles and without failure prone mechanical valves used in other traditional IV systems.

ICU products are used in hospitals, nursing homes, emergency units, physicians offices, convalescent centers, and home health care.

The Clave product line accounts for about 65 percent of ICU's total revenue.

The firm also offers several other related products, including the McGaw protected needle, which ICU distributes as part of a marketing agreement with McGaw, Inc. ICU also offers the Lopez Valve, a small valve designed to be connected into nasogastric tube systems; a line of inexpensive, single-use needleless connectors; and the CLC 2000, a one-piece connector designed to prevent the backflow of blood into the catheter.

The company markets its products through 19 independent distributors (with about 150 salespeople) in the United States. The firm also has about 30 product specialists who support its sales force.

The San Clemente, California operation went public with its initial stock offering in 1992. The firm has 130 employees and a market capitalization of about $180 million.

EARNINGS PER SHARE GROWTH   ★ ★ ★

Past four years: 110 percent (20 percent per year)

REVENUE GROWTH   ★ ★ ★

Past four years: 141 percent (25 percent per year)

STOCK GROWTH

Past three years: 29 percent (9 percent per year)
Dollar growth: $10,000 over the past three years would have grown to about $13,000.

CONSISTENCY   ★ ★ ★ ★

Increased earnings per share: four of the past four years
Increased revenue: four of the past four years

ICU MEDICAL AT A GLANCE

Fiscal year ended: Dec. 31
Revenue and net income in $ millions

	1994	1995	1996	1997	1998	4-Year Growth Avg. Annual (%)	4-Year Growth Total (%)
Revenue ($)	16.5	21.3	24.6	30.4	39.8	25	141
Net income ($)	2.9	4.2	4.7	5.7	7.22	26	149
Earnings/share ($)	0.41	0.53	0.54	0.71	0.86	20	110
Avg. PE ratio	38	27	28	15	20	—	—

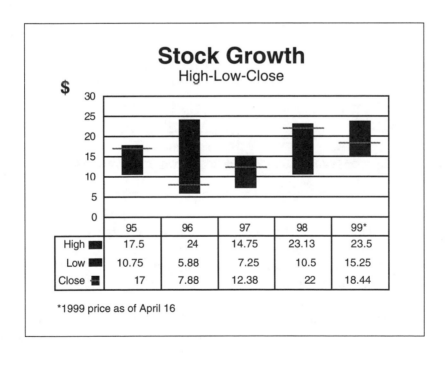

Stock Growth
High-Low-Close

	95	96	97	98	99*
High	17.5	24	14.75	23.13	23.5
Low	10.75	5.88	7.25	10.5	15.25
Close	17	7.88	12.38	22	18.44

*1999 price as of April 16

Xeta Corporation

4500 South Garnett
Suite 1000
Tulsa, OK 74146
918-664-8200

President and CEO:
Jack R. Ingram

Earnings Growth	★ ★ ★
Revenue Growth	★ ★ ★ ★
Stock Growth	
Consistency	★ ★ ★
Nasdaq: XETA	**10 points**

Xeta is a distributor of phone systems for hotels and motels.

Xeta's leading product line is the Hitachi 5000 Series Digital Communications system. The system, known as a private branch exchange (PBX), connects the hotel to outside telephone networks and routes calls to, from, and between extensions within the hotel.

The Tulsa, Oklahoma distributor also sells a variety of other PBX products for use at hotels, such as voice mail systems, analog telephones, uninterruptable power supplies, and announcement systems.

Xeta also has developed its own proprietary PBX product, called the Xpander, that is used in hotels and motels to increase their phone line capacity to accommodate guests who need an extra phone line to connect their portable computers to networks or the Internet.

The company's call accounting systems are used by hotels and motels to automatically record and bill guests for calls.

Service is a key element of Xeta's offerings. The hotel industry is a 24-hour-per-day business that relies heavily on phone systems. Xeta has built a national network of technicians and third party providers who can respond quickly to solve any phone problems at any of the company's facilities. Xeta also has developed an advanced remote service operation that can quickly diagnose and, in most cases, correct system malfunctions without an on-site service call.

Xeta recently began offering a variety of MCI long distance services to its lodging customers, under which Xeta earns commissions on all calls made by guests at those hotels.

Xeta's leading customer is Marriott International, including Marriott Hotels, Residence Inn, Courtyard, and Fairfield Inns. Marriott has been a customer of the company's since 1986.

The firm markets its products through an 11-person sales staff and an independent sales agent.

Xeta, which was founded in 1981, has about 110 employees and a market capitalization of about $35 million.

EARNINGS PER SHARE GROWTH   ★ ★ ★

Past four years: 154 percent (26 percent per year)

REVENUE GROWTH   ★ ★ ★ ★

Past four years: 248 percent (36 percent per year)

STOCK GROWTH

Past three years: 6 percent (2 percent per year)
Dollar growth: $10,000 over the past three years would have grown to $10,600.

CONSISTENCY   ★ ★ ★

Increased earnings per share: three of the past four years
Increased revenue: four of the past four years

XETA AT A GLANCE

Fiscal year ended: Oct. 31
Revenue and net income in $ millions

	1994	1995	1996	1997	1998	4-Year Growth Avg. Annual (%)	Total (%)
Revenue ($)	7.3	12.4	13.4	18.8	25.4	36	248
Net income ($)	1.1	1.5	1.6	2.1	3.1	28	182
Earnings/share ($)	0.51	0.68	0.68	0.91	1.30	26	154
Avg. PE ratio	4	17	17	18	12	—	—

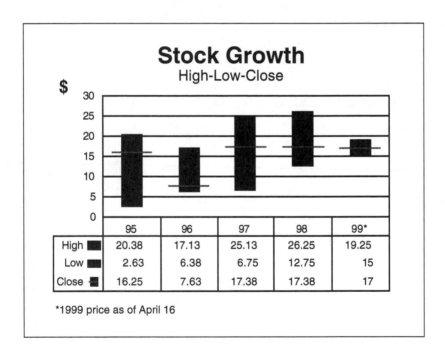

Stock Growth
High-Low-Close

	95	96	97	98	99*
High	20.38	17.13	25.13	26.25	19.25
Low	2.63	6.38	6.75	12.75	15
Close	16.25	7.63	17.38	17.38	17

*1999 price as of April 16

67
STV Group, Inc.

STV Group

205 West Welsh Drive
Douglassville, PA 19518
610-385-8200
www.stvinc.com

Chairman and CEO:
Michael Haratunian
President:
Dominick M. Servedio

Earnings Growth	★ ★ ★ ★
Revenue Growth	
Stock Growth	★ ★ ★ ★
Consistency	★ ★
Nasdaq: STVI	**10 points**

STV Group is an engineering and architectural company that helps build roads, bridges, prisons, hospitals, churches, office buildings, and a wide range of other projects.

The Douglassville, Pennsylvania operation does most of its work for state and local governments, which account for about 56 percent of its total revenue. Other leading clients include the U.S. government, 16 percent; private contractors, 27 percent; and foreign governments, 1 percent.

STV does business in several different segments, including,

- *Transportation engineering* (37 percent of total revenue). The company designs track, terminals, stations, yards, and shops for the railway industry.

- *Architectural engineering* (24 percent of revenue). STV designs commercial, industrial, and government buildings; medical and educational facilities; laboratories, recreational, religious, and cultural centers; military installations; penal institutions; and public utility facilities.
- *Civil, highway, bridge, airport, and port* (24 percent). The company designs highways, bridges, airports, seaports, lighting, toll and service facilities, drainage and erosion control systems, aircraft hangars, and control towers.
- *Defense systems engineering* (4 percent). STV designs and tests equipment and hardware for the U.S. Department of Defense. Its projects involve naval aircraft, weapons systems, aircraft carriers, support ships, mobile weapon loaders, munition trailers, and aircraft catapults and stopping systems on aircraft carriers.
- *Industrial process engineering* (2 percent). STV designs various manufacturing equipment and process systems. The firm also offers technical analyses, feasibility studies, plant layouts, and machinery and construction inspection services.

The company also performs some other engineering and consulting work outside of its core areas, which account for about 7 percent of revenue. One of its faster-growing segments is its design-build service, in which the company not only designs the projects but also handles the subcontracting and supervision of the construction phase.

STV has about 1,000 employees and a market capitalization of about $33 million.

EARNINGS PER SHARE GROWTH ★ ★ ★ ★

Past four years: 244 percent (36 percent per year)

REVENUE GROWTH

Past four years: 3 percent (18 percent per year)

STOCK GROWTH

Past three years: 176 percent (40 percent per year)
Dollar growth: $10,000 over the past three years would have grown to about $28,000.

CONSISTENCY

Increased earnings per share: three of the past four years
Increased revenue: three of the past four years

STV GROUP AT A GLANCE

Fiscal year ended: Sept. 31
Revenue and net income in $ millions

	1994	1995	1996	1997	1998	4-Year Growth Avg. Annual (%)	Total (%)
Revenue ($)	89.5	89.2	94.1	94.7	105.3	3	18
Net income ($)	0.563	0.394	0.595	0.860	2.2	41	291
Earnings/share ($)	0.16	0.11	0.16	0.23	0.55	36	244
Avg. PE ratio	16	26	22	18	16	—	—

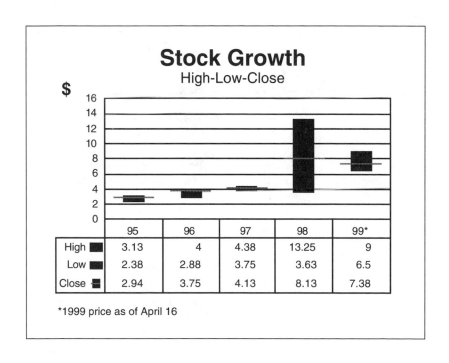

Stock Growth
High-Low-Close

$

	95	96	97	98	99*
High	3.13	4	4.38	13.25	9
Low	2.38	2.88	3.75	3.63	6.5
Close	2.94	3.75	4.13	8.13	7.38

*1999 price as of April 16

68

Newport Corp.

1791 Deere Avenue
Irvine, CA 92606
946-863-3144
www.newport.com

Chairman, President, and CEO:
Robert G. Deuster

Earnings Growth	★ ★ ★
Revenue Growth	
Stock Growth	★ ★ ★
Consistency	★ ★ ★ ★
Nasdaq: NEWP	**10 points**

Newport manufactures a line of instruments and testing equipment designed to help manufacturers of fiber-optic equipment, computer peripherals, and semiconductor equipment produce more precisely engineered products.

The trend toward miniaturization in the computer and telecommunications industries has required that manufacturers produce their products with greater precision within extremely narrow tolerances. Newport's equipment helps manufacturers make and test reduced-size components of such products as hard disk drives, semiconductor wafers, and fiber-optic communications equipment with increased functionality.

The Irvine, California operation is a leading supplier of high precision optics, instruments, micropositioning, and measurement products and systems. It also continues to focus on developing more precise research test and measurement equipment to provide ultraprecision motion and measurement technologies for research applications. Its AutoAlign, Orion, and LaserWeld systems permit automated alignment and connection of optical fibers within extremely narrow tolerances.

Newport also manufactures laser diode burn-in and characterization equipment that allows diode manufacturers to more effectively age and test laser diodes used as the light source in fiber-optic networks.

For the computer peripherals market, Newport makes high precision optical and mechanical testing equipment, as well as precision motion sub-assemblies and integrated systems used by manufacturers of disk drives and other devices for test, measurement, inspection, and calibration applications.

Newport uses a multipronged marketing approach to sell its products, including a comprehensive set of product catalogs mailed to more than 100,000 prospects, an internal marketing staff, 20 field salespersons, a nationwide network of distributors and sales representatives, and a tele-marketing operation. In the international market, products are sold through a network of company-employed field sales personnel and independent representatives. International sales account for about 35 percent of total revenue.

Newport was founded in 1967. It has about 800 employees and a market capitalization of about $150 million.

EARNINGS PER SHARE GROWTH ★ ★ ★

Past four years: 153 percent (26 percent per year)

REVENUE GROWTH

Past four years: 43 percent (9 percent per year)

STOCK GROWTH ★ ★ ★

Past three years: 107 percent (27 percent per year)
Dollar growth: $10,000 over the past three years would have grown to about $21,000.

CONSISTENCY ★ ★ ★ ★

Increased earnings per share: four of the past four years
Increased revenue: four of the past four years

NEWPORT AT A GLANCE

Fiscal year ended: Dec. 31
Revenue and net income in $ millions

| | 1994 | 1995 | 1996 | 1997 | 1998 | 4-Year Growth | |
						Avg. Annual (%)	Total (%)
Revenue ($)	94.2	102	119.8	132.6	134.4	9	43
Net income ($)	3.18	3.88	4.7	7.06	8.98	30	182
Earnings/share ($)	0.38	0.47	0.54	0.80	0.96	26	153
Avg. PE ratio	18	21	17	16	17	—	—

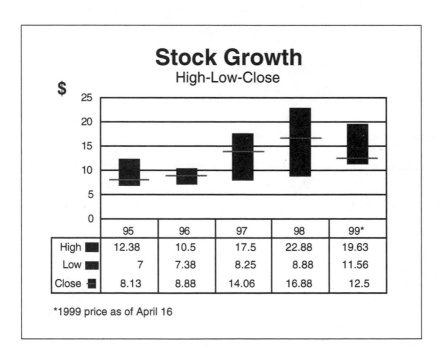

Stock Growth
High-Low-Close

	95	96	97	98	99*
High	12.38	10.5	17.5	22.88	19.63
Low	7	7.38	8.25	8.88	11.56
Close	8.13	8.88	14.06	16.88	12.5

*1999 price as of April 16

69
Century Business Services, Inc.

6480 Rockside Woods Boulevard
Suite 330
Cleveland, OH 44131
216-447-9000

Chairman, President, and CEO:
Michael G. Groote

Earnings Growth	★ ★ ★
Revenue Growth	★ ★ ★ ★
Stock Growth	
Consistency	★ ★ ★
Nasdaq: CBIZ	**10 points**

Century Business Services is an outsourcing operation that provides specialty temporary workers for corporations throughout the United States.

Its leading areas of expertise are accounting systems, advisory and tax services, employee benefits design and administration, human resources, information technology, payroll, specialty insurance, valuation, and workers comp.

Based in Valley View, Ohio, Century operates its primary business through 82 branch offices in 26 states. Cenury also owns Comprehensive Business Services, which is a franchisor of accounting services with about 250 franchisee offices in 40 states.

In all, the company serves more than 60,000 clients a year. Its clients employ more than a million Century workers, including about 250,000 through its Comprehensive Business Services subsidiary.

Most of Century's clients are businesses with fewer than 500 employees that prefer to focus their resources on their core business. They contract with Century to fill in in noncore administrative functions, such as accounting, employee benefits, payroll, and workers compensation administration.

Century also operates a speciality insurance division that provides commercial liability insurance, bonding services, and workers compensation coverage to small and medium-size businesses. Its leading insurance customers include small construction contractors, restaurants, bars and taverns, tanning salons, and small commercial and retail establishments.

Century plans to continue its rapid growth through internal expansion and a series of acquisitions of similar companies.

Century was formed in 1987, primarily as a hazardous waste service company under the name Stout Associates. The firm was acquired by Republic Industries in 1992 and spun off in 1995. In 1997, the company changed its name to Century Business Services and sold off its hazardous waste service. In its current incarnation, Century went public with its initial public stock offering in 1997. The firm has about 1,200 employees and a market capitalization of about $900 million.

EARNINGS PER SHARE GROWTH   ★ ★ ★

Past four years: 125 percent (23 percent per year)

REVENUE GROWTH   ★ ★ ★ ★

Past four years: 1,163 percent (89 percent per year)

STOCK GROWTH

Past one year: −16 percent
Dollar growth: $10,000 over the past year would have declined to $8,400.

CONSISTENCY   ★ ★ ★

Increased earnings per share: three of the past four years
Increased revenue: four of the past four years

CENTURY BUSINESS SERVICES AT A GLANCE

Fiscal year ended: Dec. 31
Revenue and net income in $ millions

	1994	1995	1996	1997	1998	4-Year Growth Avg. Annual (%)	4-Year Growth Total (%)
Revenue ($)	27.3	30.9	35.8	108.3	344.7	89	1,163
Net income ($)	3.50	3.47	4.42	12.8	38.7	82	1,006
Earnings/share ($)	0.24	0.24	0.25	0.35	0.54	23	125
Avg. PE ratio	—	—	—	36	32	—	—

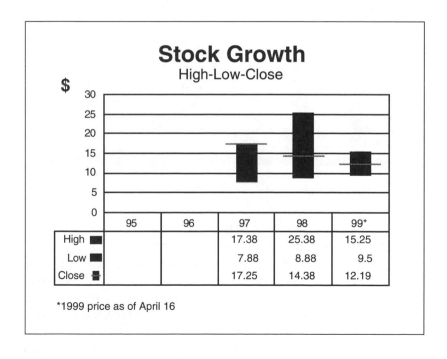

Stock Growth
High-Low-Close

	95	96	97	98	99*
High			17.38	25.38	15.25
Low			7.88	8.88	9.5
Close			17.25	14.38	12.19

*1999 price as of April 16

Medialink Worldwide, Inc.

708 Third Avenue
New York, NY 10017
212-682-8300
www.medialink.com

Chairman, President, and CEO:
Laurence Moskowitz

Earnings Growth	
Revenue Growth	★ ★ ★ ★
Stock Growth	★ ★ ★
Consistency	★ ★ ★
Nasdaq: MDLK	**10 points**

When Burger King executives wanted to get the message out that their french fries topped McDonald's fries in a nationwide taste test, they hired Medialink Worldwide to create video and audio promotional tapes to send to television and radio stations around the country. When Intel executives wanted to educate consumers about the Pentium computer chip, they hired Medialink to stage one-on-one interviews via satellite between Intel specialists and television news stations around the country.

Medialink is the leading provider of video and audio production and satellite distribution for corporations seeking to communicate their news through television, radio, the Internet, and other media.

The company also provides press release distribution services for clients, as well as tracking and analysis of print and broadcast news coverage to help its corporate clients gauge the effectiveness of their public relations efforts.

The company's core business is satellite distribution of video news releases and the electronic monitoring of their broadcast on television. The New York–based operation has more than 1,500 clients, including AT&T, General Motors, IBM, Johnson & Johnson, Microsoft, Philip Morris, Sony, and Compaq. Medialink recently signed an agreement with broadcast.com to provide Internet broadcast and production services for broadcast.com's business clients. The productions will be aired on the World Wide Web.

Medialink began offering production of video news releases in 1994 and has since developed a full range of video, audio, Internet, and print services it offers on a global basis. The company markets its releases to more than 3,000 newsrooms at television and radio networks, local stations, cable channels, direct broadcast satellite systems, and online services on the Internet.

The firm also coordinates live television interviews through satellite media tours and produces live broadcasts of newsworthy events for its clients.

Medialink went public with its initial stock offering in 1997. The company has about 200 employees and a market capitalization of about $90 million.

EARNINGS PER SHARE GROWTH

Past four years: 36 percent (8 percent per year)

REVENUE GROWTH   ★ ★ ★ ★

Past four years: 423 percent (52 percent per year)

STOCK GROWTH   ★ ★ ★

Past one year: 25 percent
Dollar growth: $10,000 over the past year would have grown to $12,500.

CONSISTENCY   ★ ★ ★

Increased earnings per share: three of the past four years
Increased revenue: four of the past four years

MEDIALINK WORLDWIDE AT A GLANCE

Fiscal year ended: Dec. 31
Revenue and net income in $ millions

	1994	1995	1996	1997	1998	4-Year Growth Avg. Annual (%)	4-Year Growth Total (%)
Revenue ($)	7.55	10.6	15.8	26.8	39.5	52	423
Net income ($)	1.46	0.382	0.844	2.38	3.32	23	127
Earnings/share ($)	0.42	0.11	0.25	0.49	0.57	8	36
Avg. PE ratio	—	—	—	28	34	—	—

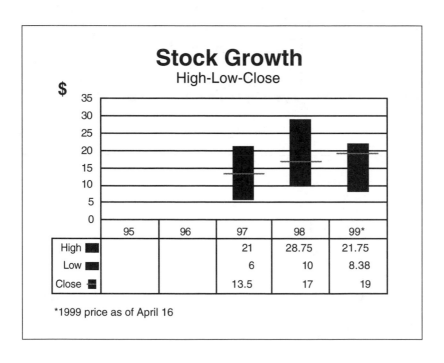

Stock Growth
High-Low-Close

$	95	96	97	98	99*
High			21	28.75	21.75
Low			6	10	8.38
Close			13.5	17	19

*1999 price as of April 16

LINC CAPITAL

303 East Wacker Drive
Suite 1000
Chicago, IL 60601
312-946-1000
www.linccapital.com

Chairman and CEO:
Martin E. Zimmerman
President:
Robert E. Laing

Earnings Growth	★ ★ ★ ★
Revenue Growth	★ ★
Stock Growth	
Consistency	★ ★ ★ ★
Nasdaq: LNCC	**10 points**

LINC Capital is in the equipment leasing business. The company specializes in leasing equipment to emerging growth companies in the health care and information technology industries. It also focuses on the rental and distribution of analytical instruments to companies serving the environmental, chemical, pharmaceutical, and biotechnology industries.

The Chicago-based operation also acquires lease portfolios originated by other lessors.

The company entered the instrument rental and distribution business in the early 1990s with the acquistition of a couple of companies in the business.

The firm focuses primarily on complex analytical instruments, such as gas and liquid chromatographs, mass spectrometers, and atomic absorption systems. Most of the instruments cost between $15,000 and $60,000. Among its leading customers are Bausch & Lomb, Western Digital, Quanterra Environmental Services, Onsite Environmental Laboratories, and Core Laboratories.

LINC Capital usually is able to deliver its equipment—customized, calibrated, and ready for use—within 24 hours of receipt of the order. The firm services more than 2,500 analytical instrument customers through its sales force of product specialists.

LINC's select growth leasing division focuses on equipment leases to middle- and late-stage emerging growth companies in the health care and information technology industries, such as physician practice management organizations, rehabilitation service companies, extended care providers, health care claims administrators, information services providers, and Internet and telecommunications service companies.

Most of its leases are for essential operating equipment, including data processing equipment, production equipment, analytical instruments, and medical equipment. Leases typically include items with an aggregate cost ranging from $250,000 to $2.5 million, although most items individually would cost less than $100,000.

LINC Capital was founded in 1975 and went public with its initial stock offering in 1997. The company has about 90 employees and a market capitalization of about $50 million.

EARNINGS PER SHARE GROWTH ★ ★ ★ ★

Past four years: 975 percent (82 percent per year)

REVENUE GROWTH ★ ★

Past four years: 115 percent (21 percent per year)

STOCK GROWTH

Past year: −57 percent
Dollar growth: $10,000 over the past year would have declined to $4,300.

CONSISTENCY ★ ★ ★ ★

Increased earnings per share: four of the past four years
Increased revenue: four of the past four years

LINC CAPITAL AT A GLANCE

Fiscal year ended: Dec. 31
Revenue and net income in $ millions

	1994	1995	1996	1997	1998	4-Year Growth Avg. Annual (%)	4-Year Growth Total (%)
Revenue ($)	25.6	27.6	36.1	41.7	55	21	115
Net income ($)	0.335	0.797	1.56	2.47	4.59	91	1,270
Earnings/share ($)	0.08	0.25	0.48	0.73	0.86	82	975
Avg. PE ratio	—	—	—	23	16	—	—

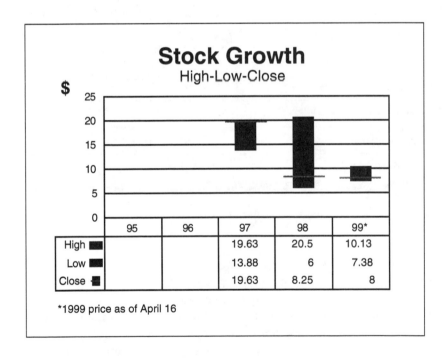

Stock Growth
High-Low-Close

	95	96	97	98	99*
High			19.63	20.5	10.13
Low			13.88	6	7.38
Close			19.63	8.25	8

*1999 price as of April 16

72

Mercury Computer Systems, Inc.

199 Riverneck Road
Chelmsford, MA 01824
978-256-1300
www.mc.com

President and CEO:
James R. Bertelli

Earnings Growth	★ ★ ★
Revenue Growth	★ ★
Stock Growth	
Consistency	★ ★ ★ ★
Nasdaq: MRCY	**9 points**

Mercury Computer Systems helps its customers see images that are invisible to the naked eye. The company's systems help doctors see inside the human body, and military commanders see behind enemy lines.

The Chelmsford, Massachusetts operation designs and manufactures digital signal processing computer systems that transform sensor generated data into information that can be displayed as images for human interpretation or subjected to additional computer analysis.

In the medical field, Mercury's computer systems are embedded in magnetic resonance imaging (MRI), computed tomography, and digital X-ray machines. The systems process the continuous stream of data provided by the machines to create an image a physician may use to diagnose a patient's ailment. The company supplies technology for some of the MRIs and similar machines developed by General Electric Medical Systems, Siemens, and Toshiba.

In the defense field, Mercury's systems process the stream of data from sensors attached to radar or sonar equipment to enable military commanders to "see" the battle through natural barriers such as clouds, darkness, water, or foliage, so that the position and strength of the enemy can be analyzed.

Mercury is the dominant player in the military segment of its industry with a 40 percent stake, supplying technology to many of the leading defense contractors, such as Lockheed Martin, Hughes Aircraft, Raytheon/E-Systems, Northrop-Grumman, and Mitsubishi Heavy Industries.

Analysts forecast strong growth for the military imaging industry. Although military spending in general is expected to continue to decline, spending on defense electronics is expected to rise more than $7 billion in the next decade.

Military electronics sales account for more than 80 percent of the company's $85 million in annual revenue.

Mercury went public in 1998 with its initial stock offering. The company has about 380 employees and a market capitalization of about $170 million.

EARNINGS PER SHARE GROWTH   ★ ★ ★

Past four years: 142 percent (25 percent per year)

REVENUE GROWTH   ★ ★

Past four years: 105 percent (20 percent per year)

STOCK GROWTH

The company just issued its stock in 1998.

CONSISTENCY   ★ ★ ★ ★

Increased earnings per share: four of the past four years
Increased revenue: four of the past four years

MERCURY COMPUTER SYSTEMS AT A GLANCE

Fiscal year ended: June 30
Revenue and net income in $ millions

	1994	1995	1996	1997	1998	4-Year Growth Avg. Annual (%)	Total (%)
Revenue ($)	41.7	54.3	58.3	64.6	85.5	20	105
Net income ($)	4.12	6.34	4.43	4.61	8.73	21	112
Earnings/share ($)	0.50	0.77	0.88	0.90	1.21	25	142
Avg. PE ratio	—	—	—	—	12	—	—

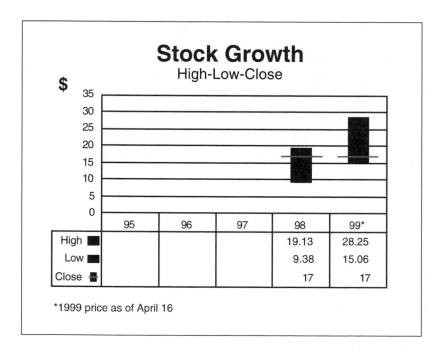

Stock Growth
High-Low-Close

$	95	96	97	98	99*
High				19.13	28.25
Low				9.38	15.06
Close				17	17

*1999 price as of April 16

73
Vicon Industries, Inc.

89 Arkay Drive
Hauppauge, NY 11788
516-952-2288
www.vicon-cctv.com

Chairman:
Donald N. Horn
President:
Kenneth M. Darby

Earnings Growth	★ ★ ★ ★
Revenue Growth	
Stock Growth	★ ★ ★ ★
Consistency	★
AMEX: VII	**9 points**

Vicon Industries manufactures a wide range of closed circuit television components and systems used for security, surveillance, and safety.

A closed circuit television system is a video system that can transmit and receive video, audio, and data signals in a private system. Vicon's systems are typically used for crime deterrence, visual documentation, and observation of inaccessible or hazardous areas. They also are used to enhance safety, manage control systems, and improve efficiency of personnel.

Its closed circuit equipment is used in office buildings, manufacturing plants, apartment complexes, large retail stores, government facilities, prisons, casinos, sports arenas, health care facilities, and banks.

You'll find its surveillance systems at O'Hare International Airport in Chicago, Xiamen International Airport in China, the Henry Ford Hospital in Detroit, Fort Bragg military base in North Carolina, and at several U.S. Postal Services offices throughout the country.

Prior to 1993, the company had focused entirely on closed circuit hardware components. Since 1993, it has concentrated more on software-based systems and digital systems.

The Hauppauge, New York operation sells primarily to installing dealers and integrators of various types of security systems, to government agencies, and to distributors. U.S. sales are done through its in-house sales staff and several independent manufacturer's representatives. Outside the United States, sales are handled by the company's British subsidiary, Vicon Industries, Ltd.

International sales account for about 36 percent of the company's revenue.

Among Vicon's leading products are the DigiTek intrusion detector that senses motion in the video image, triggering alarms, recording activity, and alerting security; the ProTech PC-based graphic command and control software package; the Matrix 66 video switchers that enable multiple cameras to be routed to any system monitor; and the ViStar and Surveyor remote surveillance systems that can be moved and controlled from remote locations.

Vicon has about 220 employees and a market capitalization of $40 million.

EARNINGS PER SHARE GROWTH ★ ★ ★ ★

Past four years: 7,950 percent (120 percent per year)

REVENUE GROWTH

Past four years: 33 percent (7 percent per year)

STOCK GROWTH ★ ★ ★ ★

Past three years: 490 percent (81 percent per year)
Dollar growth: $10,000 over the past three years would have grown to $59,000.

CONSISTENCY ★

Increased earnings per share: three of the past four years
Increased revenue: two of the past four years

VICON INDUSTRIES AT A GLANCE

Fiscal year ended: Sept. 30
Revenue and net income in $ millions

	1994	1995	1996	1997	1998	4-Year Growth Avg. Annual (%)	Total (%)
Revenue ($)	47.7	43.8	43.2	51.5	63.3	7	33
Net income ($)	0.045	−1.3	0.300	1.6	5.8	232	12,900
Earnings/share ($)	0.02	−0.49	0.11	0.56	1.61	120	7,950
Avg. PE ratio	116	—	32	11	6	—	—

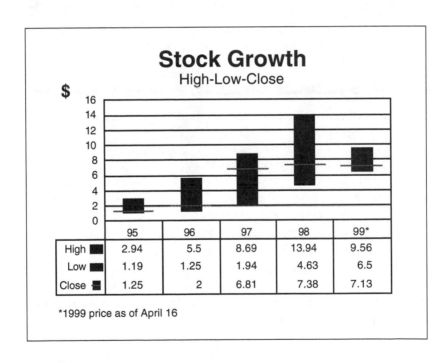

Stock Growth
High-Low-Close

	95	96	97	98	99*
High	2.94	5.5	8.69	13.94	9.56
Low	1.19	1.25	1.94	4.63	6.5
Close	1.25	2	6.81	7.38	7.13

*1999 price as of April 16

NFO Worldwide, Inc.

Two Pickwick Plaza
Greenwich, CT 06830
203-629-8888
www.nfor.com

Chairman, President, and CEO:
William Lipner

Earnings Growth	★
Revenue Growth	★ ★ ★ ★
Stock Growth	
Consistency	★ ★ ★ ★
NYSE: NFO	**9 points**

Think of NFO Worldwide as your Big Brother.

Big Brother is watching you (or others like you), analyzing your buying habits, attitudes, needs, and behaviors, and then selling that data to other companies who want to market their goods or services to you.

NFO Worldwide has more than 50 years in the business of conducting consumer research for the nation's major marketers. The company invented the panel-based market research approach and is the market leader in collecting and interpreting consumer attitudes, perceptions, and behaviors. In fact, the Conference Board's periodic Consumer Confidence ratings are provided by NFO Worldwide.

The Greenwich, Connecticut operation conducts more than 3,500 custom and syndicated research studies a year for more than 2,000 corporate clients in such industries as packaged goods, foods, health care, financial services, high tech, telecommunications, and travel and leisure. As its name implies, the company is worldwide in scope, with services offered in more than 30 countries.

To gather its consumer attitude information, NFO uses a carefully selected panel of about 575,000 U.S. households representing about 1.5 million people. Through a joint venture, it also has access to 100,000 European households.

NFO has brought market research into the cyberage with its network of about 50,000 "wired" households who can be quickly polled online. Through its NFO//net.source program, the company can complete and tabulate an online survey with its wired panelists in just a few days—or as little as 48 hours. With the company's NFO//net.query service, clients can submit a question for wired consumer panelists on Tuesday and get an answer back by the following Wednesday.

Among its leading services are custom market research, financial research and consulting, Yellow Pages usage tracking and measurement, pharmaceutical marketing research, consumer health research, and travel and leisure marketing research.

NFO went public with its initial stock offering in 1993. It has about 2,000 employees and a market capitalization of about $255 million.

EARNINGS PER SHARE GROWTH ★

Past four years: 72 percent (14 percent per year)

REVENUE GROWTH ★ ★ ★ ★

Past four years: 348 percent (45 percent per year)

STOCK GROWTH

Past three years: −2 percent
Dollar growth: $10,000 over the past three years would have declined to $9,800.

CONSISTENCY ★ ★ ★ ★

Increased earnings per share: four of the past four years
Increased revenue: four of the past four years

NFO WORLDWIDE AT A GLANCE

Fiscal year ended: Dec. 31
Revenue and net income in $ millions

	1994	1995	1996	1997	1998	4-Year Growth Avg. Annual (%)	4-Year Growth Total (%)
Revenue ($)	61.5	113.1	154.9	190.2	275.4	45	348
Net income ($)	5.58	10.6	12	13.5	14.9	28	167
Earnings/share ($)	0.39	0.49	0.53	0.62	0.67	14	72
Avg. PE ratio	17	19	27	27	21	—	—

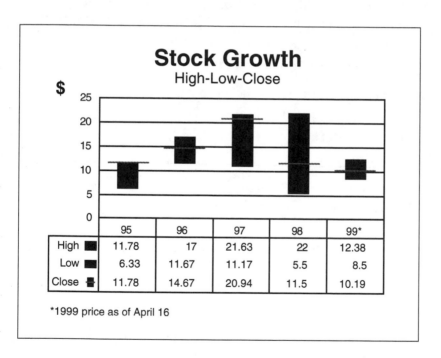

Stock Growth
High-Low-Close

$	95	96	97	98	99*
High	11.78	17	21.63	22	12.38
Low	6.33	11.67	11.17	5.5	8.5
Close	11.78	14.67	20.94	11.5	10.19

*1999 price as of April 16

75

Corrpro Companies Incorporated

1090 Enterprise Drive
Medina, OH 44256
330-723-5082
www.corrpro.com

Chairman, President, and CEO:
Joseph W. Rog

Earnings Growth	
Revenue Growth	★ ★ ★
Stock Growth	★ ★ ★ ★
Consistency	★ ★
NYSE: CO	**9 points**

Corrpro provides corrosion control engineering and monitoring services, as well as systems and equipment to the infrastructure, environmental, and energy markets. Its corrosion control products help protect water towers, power plants, storage tanks, bridges, and pipelines.

The firm specializes in cathodic protection systems, which use an electrochemical process that prevents corrosion in new structures and mitigates the corrosion process in existing structures. The cathodic process is used on such applications as offshore platforms, ships, electric power plants, bridges, oil and gas pipelines, underground storage tanks, parking garages, transit systems, and water and waste treatment equipment.

The company has grown rapidly in the past few years through a series of acquisitions of related companies.

The Medina, Ohio operation maintains advanced corrosion research and testing laboratories in order to analyze the scope of a corrosion problem and to recommend appropriate methods of corrosion control.

223

Corrpro also offers engineering services to private sector customers in the aerospace, defense, marine, chemicals, petroleum, and utilities industries, and to government agencies involved in water treatment and delivery systems, marine vessels, transit systems, and weapons.

The firm also sells material and equipment both to its customers and to other engineering and construction firms involved in corrosion control projects. Among its leading products are various cathodic protection anodes, rectifier units and instrumentation, computer hardware and software for monitoring corrosion, and related accessories.

Corrpro operates in the United States and Canada through several subsidiaries, such as Corrpro Canada, Good-All Products, and WWGL Services. It does very limited business outside North America.

The company was founded in 1984 and went public with its initial stock offering in 1993. The firm has about 1,100 employees and a market capitalization of about $100 million.

EARNINGS PER SHARE GROWTH

Past four years: 12 percent (2 percent per year)

REVENUE GROWTH   ★ ★ ★

Past four years: 148 percent (25 percent per year)

STOCK GROWTH   ★ ★ ★ ★

Past three years: 143 percent (35 percent per year)
Dollar growth: $10,000 over the past three years would have grown to about $24,000.

CONSISTENCY   ★ ★

Increased earnings per share: two of the past four years
Increased revenue: four of the past four years

CORRPRO COMPANIES AT A GLANCE

Fiscal year ended: March 31
Revenue and net income in $ millions

	1994	1995	1996	1997	1998	Avg. Annual (%)	Total (%)
						4-Year Growth	
Revenue ($)	69.5	118.5	127.8	139.6	172.7	25	148
Net income ($)	2.71	3.29	−3.41	4.81	6.89	26	154
Earnings/share ($)	0.74	0.46	−0.44	0.58	0.85	2	12
Avg. PE ratio	31	—	11	12	11	—	—

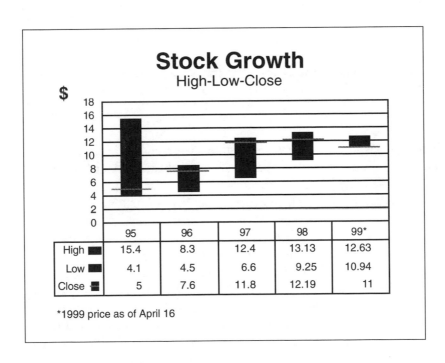

Stock Growth
High-Low-Close

$

	95	96	97	98	99*
High	15.4	8.3	12.4	13.13	12.63
Low	4.1	4.5	6.6	9.25	10.94
Close	5	7.6	11.8	12.19	11

*1999 price as of April 16

Covenant Transport

Covenant Transport, Inc.

400 Birmingham Highway
Chattanooga, TN 37419
423-821-1212

Chairman, President, and CEO:
David R. Parker

Earnings Growth	★ ★
Revenue Growth	★ ★ ★
Stock Growth	★
Consistency	★ ★ ★
Nasdaq: CVTI	**9 points**

Covenant Transport trucks a wide range of cargo coast to coast. It is one of the nation's longest-haul shippers. Its average haul of about 1,650 miles is the longest of any publicly traded truckload carrier. The firm often uses two-person driver teams to help expedite delivery of its long-haul jobs.

The Chattanooga-based operation's primary customers include retailers and manufacturers of goods, such as garments, consumer electronics, appliances, carpet, textiles, tires, and frozen food. The firm also transports freight that has been consolidated into truckload quantities by consolidators, such as less-than-truckload and air freight carriers, third party freight consolidators, and freight forwarders.

The company attempts to distinguish itself in the market by offering premium transport services, including just-in-time delivery, transcontinental express, and specific scheduling for shippers with exacting transportation requirements.

Covenant conducts its dry van dispatch from its Chattanooga headquarters, and its temperature-controlled dispatch from its Bud Meyer Truck Lines subsidiary headquarters in Lake City, Minnesota.

The firm uses the latest technology to monitor and communicate with its truckers. Its "Omnitracs" system is a satellite-based tracking and communications system that permits direct communication between drivers and fleet managers. It also updates the tractor's position every 30 minutes to help shippers locate freight and estimate pickup and delivery times.

Covenant was founded in 1985 by David Parker (who still serves as chairman, president, and CEO) and Jacqueline Parker. The firm began with 25 tractors and 50 trailers. It now has well over 2,000 tractors and more than 4,000 trailers. Although most of its early growth was through internal expansion, in recent years Covenant has bolstered its business by making some key acquisitions of other trucking companies. It recently acquired Trans-Roads, based near Atlanta, Georgia, and Bud Meyer Truck Lines of Minnesota.

The firm went public with its initial stock offering in 1994. It has about 4,000 employees and a market capitalization of about $225 million.

EARNINGS PER SHARE GROWTH ★ ★

Past four years: 83 percent (16 percent per year)

REVENUE GROWTH ★ ★ ★

Past four years: 181 percent (29 percent per year)

STOCK GROWTH ★

Past three years: 49 percent (14 percent per year)
Dollar growth: $10,000 over the past three years would have grown to about $15,000.

CONSISTENCY ★ ★ ★

Increased earnings per share: three of the past four years
Increased revenue: four of the past four years

COVENANT TRANSPORT AT A GLANCE

Fiscal year ended: Dec. 31
Revenue and net income in $ millions

	1994	1995	1996	1997	1998	4-Year Growth Avg. Annual (%)	4-Year Growth Total (%)
Revenue ($)	131.9	180.3	236.3	297.9	370.5	29	181
Net income ($)	7.26	9.28	8.98	13.7	18.3	26	152
Earnings/share ($)	0.69	0.70	0.67	1.03	1.26	16	83
Avg. PE ratio	27	22	24	16	13	—	—

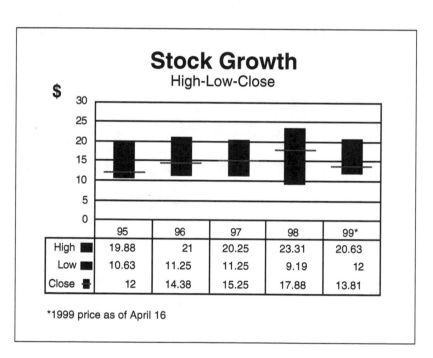

Stock Growth
High-Low-Close

$	95	96	97	98	99*
High	19.88	21	20.25	23.31	20.63
Low	10.63	11.25	11.25	9.19	12
Close	12	14.38	15.25	17.88	13.81

*1999 price as of April 16

Webco Industries, Inc.

9101 West 21st Street
Sand Springs, OK 74063
918-241-1000
www.webcoindustries.com

Chairman and CEO:
F. William Weber
President:
Dana S. Weber

Earnings Growth	★ ★ ★ ★
Revenue Growth	★
Stock Growth	
Consistency	★ ★ ★ ★
AMEX: WEB	**9 points**

It may sound like another hot Internet stock, but Webco Industries has nothing to do with the World Wide Web.

The Sand Springs, Oklahoma operation manufactures high-quality carbon steel tubing and stainless steel tubing products used by manufacturers for a wide variety of products, including automotive components, bicycles, lawnmowers, and other metal products.

Webco's subsidiary, Phillips & Johnston, also distributes products from other manufacturers in the mechanical and specialty metal tubular market, including products made from copper, brass, aluminum, and stainless and carbon steel. That gives Webco a broader selection of products to offer its customers.

Webco also has a QuikWater division that manufactures a direct contact water heater for commercial and industrial applications, such as food processing, manufacturing, health care, construction, and other operations that require a high volume of hot water. The QuikWater system provides hot water on demand at significant energy savings.

One of Webco's leading products is carbon heat exchanger tubing, which is used in systems that dissipate heat generated by industrial processes.

The company also makes boiler tubing used for the manufacture and maintenance of boiler systems for utilities, waste-heat recovery units, industrial and commercial facilities, and cogeneration plants.

The company sells its products to a diverse group of more than 1,300 customers. About 86 percent of its sales are direct to industrial customers, including manufacturers of heat exchangers, high-efficiency home heating furnaces, appliances, automotive companies, power generation equipment, waste heat recovery systems, industrial and commercial boilers, and other consumer durables. The remaining 14 percent of sales are to steel service centers and distributors.

The company was founded in 1969 by F. William Weber, who still serves as chairman of the board and CEO. Webco went public with its initial stock offering in 1994. The company has about 800 employees and a market capitalization of about $50 million.

EARNINGS PER SHARE GROWTH ★ ★ ★ ★

Past three years: 412 percent (51 percent per year)

REVENUE GROWTH ★

Past four years: 71 percent (14 percent per year)

STOCK GROWTH

Past three years: 15 percent (4 percent per year)
Dollar growth: $10,000 over the past three years would have grown to $11,500.

CONSISTENCY ★ ★ ★ ★

Increased earnings per share: four of the past four years
Increased revenue: four of the past four years

WEBCO INDUSTRIES AT A GLANCE

Fiscal year ended: July 31
Revenue and net income in $ millions

	1994	1995	1996	1997	1998	4-Year Growth Avg. Annual (%)	Total (%)
Revenue ($)	88.7	108.3	112.5	128.6	151.4	14	71
Net income ($)	−2.4	1.2	3.7	3.9	6.2	49*	417*
Earnings/share ($)	−0.43	0.17	0.53	0.55	0.87	51*	412*
Avg. PE ratio	—	—	13	13	8	—	—

*Net income and earnings per share returns are based on three-year performance.

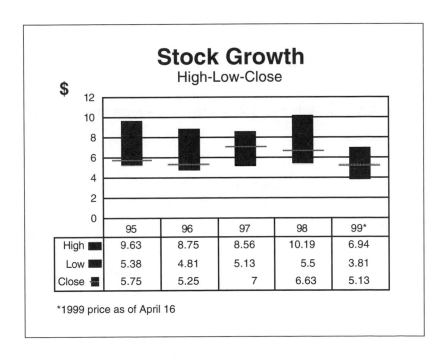

Stock Growth
High-Low-Close

$		95	96	97	98	99*
High ■		9.63	8.75	8.56	10.19	6.94
Low ■		5.38	4.81	5.13	5.5	3.81
Close ▤		5.75	5.25	7	6.63	5.13

*1999 price as of April 16

Vari-L Company, Inc.

4895 Peoria Street
Denver, CO 80239
303-371-1560
www.vari-l.com

Chairman:
Joseph H. Kiser
President and CEO:
David G. Sherman

Earnings Growth	★ ★ ★
Revenue Growth	★ ★
Stock Growth	
Consistency	★ ★ ★ ★
Nasdaq: VARL	**9 points**

Vari-L makes the building blocks of wireless communications.

One of its major product lines is a low-voltage oscillator used for transmitting and receiving a signal source within a specific frequency range. They are used in cellular phones and other communications equipment. Because of their low voltage requirements, Vari-L's oscillators operate with about 20 percent of the input power requirements of most of its competitors.

The Denver-based operation also makes oscillators for personal communications systems, local area computer networks, satellite communications, global positioning systems, and direct broadcast systems.

Until recently, the U.S. military had accounted for most of Vari-L's sales revenue and still remains its leading customer. The company produces radio frequency and microwave signal processing components used in defense and space applications, including radar systems for military aircraft, guidance systems of antiaircraft and antimissile missiles, and military and commercial satellites. Vari-L systems are used to guide Patriot missiles, AMRAAM missiles, Harm missiles, Phoenix missiles, and F14, F15, and F18 fire control systems.

In the past few years, the company has made an effort to focus more on the commercial marketplace to lessen its reliance on military spending. In 1993, 75 percent of its revenue came from military orders. Now less than 20 percent of revenue comes from military applications, with more than 80 percent coming from commercial customers, such as cell phone manufacturers.

About 50 percent of Vari-L's revenue comes from foreign customers. The firm has sales in Sweden, Germany, France, Japan, England, India, China, South Korea, and other countries.

The company sells primarily to communications equipment manufacturers, including Motorola, Nokia, Ericsson, Lucent Technologies, Samsung, Uniden Hughes, Network Systems, Lockheed Martin, and Northrop Grumman.

Vari-L was founded in 1953 and went public with its initial stock offering in 1994. The firm has about 200 employees and a market capitalization of about $35 million.

EARNINGS PER SHARE GROWTH   ★ ★ ★

Past four years: 167 percent (28 percent per year)

REVENUE GROWTH   ★ ★

Past four years: 150 percent (20 percent per year)

STOCK GROWTH

Past three years: –46 percent
Dollar growth: $10,000 over the past three years would have declined to $5,400.

CONSISTENCY   ★ ★ ★ ★

Increased earnings per share: four of the past four years
Increased revenue: four of the past four years

VARI-L AT A GLANCE

Fiscal year ended: Dec. 31
Revenue and net income in $ millions

	1994	1995	1996	1997	1998	4-Year Growth Avg. Annual (%)	Total (%)
Revenue ($)	7.23	9.47	12.2	17.4	18.1	20	150
Net income ($)	0.436	0.859	1.18	2.03	2.70	58	519
Earnings/share ($)	0.18	0.27	0.32	0.45	0.48	28	167
Avg. PE ratio	28	41	38	22	18	—	—

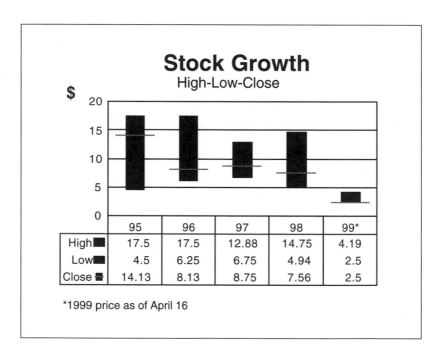

Stock Growth
High-Low-Close

	95	96	97	98	99*
High	17.5	17.5	12.88	14.75	4.19
Low	4.5	6.25	6.75	4.94	2.5
Close	14.13	8.13	8.75	7.56	2.5

*1999 price as of April 16

Ontrack Data International, Inc.

Ontrack.®

6321 Bury Drive
Eden Prairie, MN 55346
612-937-1107
www.ontrack.com

Chairman and CEO:
Michael W. Rogers
President:
John E. Pence

Earnings Growth	★ ★ ★
Revenue Growth	★ ★ ★
Stock Growth	
Consistency	★ ★ ★
Nasdaq: ONDI	**9 points**

Your computer crashes. All your data is lost. To whom do you turn? The worldwide leader in the industry is Ontrack Data International.

Ontrack has performed more than 50,000 data recoveries since its inception. The firm works with large corporations, government agencies, educational and financial institutions, and individuals and small businesses.

Data recovery services make up about 76 percent of the firm's total revenue. The company has the capability to recover data stored in nearly all types of storage media and operating systems, regardless of the sophistication or age of the storage media or the system.

Ontrack has a staff of data recovery engineers who retrieve lost data by performing a diagnostic evaluation to determine the nature and cause of the data loss, the quantity of the data that can be recovered, and the prescribed course of action. Customers are then given a price quote on the cost of recovery, depending on the difficulty of the specific process required. If customers elect to proceed, Ontrack performs the recovery, stores the data on the medium of the customer's choice, and returns the data along with the customer's original equipment.

The firm also has developed a remote recovery process under which certain non-hardware-related data losses can be recovered through a modem line. The service works only for a few select applications, including DOS, Windows, Windows 95, Windows NT, and OS2.

Ontrack also develops related software for sale to customers. Its leading software package is Disk Manager, which is a hard disk drive installation and partitioning utility for personal computers. It optimizes storage capacity on a wide range of hard disk drives and facilitates the process of installing replacement or upgrade drives by linking operating system software with the drives. Software product sales account for about 24 percent of total revenue.

The Eden Prairie, Minnesota operation has branch offices in California, New Jersey, Washington, D.C., London, and Germany.

Ontrack went public with its initial stock offering in 1996. The company has about 300 employees and a market capitalization of about $55 million.

EARNINGS PER SHARE GROWTH ★ ★ ★

Past four years: 174 percent (29 percent per year)

REVENUE GROWTH ★ ★ ★

Past four years: 206 percent (31 percent per year)

STOCK GROWTH

Past two years: −57 percent
Dollar growth: $10,000 over the past two years would have declined to $4,300.

CONSISTENCY ★ ★ ★

Increased earnings per share: three of the past four years
Increased revenue: four of the past four years

ONTRACK DATA INTERNATIONAL AT A GLANCE

Fiscal year ended: Dec. 31
Revenue and net income in $ millions

	1994	1995	1996	1997	1998	4-Year Growth Avg. Annual (%)	Total (%)
Revenue ($)	11.7	17.1	26.8	35.2	35.8	31	206
Net income ($)	1.51	2.21	3.12	5.66	5.2	36	244
Earnings/share ($)	0.19	0.28	0.38	0.58	0.52	29	174
Avg. PE ratio	—	—	35	36	18	—	—

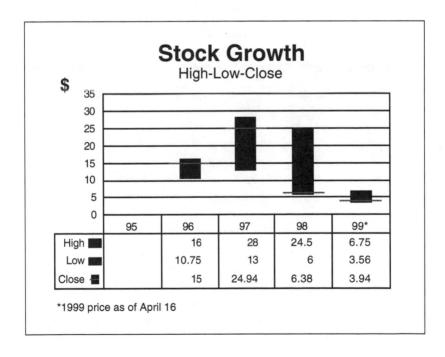

Stock Growth
High-Low-Close

	95	96	97	98	99*
High		16	28	24.5	6.75
Low		10.75	13	6	3.56
Close		15	24.94	6.38	3.94

*1999 price as of April 16

80

Winfield Capital Corp.

237 Mamaroneck Avenue
White Plains, NY 10605
914-949-2600

Chairman, President, and CEO:
Paul A. Perlin

Earnings Growth	★ ★ ★
Revenue Growth	★ ★ ★
Stock Growth	
Consistency	★ ★
Nasdaq: WCAP	**8 points**

Winfield Capital is a venture capital firm that invests in growing young companies in the high-flying high-tech sectors.

The White Plains, New York operation uses funds borrowed from the Small Business Administration along with its own capital to invest in and provide loans to small, young companies. In return, Winfield receives an equity position in the companies it helps finance. If those companies begin to flourish, Winfield reaps the rewards through the stock warrants it holds.

Winfield uses about one-third of its assets for straight loans or debt securities, and the other two-thirds for investments involving debt securities with equity features, such as conversion rights and warrants and common and preferred stock.

The firm focuses most of its loans on companies in the fastest growing segments of the economy, such as communications, transportation, consumer products, and information processing. Most of the companies in Winfield's investment portfolio are expansion stage businesses and start-up or development stage companies. The company receives referrals for potential investments from venture capitalists, investment bankers, attorneys, accountants, and commercial bankers.

In evaluating potential investments, Winfield analysts consider several key factors. They want companies that are profitable or show potential for becoming profitable; they want companies with products or services that are beyond the testing stage; and they prefer companies with an experienced management team. They also analyze the company's potential for growth and the liquidation value of its assets.

Winfield limits its loans to companies with a net worth of no more than $18 million and net income of no more than $6 million.

Founded in 1972, Winfield went public with its initial stock offering in 1995. The company has just three full-time employees and a market capitalization of $110 million.

EARNINGS PER SHARE GROWTH ★ ★ ★

Past four years: Figures cannot be properly calculated.

REVENUE GROWTH ★ ★ ★

Past four years: 178 percent (29 percent per year)

STOCK GROWTH

Past three years: −1 percent
Dollar growth: $10,000 over the past three years would have declined to $9,900.

CONSISTENCY ★ ★

Increased earnings per share: three of the past four years
Increased revenue: three of the past four years

WINFIELD CAPITAL AT A GLANCE

Fiscal year ended: March 31
Revenue and net income in $ millions

	1995	1996	1997	1998	1999*	4-Year Growth Avg. Annual (%)	Total (%)
Revenue ($)	0.291	0.600	1.44	1.12	0.629*	29**	178**
Net income ($)	−0.53	−0.45	0.345	−1.98	24.3*	—	—
Earnings/share ($)	−0.90	−0.13	0.07	−0.40	4.37*	—	—
Avg. PE ratio	—	—	91	—	7	—	—

*1999 figures are for nine months through Dec. 31, 1998.
**Revenue growth figures are for fiscal years 1994 through 1998.

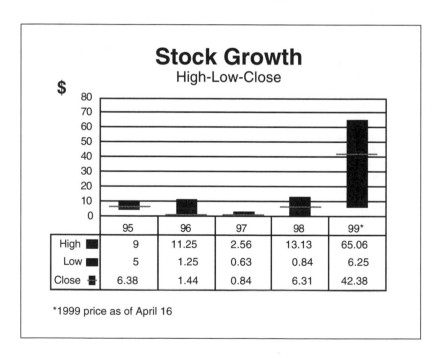

Stock Growth
High-Low-Close

$

	95	96	97	98	99*
High	9	11.25	2.56	13.13	65.06
Low	5	1.25	0.63	0.84	6.25
Close	6.38	1.44	0.84	6.31	42.38

*1999 price as of April 16

81
Ansys, Inc.

ANSYS

275 Technology Drive
Canonsburg, PA 15317
724-746-3304
www.ansys.com

Chairman, President, and CEO:
Peter J. Smith

Earnings Growth	★ ★ ★ ★
Revenue Growth	★
Stock Growth	
Consistency	★ ★ ★
Nasdaq: ANSS	**8 points**

Ansys creates software designed to help engineers operate more efficiently. Design engineers use Ansys software to accelerate product time to market, reduce production costs, improve engineering processes, and optimize product quality and safety.

The Canonsburg, Pennsylvannia operation offers a wide range of computer-aided engineering (CAE) analysis software and computer-aided design (CAD) software for a variety of industries. Leading customers come from the automotive, aerospace, and electronics industries. Its software also is used by universities around the world.

Ansys software enables engineers to construct computer models of structures, compounds, components, or systems to simulate performance conditions and physical responses to varying levels of stress, pressure, temperature, and velocity. The computer-simulated testing helps reduce the time and expense of physical prototyping and testing.

The firm markets its products through a global network of 35 independent regional Ansys distributors, who operate 64 offices in 31 countries. Ansys also markets its products through alliances with a variety of computer makers, such as Hewlett-Packard, Compaq, Silicon Graphics, Sun Microsystems, IBM, and Intel.

The company utilitzes strategic corporate alliances in the development of its software. For instance, Ansys worked with Livermore Software Corp. to perfect crash test simulations for the automotive and related industries. The firm also has technical and marketing relationships with a number of other leading CAD creators, such as Parametric Technology, Autodesk, Computervision, and Intergraph.

The firm's design and analysis software programs, all of which are included in its Ansys/Multiphysics program, are available as subsets or as stand-alone products. Its multiphysics products account for all of the company's approximately $57 million in annual revenue.

Ansys was founded in 1970 as Swanson Analysis Systems. It went public with its initial stock offering in 1996. The firm has about 250 employees and a market capitalization of about $140 million.

EARNINGS PER SHARE GROWTH ★ ★ ★ ★

Past two years: 580 percent (62 percent per year)

REVENUE GROWTH ★

Past four years: 73 percent (15 percent per year)

STOCK GROWTH

Past two years: −18 percent
Dollar growth: $10,000 over the past two years would have declined to $8,200.

CONSISTENCY ★ ★ ★

Increased earnings per share: three of the past four years
Increased revenue: four of the past four years

ANSYS AT A GLANCE

Fiscal year ended: Dec. 31
Revenue and net income in $ millions

	1994	1995	1996	1997	1998	4-Year Growth Avg. Annual (%)	Total (%)
Revenue ($)	32.8	39.6	47.1	50.5	56.6	15	73
Net income ($)	0.26	–1.6	1.6	7.4	11. 3	245*	4,246*
Earnings/share ($)	–0.01	–0.18	0.10	0.47	0.68	62*	580*
Avg. PE ratio	—	—	128	20	14	—	—

*Net income and earnings per share returns are based on two-year performance.

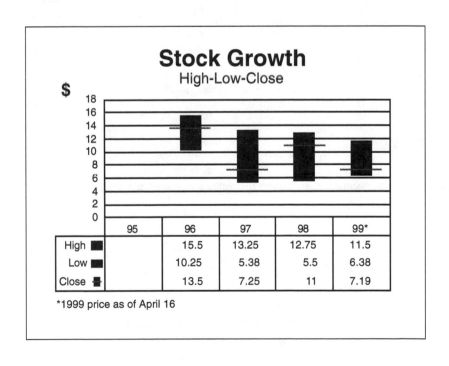

	95	96	97	98	99*
High		15.5	13.25	12.75	11.5
Low		10.25	5.38	5.5	6.38
Close		13.5	7.25	11	7.19

*1999 price as of April 16

Made2Manage, Inc.

MADE 2 MANAGE®

9002 Purdue Road
Indianapolis, IN 46268
317-532-7000
www.made2manage.com

Chairman:
Ira Coron
President:
David B. Wortman

Earnings Growth	
Revenue Growth	★ ★ ★ ★
Stock Growth	★ ★ ★
Consistency	★
Nasdaq: MTMS	**8 points**

Made2Manage is a small, upstart software maker that designs Windows-based programs specifically to handle the management and operations of manufacturing businesses.

With its wide range of applications, the Made2Manage package is designed to be the only software needed to handle all the management functions of a small or midsize manufacturing operation.

The software features are organized into five basic categories, including the following:

1. *Executive information system.* The program includes reports and graphs, system overviews, sales performance, production performance, and financial performance.

2. *Sales management.* Includes applications for quotations, sales order processing, customer service, sales reports and graphs, and sales overview.
3. *Production management.* Includes applications for job order entry and release, labor entry, purchasing and inventory, shipping and receiving, bar code data, production scheduling, bill of materials and routing, production reports, and related matters.
4. *Financial management.* Includes accounts receivable, accounts payable, general ledger, cash flow projections, order costing, payroll and human services, financial reports and graphs, and financial overview.
5. *Systemwide capabilities.* Includes networking systems, Internet applications, user-defined reports, and user permissions and preferences.

Made2Manage markets its software directly to customers or through a network of resellers. Customers typically have annual revenues of $5 million to $50 million. Its leading customers include manufacturers of fabricated metal products, industrial machinery and equipment, computer and office equipment, and transportation products. The software is used at nearly 1,000 sites throughout the United States.

In addition to its software, Made2Manage also offers related services, including implementation and assistance in using its software and ongoing customer support and education programs.

Founded in 1986, the Indianapolis-based operation went public with its initial stock offering in 1997. Made2Manage has about 150 employees and a market capitalization of about $60 million.

EARNINGS PER SHARE GROWTH

Past four years: Loss in 1998

REVENUE GROWTH   ★ ★ ★ ★

Past four years: 511 percent (58 percent per year)

STOCK GROWTH   ★ ★ ★

Past one year: 96 percent
Dollar growth: $10,000 over the past year would have grown to about $20,000.

CONSISTENCY   ★

Increased earnings per share: one of the past four years
Increased revenue: four of the past four years

MADE2MANAGE AT A GLANCE

Fiscal year ended: Dec. 31
Revenue and net income in $ millions

	1994	1995	1996	1997	1998	4-Year Growth Avg. Annual (%)	Total (%)
Revenue ($)	4.45	5.94	9.38	16.2	27.2	58	511
Net income ($)	0.443	0.392	1.61	0.613	−0.858	—	—
Earnings/share ($)	0.16	0.14	0.56	0.21	−0.025	—	—
Avg. PE ratio	—	—	—	37	30	—	—

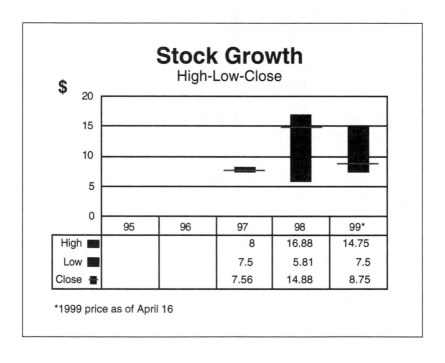

Stock Growth
High-Low-Close

	95	96	97	98	99*
High			8	16.88	14.75
Low			7.5	5.81	7.5
Close			7.56	14.88	8.75

*1999 price as of April 16

Dawson Geophysical Company

Dawson Geophysical Company

508 West Wall
Suite 800
Midland, TX 79701
915-684-3000
www.dawson3d.com

President and CEO:
L. Decker Dawson

Earnings Growth	★ ★
Revenue Growth	★ ★ ★
Stock Growth	
Consistency	★ ★ ★
Nasdaq: DWSN	**8 points**

Dawson Geophysical helps energy companies explore for new oil and natural gas reservoirs by analyzing 3-D seismic data collected at promising sites to determine whether those sites are likely to yield a new pocket of gas or oil.

The company does not do its own energy exploration, drilling, and processing, but rather helps large and intermediate-size oil companies collect and analyze information to help them drill more successfully. All of its operations are land-based (rather than ocean drilling), and the vast majority of its work is in the western United States.

Dawson's fortunes do indeed swing with the tide of the energy industry. And that industry has been as volatile as any sector of the economy over the past two decades. When oil prices are on the rise, Dawson and other energy-related stocks tend to perform well. But in recent years, when an oversupply of oil glutted the market and drove gas prices down

30 to 40 percent, Dawson's earnings and stock price suffered along with the rest of the energy industry.

By utilizing a powerful parallel processor supercomputer to process field data, geophysicists at Dawson's computer center in Midland, Texas, analyze seismic data. The company has been able to help its clients approach a drilling success rate of 50 percent or more. That's a rate that far exceeds earlier drilling technology figures (generally less than one successful well out of every seven drilled).

In the past couple of years, Dawson has stepped up to an even more advanced 4-D seismic data acquisition and analysis system, which adds the dimensions of time and reservoir analysis to its 3-D seismic surveys. Clients can visit the same site at successive intervals to determine the status of existing oil or gas reservoirs.

Founded in 1952, Dawson maintains a staff of nearly 400 employees and has a market capitalization of $42 million.

EARNINGS PER SHARE GROWTH   ★ ★

Past four years: 72 percent (15 percent per year)

REVENUE GROWTH   ★ ★ ★

Past four years: 167 percent (28 percent per year)

STOCK GROWTH

Past three years: −23 percent
Dollar growth: $10,000 over the past three years would have declined to $7,700.

CONSISTENCY   ★ ★ ★

Increased earnings per share: two of the past four years
Increased revenue: four of the past four years

DAWSON GEOPHYSICAL AT A GLANCE

Fiscal year ended: Dec. 31
Revenue and net income in $ millions

	1994	1995	1996	1997	1998	4-Year Growth Avg. Annual (%)	4-Year Growth Total (%)
Revenue ($)	23.0	28.2	33.5	48.2	61.4	28	167
Net income ($)	2.27	2.17	1.89	4.57	6.63	30	192
Earnings/share ($)	0.74	0.54	0.45	1.09	1.27	15	72
Avg. PE ratio	14	22	22	17	11	—	—

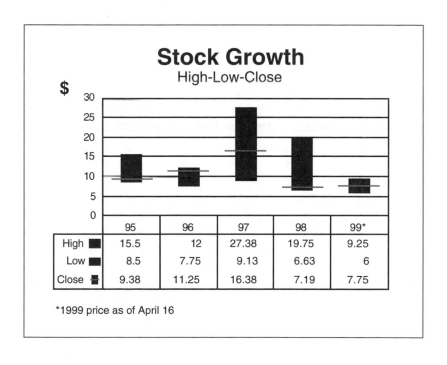

Stock Growth
High-Low-Close

	95	96	97	98	99*
High	15.5	12	27.38	19.75	9.25
Low	8.5	7.75	9.13	6.63	6
Close	9.38	11.25	16.38	7.19	7.75

*1999 price as of April 16

84

Nature's Sunshine Products, Inc.

75 East 1700 South
Provo, UT 84606
801-342-4300

Chairman:
Kristine F. Hughes
President:
Daniel P. Howells

Earnings Growth	★ ★ ★
Revenue Growth	★
Stock Growth	
Consistency	★ ★ ★ ★
Nasdaq: NATR	**8 points**

Nature's Sunshine Products is a maker and multilevel distributor of vitamins, herbs, food supplements, skin care lotions, and related products.

The company's multilevel distribution system involves about 700,000 salespeople around the world who pitch the products to their friends, family members, and other acquaintances.

Unlike many multilevel marketing operations, Nature's Sunshine does not compensate its people for recruiting new distributors but does pay them generous commissions on products sold by those they recruit. That policy has helped Nature's Sunshine maintain a more stable base of distributors than many other multilevel operations. Its distributor retention rate of about 33 percent may seem low, but it's much better than the roughly 10 percent retention rate of many of the other companies in the industry.

Higher commission fees also help the company retain its salespeople. The average commission for Nature's Sunshine salespeople is about 47 percent, compared with about 39 percent for NuSkin and 30 percent for Herbalife.

The Provo, Utah operation sells hundreds of herbs and vitamin supplements and introduces about 30 to 40 new products each year. Its leading category is herbs, which accounts for about 67 percent of total revenue. Other categories include vitamins (23 percent of revenue), personal care (3 percent), diet (2 percent), homeopathics (1 percent), and other products (4 percent).

Most of the company's products are developed and manufactured at the company's own facilities.

Nature's Sunshine has marketing operations in about 20 countries, primarily in North and South America. It also has operations in the United Kingdom, Japan, and South Korea, and it has exclusive distribution agreements with companies in Australia, New Zealand, Malaysia, and Norway.

Nature's Sunshine was founded in 1972. The company has about 1,000 employees and a market capitalization of about $265 million.

EARNINGS PER SHARE GROWTH ★ ★ ★

Past four years: 172 percent (28 percent per year)

REVENUE GROWTH ★

Past four years: 84 percent (16 percent per year)

STOCK GROWTH

Past three years: −9 percent
Dollar growth: $10,000 over the past three years would have declined to about $9,000.

CONSISTENCY ★ ★ ★ ★

Increased earnings per share: four of the past four years
Increased revenue: four of the past four years

NATURE'S SUNSHINE PRODUCTS AT A GLANCE

Fiscal year ended: Dec. 31
Revenue and net income in $ millions

	1994	1995	1996	1997	1998	4-Year Growth Avg. Annual (%)	4-Year Growth Total (%)
Revenue ($)	160.9	205.6	249	280.9	296.1	16	84
Net income ($)	8.45	11.9	16.8	20.1	23.3	29	176
Earnings/share ($)	0.46	0.65	0.90	1.08	1.25	28	172
Avg. PE ratio	19	20	26	19	14	—	—

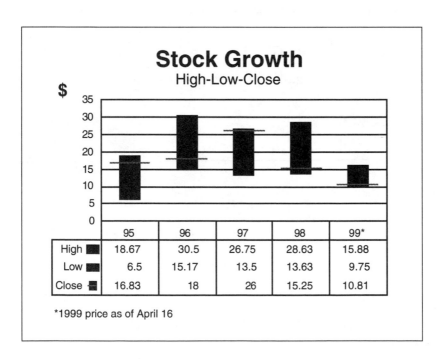

Stock Growth
High-Low-Close

	95	96	97	98	99*
High	18.67	30.5	26.75	28.63	15.88
Low	6.5	15.17	13.5	13.63	9.75
Close	16.83	18	26	15.25	10.81

*1999 price as of April 16

RF Monolithics, Inc.

4441 Sigma Road
Dallas, TX 75244
214-233-2903
www.rfm.com

President and CEO:
Sam L. Densmore

Earnings Growth	
Revenue Growth	★ ★
Stock Growth	★ ★
Consistency	★ ★ ★
Nasdaq: RFMI	7 points

Ominous as it may sound, radio waves are taking over our lives.

They're used to lock and unlock our cars, start the engine, open the garage door, change the channel, raise the volume, talk on cellular and cordless phones, and open the front door. In the years ahead, who knows how many more of life's daily functions will be commandeered by radio waves.

RF Monolithics (RFM) makes radio frequency–related products and components used in a broad range of applications. The company breaks its product line into four areas: low-power components, low-power Virtual Wire radio systems, frequency control modules, and filters.

The Dallas-based operation bases its products on a technology known as surface acoustic waves, which focus on the higher end of the frequency range—from 200 MHz to 2,400 MHz and above.

Concentrating on the higher frequency range is a strategy the company believes will pay off in the long term. As electronic applications from keyless entries for cars to digital cell phones migrate to higher operating frequencies, they'll face tighter tolerances and more stringent specifications. The firm's products are geared to serve that end of the market.

RFM markets its line of more than 500 resonators, filters, clocks, oscillators, transmitters, and receivers to original equipment manufacturers around the world.

Most of its customers are in the automotive, computer, commercial and consumer, industrial, or telecommunications industries. Among its leading customers are Northern Telecom, Siemens, Silicon Graphics, Delco Electronics, and Nokia Telecommunications.

The company has significant international sales, which account for about 50 percent of its total revenue.

RFM's devices are used for keyless entry systems, security systems, meter reading and bar code reading devices, medical systems, wireless headphones and loudspeakers, wireless door chimes, home automation systems, cellular phones, and wireless thermostats.

The company was founded in 1979 and went public with its initial stock offering in 1994. RFM has about 450 employees and a market capitalization of about $50 million.

EARNINGS PER SHARE GROWTH

Past four years: 32 percent (7 percent per year)

REVENUE GROWTH ★ ★

Past four years: 123 percent (22 percent per year)

STOCK GROWTH ★ ★

Past three years: 55 percent (16 percent per year)
Dollar growth: $10,000 over the past three years would have grown to about $16,000.

CONSISTENCY ★ ★ ★

Increased earnings per share: three of the past four years
Increased revenue: four of the past four years

RF MONOLITHICS AT A GLANCE

Fiscal year ended: Aug. 31
Revenue and net income in $ millions

	1994	1995	1996	1997	1998	4-Year Growth Avg. Annual (%)	Total (%)
Revenue ($)	24.8	32.1	35.7	47.7	55.2	22	123
Net income ($)	2.26	1.52	1.89	3.81	4.76	20	111
Earnings/share ($)	0.65	0.31	0.37	0.71	0.86	7	32
Avg. PE ratio	16	28	25	27	14	—	—

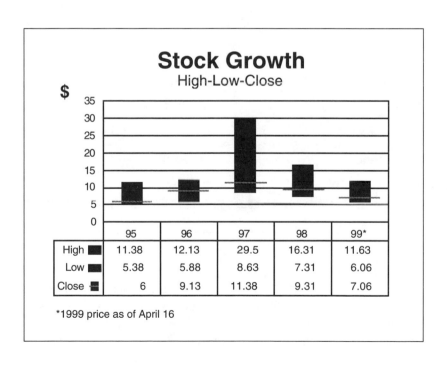

Stock Growth
High-Low-Close

	95	96	97	98	99*
High	11.38	12.13	29.5	16.31	11.63
Low	5.38	5.88	8.63	7.31	6.06
Close	6	9.13	11.38	9.31	7.06

*1999 price as of April 16

Recoton Corporation

RECOTON

2950 Lake Emma Road
Lake Mary, FL 32746
407-333-8900
www.rcot.com

Co-Chairman, President, and CEO:
Robert L. Borchardt
Co-Chairman:
Herbert H. Borchardt

Earnings Growth	
Revenue Growth	★ ★ ★ ★
Stock Growth	
Consistency	★ ★ ★
Nasdaq: RCOT	**7 points**

Recoton can make your world rock.

The Lake Mary, Florida operation makes some of the finest speaker systems in the world. Among its better-known lines are Advent, Acoustic Research, Jensen, MacAudio, Magnat, Ross, Rembrandt, and Sound Quest.

In addition to the standard stereo speakers, Recoton makes home theater speakers, multimedia speakers, car audio systems, and a variety of audio and video accessories. It makes a complete line of antennas, audio and video cables and connectors, power adapters, inverters, microphones, surge protection devices, and blank audiocasettes.

Recoton also makes a line of camcorder accessories, such as tripods, batteries, carry cases, chargers, cables, lights, and microphones. It also makes telephone and cellular phone accessories, video and computer game accessories (such as joy sticks, cables, and control pads), and a line of universal remote controls for televisions, VCRs, and other electronics products.

The company's high-end 900 MHz wireless systems use radio signals to transmit pictures and sound signals through walls, floors, and ceilings from a TV, VCR, cable box, satellite box, stereo, or sound system to speakers, headphones, or televisions. The systems have a range of about 150 feet.

Recoton sells its more than 4,000 products through a wide range of retail channels, including consumer electronics stores, computer and office supply superstores, department stores, mass merchants, catalog showrooms, direct mail, TV shopping channels, warehouse clubs, and music and video chains. In all, its products are sold at more than 30,000 outlets in the United States and Canada.

It also has marketing subsidiaries in Asia and Europe, although foreign sales account for less than 10 percent of Recoton's total revenue.

In addition to the retail market, Recoton has significant sales to other manufacturers who use its speakers, cables, remote control devices, and other products as part of larger systems.

Founded in 1936, Recoton has about 4,000 employees and a market capitalization of about $230 million.

EARNINGS PER SHARE GROWTH

Past four years: 40 percent (9 percent per year)

REVENUE GROWTH   ★ ★ ★ ★

Past four years: 326 percent (43 percent per year)

STOCK GROWTH

Past three years: −4 percent
Dollar growth: $10,000 over the past three years would have declined to $9,600.

CONSISTENCY   ★ ★ ★

Increased earnings per share: three of the past four years
Increased revenue: four of the past four years

RECOTON AT A GLANCE

Fiscal year ended: Dec. 31
Revenue and net income in $ millions

	1994	1995	1996	1997	1998	4-Year Growth Avg. Annual (%)	Total (%)
Revenue ($)	164	212.7	331.7	502	700.4	43	326
Net income ($)	11.8	15.1	8.38	13.6	19.1	13	61
Earnings/share ($)	1.12	1.39	0.74	1.19	1.57	9	40
Avg. PE ratio	16	16	24	12	30	—	—

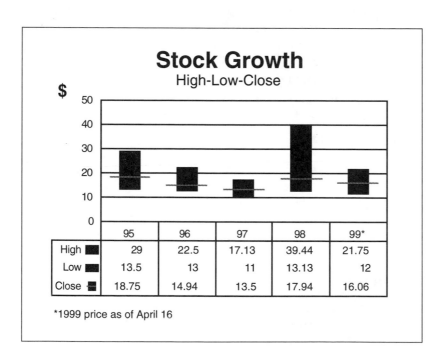

Stock Growth
High-Low-Close

$	95	96	97	98	99*
High	29	22.5	17.13	39.44	21.75
Low	13.5	13	11	13.13	12
Close	18.75	14.94	13.5	17.94	16.06

*1999 price as of April 16

87

PFF Bancorp, Inc.

350 South Garey Avenue
Pomona, CA 91766
909-623-2323
www.pffbank.com

President and CEO:
Larry M. Rinehart

Earnings Growth	★ ★ ★ ★
Revenue Growth	
Stock Growth	
Consistency	★ ★ ★
Nasdaq: PFFB	**7 points**

Formerly known as the Pomona First Federal Savings and Loan Association, PFF Bancorp focuses on retail customers interested in savings and checking accounts and home mortgages.

The California institution made the switch from savings and loan to bank—technically known as changing from a mutual form of ownership to a stock form—in 1996. The company raised about $200 million in its initial public stock offering in 1996. After the changeover, the bank saw its earnings grow from $.11 a share in fiscal 1996 to $1.00 in fiscal 1998.

PFF remains a fairly small bank by industry standards, with 24 full-service branches, three trust offices, and a regional loan center in the Pomona area. It serves the eastern Los Angeles area, San Bernardino, Riverside, and northern and central Orange County.

Most of the company's deposits have come from the general public rather than business or commercial accounts. Home mortgages (for one- to four-family residences) account for about 75 percent of PFF's total gross loans.

Multifamily mortgages account for about 5 percent; commercial real estate loans make up about 7 percent; and construction and land loans account for about 10 percent. The bank handles some consumer loans and commercial business loans.

Recently, PFF has begun to put much more emphasis on attracting business deposit accounts and originating commercial business and real estate loans.

PFF is tuned into the technology age, with its own Web site and a state-of-the-art loan and telebanking center that opened in 1997. The company also recently engineered a complete overhaul of its computer operations to expedite processing of loans and other administrative and banking procedures.

The company has about 500 employees and a market capitalization of about $240 million.

EARNINGS PER SHARE GROWTH   ★ ★ ★ ★

Past two years: 809 percent (200 percent per year)

REVENUE GROWTH

Past four years: 65 percent (13 percent per year)

STOCK GROWTH

Past two years: 7 percent (3 percent per year)
Dollar growth: $10,000 over the past two years would have grown to about $11,000.

CONSISTENCY   ★ ★ ★

Increased earnings per share: four of the past four years
Increased revenue: three of the past four years

PFF BANCORP AT A GLANCE

Fiscal year ended: March 31
Revenue and net income in $ millions

	1994	1995	1996	1997	1998	4-Year Growth Avg. Annual (%)	Total (%)
Revenue ($)	115.7	108	136.2	168.5	191.4	13	65
Net income ($)	−2.91	−4.16	2.07	2.73	16	180*	673*
Earnings/share ($)	—	−0.23	0.11	0.15	1.00	200*	809*
Avg. PE ratio	—	—	82	18	16	—	—

*Net income and earnings per share returns are based on two-year performance.

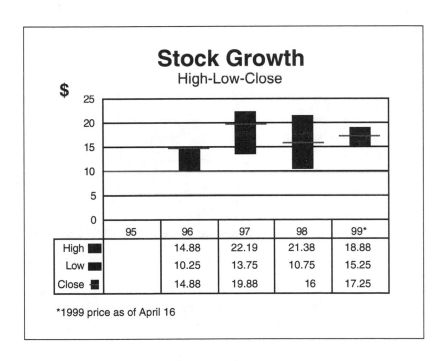

	95	96	97	98	99*
High		14.88	22.19	21.38	18.88
Low		10.25	13.75	10.75	15.25
Close		14.88	19.88	16	17.25

*1999 price as of April 16

TANDY·BRANDS
A C C E S S O R I E S ,   I N C .

690 East Lamar Boulevard
Suite 200
Arlington, TX 76011
817-548-0090
www.tandybrands.com

Chairman:
James Gaertner
President and CEO:
J. S. B. Jenkins

Earnings Growth	
Revenue Growth	★
Stock Growth	★ ★ ★ ★
Consistency	★ ★
Nasdaq: TBAC	**7 points**

You may not know the name Tandy Brands, but there's a very good chance you've owned a Tandy belt or billfold. The company is one of the nation's leading leather goods makers. It also makes socks, scarves, hats, suspenders, and neckties.

You're probably familiar with many of Tandy's apparel lines, including belts and billfolds for the Greg Norman Collection (sold at golf pro shops, specialty stores, and departments stores); handbags and other accessories for the Jones New York line (sold in department stores and specialty shops); and belts and small leather goods for Haggar.

Tandy also makes belts and small leather goods for Bugle Boy, Canterbury, Tiger, and Accessory Design Group, and small leather goods (such as men's and women's wallets) for Rolfs, Prince Gardner, Princess Gardner, and Amity.

The Arlington, Texas manufacturer also makes private label brand belts and leather goods for a number of leading retailers, including Wal-Mart, J.C. Penney, Sears, and Target. Private label sales account for about 58 percent of total revenue.

In all, the company's products are sold by more than 10,000 retailers.

Leather belts are the leading product for Tandy Brands, accounting for about 60 percent of total revenue. Wallets, purses, and other smaller leather accessories account for about 15 percent. Its other products make up the remaining 25 percent of revenue.

Men's and boys' products account for about 52 percent of sales versus 48 percent for women's and girls' products.

Tandy has grown quickly in recent years through a series of product line acquisitions, including Tiger Accessories men's and boys' belts, Amity and Rolfs wallets, and H.A. Sheldon men's belts, wallets, and suspenders. It also acquired Canterbury Belts, Ltd., which makes belts and other leather and fabric accessories.

The company has been making belts for more than 70 years. Tandy has about 1,000 employees and a market capitalization of about $100 million.

EARNINGS PER SHARE GROWTH

Past four years: 25 percent (6 percent per year)

REVENUE GROWTH   ★

Past four years: 101 percent (19 percent per year)

STOCK GROWTH   ★ ★ ★ ★

Past three years: 168 percent (39 percent per year)
Dollar growth: $10,000 over the past three years would have grown to about $27,000.

CONSISTENCY   ★ ★

Increased earnings per share: two of the past four years
Increased revenue: four of the past four years

TANDY BRANDS ACCESSORIES AT A GLANCE

Fiscal year ended: June 30
Revenue and net income in $ millions

	1994	1995	1996	1997	1998	4-Year Growth Avg. Annual (%)	Total (%)
Revenue ($)	67.3	83.7	86.7	102.5	135	19	101
Net income ($)	5.4	4.2	0.101	4.6	7.2	8	33
Earnings/share ($)	1.04	0.80	0.02	0.84	1.30	6	25
Avg. PE ratio	16	14	388	15	11	—	—

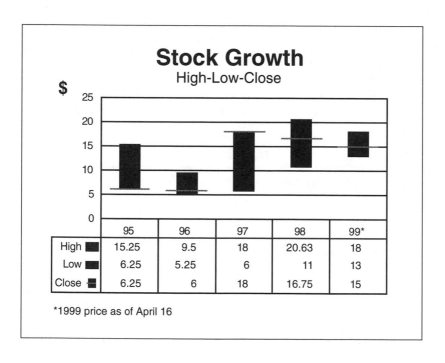

Stock Growth
High-Low-Close

$	95	96	97	98	99*
High	15.25	9.5	18	20.63	18
Low	6.25	5.25	6	11	13
Close	6.25	6	18	16.75	15

*1999 price as of April 16

Prophet 21, Inc.

Prophet 21™

19 West College Avenue
Yardley, PA 19067
215-493-8900
www.p21.com

Chairman:
John E. Miggitt
President and CEO:
Charles L. Boyle III

Earnings Growth	
Revenue Growth	
Stock Growth	★ ★ ★ ★
Consistency	★ ★
Nasdaq: PXXI	**6 points**

Prophet 21 software helps distributors and wholesalers manage their operations more efficiently.

The Yardley, Pennsylvania operation has installed software systems at nearly 2,000 companies throughout North America. Its customers vary in size from small distributors and wholesalers with a few users to larger operations with several hundred users linking multiple geographically dispersed branches.

Its customers are spread through a wide range of industries, including electrical, plumbing, electronic, hardware, heating and air-conditioning, medical, dental, janitorial, tile, and general distribution.

The company's Prophet 21 Acclaim software is used for automating order processing, inventory management and control, communications networking, and product pricing. The product also offers electronic commerce such as EDI, VMI, DMI, and Internet enabling capabilities. Prophet 21 Acclaim also allows for centralized purchasing and billing and accounting, which helps speed up the the delivery process.

The company also offers the Prophet 21 Servent software package that is used for a wide range of functions, including automating order management, order configuration, inventory management and control, product pricing, and financials. It's used by wholesalers and distributors with multibranch operations. About half of the company's clients have multiple locations connected by communications networks.

Prophet 21 sells its products and services throughout the United States using a direct sales force of about 50 people.

The company designs its software to be used on either a UNIX system or a Microsoft Windows NT environment. In addition to its software, the firm also offers training, consulting, software customization, hardware, and implementation services.

Prophet 21 was founded in 1967 under the name Programmed Control Corp. The company went public with its initial stock offering in 1994. Prophet 21 has about 300 employees and a market capitalization of about $40 million.

EARNINGS PER SHARE GROWTH

Past four years: 42 percent (9 percent per year)

REVENUE GROWTH

Past four years: 49 percent (10 percent per year)

STOCK GROWTH   ★ ★ ★ ★

Past three years: 134 percent (33 percent per year)
Dollar growth: $10,000 over the past three years would have grown to about $23,000.

CONSISTENCY   ★ ★

Increased earnings per share: three of the past four years
Increased revenue: three of the past four years

PROPHET 21 AT A GLANCE

Fiscal year ended: June 30
Revenue and net income in $ millions

	1994	1995	1996	1997	1998	4-Year Growth Avg. Annual (%)	Total (%)
Revenue ($)	37.5	31.2	33.1	36.4	46.6	10	49
Net income ($)	2.3	−0.227	1.4	2.3	3.5	11	51
Earnings/share ($)	0.69	−0.06	0.34	0.60	0.98	9	42
Avg. PE ratio	—	—	16	18	15	—	—

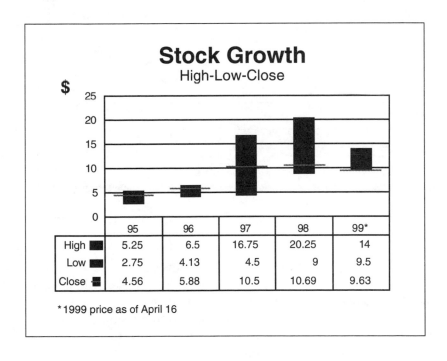

Stock Growth
High-Low-Close

$

	95	96	97	98	99*
High	5.25	6.5	16.75	20.25	14
Low	2.75	4.13	4.5	9	9.5
Close	4.56	5.88	10.5	10.69	9.63

*1999 price as of April 16

90
Advanced Neuromodulation Systems, Inc.

One Allentown Parkway
Allen, TX 75002
972-390-9800
www.ans-medical.com

President and CEO:
Thomas C. Thompson

Earnings Growth	★ ★ ★ ★
Revenue Growth	
Stock Growth	
Consistency	★ ★
Nasdaq: ANSI	**6 points**

Advanced Neuromodulation Systems (ANS) helps ease the pain for those with chronic back problems. The Allen, Texas firm makes implantable stimulation systems used by patients with chronic pain.

The company's leading product line is its electronic spinal cord stimulation devices, which are implanted in the back and used to mask the pain signals sent to the brain. ANS's CompuStim implantable devices are promoted as a cost-effective alternative to repeat back surgeries for relieving chronic severe back pain. Rather than using batteries that must be changed periodically, the CompuStim is powered by a radio frequency transmitter outside the body.

Traditional implantable pain control devices involve added costs and risk because repeat surgeries are required to replace the batteries. But in the ANS devices, there are no batteries to replace.

Its devices are used to relieve pain from failed back syndrome, peripheral neuropathy, phantom limb or stump pain, ischemic pain, reflex sympathetic dystrophy, and other related back conditions. The stimulation devices are often effective enough that patients can discontinue using their prescription pain medication.

ANS also makes a line of pressure control valves, prebypass and arterial line filters, and bubble traps used during cardiopulmonary bypass surgery. Pressure control valves are placed in the suction line to vent or decompress the heart.

The company also is working on the development of a deep brain stimulator through an agreement with Sofamor Danek Group, which will market the products worldwide.

ANS sells most of its products through a combination of specialty distributors and commissioned salespeople. About 15 percent of its sales are generated outside the United States. The firm targets anesthesiologists, neurosurgeons, and orthopedic surgeons.

ANS, formerly known as Quest Medical, was founded in 1979 as a manufacturer of intravenous fluid delivery tubing sets (although its fluid delivery system business was recently sold). The company has about 100 employees and a market capitalization of about $60 million.

EARNINGS PER SHARE GROWTH ★ ★ ★ ★

Past two years: 2,900 percent (440 percent per year)

REVENUE GROWTH

Past four years: 44 percent (9 percent per year)

STOCK GROWTH

Past three years: −39 percent
Dollar growth: $10,000 over the past three years would have declined to about $6,000.

CONSISTENCY ★ ★

Increased earnings per share: three of the past four years
Increased revenue: three of the past four years

ADVANCED NEUROMODULATION SYSTEMS AT A GLANCE

Fiscal year ended: Dec. 31
Revenue and net income in $ millions

	1994	1995	1996	1997	1998	4-Year Growth Avg. Annual (%)	Total (%)
Revenue ($)	14.0	10.4	11.4	14.7	20.1	9	44
Net income ($)	−1.72	−8.91	0.116	0.818	2.59	115*	2,133*
Earnings/share ($)	−0.33	−1.42	0.01	0.10	0.30	440*	2,900*
Avg. PE ratio	—	—	732	85	25	—	—

*Net income and earnings per share returns are based on two-year performance.

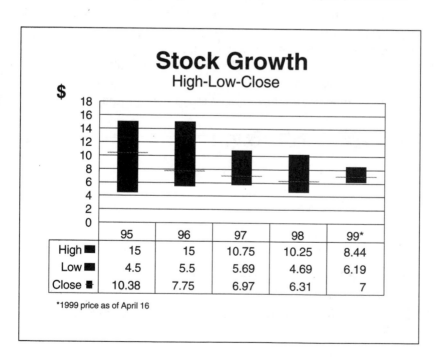

	95	96	97	98	99*
High	15	15	10.75	10.25	8.44
Low	4.5	5.5	5.69	4.69	6.19
Close	10.38	7.75	6.97	6.31	7

*1999 price as of April 16

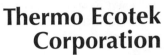

Thermo Ecotek Corporation

245 Winter Street
Suite 300
Waltham, MA 02154
781-622-1000
www.therm.com/subsid/tckl.html

President and CEO:
Brian D. Holt

Earnings Growth	★ ★ ★
Revenue Growth	
Stock Growth	
Consistency	★ ★ ★
AMEX: TCK	**6 points**

Thermo Ecotek focuses on providing environmentally clean energy through a variety of sources.

The Waltham, Massachusetts operation operates clean power plants, develops cleaner-burning alternatives to conventional fuels, and, through its Thermo Trilogy subsidiary, is also a leading manufacturer of environmentally friendly pesticides.

Thermo Ecotek's original business was operating power plants that used environmentally friendly combustion technologies. It still operates seven iomass facilities, with a generating capacity of about 140 megawatts. It also is exploring the possibility of retrofitting aging power plants, using the latest technologies to provide clean power.

The company is cultivating a growing business overseas where new regulations require stricter environmental controls. It has helped develop new clean combustion power plants in Italy, the Czech Republic, and other

European countries. The firm also is working on a new power plant in India that will be a 105-megawatt combined cycle, gas turbine electricity generation facility.

In the United States, the company is involved in a project to provide "clean coal." A new plant the company helped design and build in Gillette, Wyoming, is designed to produce more than 500,000 tons per year of clean coal to help utilities companies comply with recent clean air regulations.

Thermo Ecotek also makes a wide range of crop-protection products (through its Thermo Trilogy subsidiary), including neem-based products (from the neem tree), as well as pheromone, nematode, and virus-, fungal-, and bacteria-based products. These naturally occurring products control pests in a variety of ways, such as disrupting the mating process, luring the pests into traps, or killing the pests without harming the crops.

Thermo Electron owns about 85 percent of Thermo Ecotek's outstanding stock. The company went public with its initial stock offering in 1995. The firm has about 400 employees and a market capitalization of about $380 million.

EARNINGS PER SHARE GROWTH ★ ★ ★

Past four years: 123 percent (22 percent per year)

REVENUE GROWTH

Past four years: 56 percent (12 percent per year)

STOCK GROWTH

Past three years: −5 percent
Dollar growth: $10,000 over the past three years would have declined to $9,500.

CONSISTENCY ★ ★ ★

Increased earnings per share: four of the past four years
Increased revenue: three of the past four years

THERMO ECOTEK AT A GLANCE

Fiscal year ended: Sept. 30
Revenue and net income in $ millions

	1994	1995	1996	1997	1998	4-Year Growth Avg. Annual (%)	Total (%)
Revenue ($)	134.3	107.1	150.1	180.2	209	12	56
Net income ($)	10.8	12.5	17.8	22.5	32.9	33	205
Earnings/share ($)	0.48	0.58	0.70	0.85	1.07	22	123
Avg. PE ratio	—	21	18	16	10	—	—

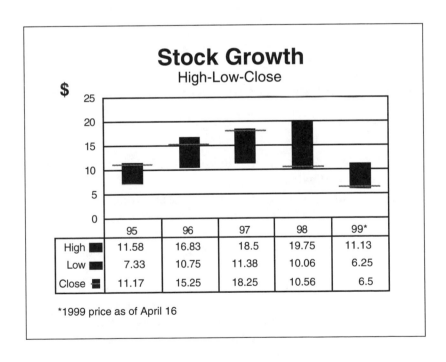

Stock Growth
High-Low-Close

	95	96	97	98	99*
High	11.58	16.83	18.5	19.75	11.13
Low	7.33	10.75	11.38	10.06	6.25
Close	11.17	15.25	18.25	10.56	6.5

*1999 price as of April 16

Maxwell Shoe Company, Inc.

101 Sprague Street
Boston, MA 02137
617-364-5090

Chairman, President, and CEO:
Mark J. Cocozza

Earnings Growth	
Revenue Growth	
Stock Growth	★ ★ ★
Consistency	★ ★ ★
Nasdaq: MAXS	**6 points**

The Maxwell Shoe Company is a long-established shoemaker that specializes in footwear for women and children.

Maxwell's leading line is the Mootsies Tootsies women's casual and dress shoes, boots, and sandals. It is a moderately priced line geared to women in the 18 to 34 age range. The line includes about 30 new styles each spring and fall season, as well as a number of core styles that are updated periodically. Mootsies Tootsies shoes sell for about $25 to $50, while the boots sell for about $35 to $60. The Mootsies Tootsies line accounts for the lion's share of the company's total annual revenue.

The firm also makes a line of Mootsies Kids shoes targeted to girls in the 8 to 12 age range. The line includes casual and party shoes, boots, and sandals that retail for about $20 to $50.

Maxwell's other lines include Sam & Libby, casual and dress footwear targeted to women ages 21 to 35; Sam & Libby Kids, geared to girls ages 8 to 14; Jones New York, which is a higher quality footwear line geared to career-oriented women age 30 and older; and Jones New York Sport, leisure footwear for career women.

The Boston-based manufacturer also offers private label brands for retailers who want their own name on the shoes.

Maxwell markets its shoes through both moderately priced retailers, such as Federated Department Stores and the Mercantile Stores, and leading department stores such as Dayton Hudson, Macy's, and Bloomingdale's. In all, the company sells to about 1,500 separate accounts with more than 5,000 retail locations. The firm also sells shoes through national catalog retailers and cable television consumer shopping channels.

The company manufactures the vast majority of its shoes in Asia. About 80 percent of the manufacturing is done in China.

Maxwell was founded by Maxwell Blum in 1949. It was first incorporated in 1976 and went public with its initial stock offering in 1994. Blum, who had managed the company for 50 years and controlled the majority of voting stock, retired in 1998 and ceded control of the company. Maxwell has about 100 employees and a market capitalization of about $100 million.

EARNINGS PER SHARE GROWTH

Past four years: 28 percent (6 percent per year)

REVENUE GROWTH

Past four years: 64 percent (13 percent per year)

STOCK GROWTH   ★ ★ ★

Past three years: 99 percent (26 percent per year)
Dollar growth: $10,000 over the past three years would have grown to about $20,000.

CONSISTENCY   ★ ★ ★

Increased earnings per share: three of the past four years
Increased revenue: four of the past four years

MAXWELL SHOE COMPANY AT A GLANCE

Fiscal year ended: Oct. 31
Revenue and net income in $ millions

	1994	1995	1996	1997	1998	4-Year Growth Avg. Annual (%)	Total (%)
Revenue ($)	100.9	101.9	104.3	134.2	165.9	13	64
Net income ($)	2.8	5.8	5.9	9.0	13.3	47	375
Earnings/share ($)	1.12	0.70	0.72	1.06	1.43	6	28
Avg. PE ratio	9	11	9	10	12	—	—

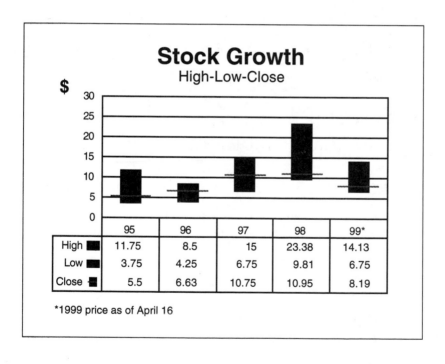

Stock Growth
High-Low-Close

	95	96	97	98	99*
High	11.75	8.5	15	23.38	14.13
Low	3.75	4.25	6.75	9.81	6.75
Close	5.5	6.63	10.75	10.95	8.19

*1999 price as of April 16

93

Daktronics, Inc.

DAKTRONICS, INC.

331 32nd Avenue
Brookings, SD 57006
605-697-4000
www.daktronics.com

President and CEO:
Aelred J. Kurtenbach

Earnings Growth	
Revenue Growth	
Stock Growth	★ ★ ★ ★
Consistency	★ ★
Nasdaq: DAKT	**6 points**

Daktronics has reaped the rewards of the recent boom in spectator sports. The Brookings, South Dakota operation specializes in signs and scoreboards, including the giant electronic scoreboards used at major stadiums and arenas. Daktronics has installed thousands of scoreboards and display systems in more than 60 countries.

Daktronics offers the most complete line of scoreboards and display systems in the industry, from the smaller indoor scoreboards to highway and airport electronic information display signs to the huge multi-million-dollar outdoor video display systems. Prices of its products range from less than $1,000 to more than $7 million.

The firm also sells scoreboards and message centers to elementary, middle, and high schools and to park and recreation departments. It manufactures display boards for motor racing venues, swimming pools, and track and field stadiums.

The company also sells indoor and outdoor programmable signs for businesses, including information and advertising panels, time and temperature and price display signs, and spectacular multi-million-dollar video display advertising signs.

In addition to its sports and business customer base, Daktronics has sales to government agencies, including signs for transportation terminals, over-the-road systems for motorist information, and legislative voting systems.

Most of its signs can be reprogrammed through Windows-based control systems. Daktronics not only designs and manufactures the displays it sells, it also provides the installation and servicing for most of its products.

Daktronics sells its products through both its own sales staff and a network of independent resellers throughout the world. Its leading customers include schools, universities, recreation centers, convention centers, professional sports teams, banks, auto dealers, shopping malls, casinos, departments of transportation, financial exchanges, airlines, and transit centers.

Founded in 1968, the company went public with its initial stock offering in 1994. It has about 525 employees and a market capitalization of about $50 million.

EARNINGS PER SHARE GROWTH

Past four years: 25 percent (6 percent per year)

REVENUE GROWTH

Past four years: 70 percent (14 percent per year)

STOCK GROWTH   ★ ★ ★ ★

Past three years: 164 percent (38 percent per year)
Dollar growth: $10,000 over the past three years would have grown to about $26,000.

CONSISTENCY   ★ ★

Increased earnings per share: two of the past four years
Increased revenue: four of the past four years

DAKTRONICS AT A GLANCE

Fiscal year ended: April 30
Revenue and net income in $ millions

	1994	1995	1996	1997	1998	4-Year Growth Avg. Annual (%)	4-Year Growth Total (%)
Revenue ($)	41.1	41.9	52.5	62.6	69.9	14	70
Net income ($)	1.98	0.967	−0.215	1.51	3.39	14	71
Earnings/share ($)	0.63	0.23	−0.05	0.36	0.79	6	25
Avg. PE ratio	—	—	12	7	11	—	—

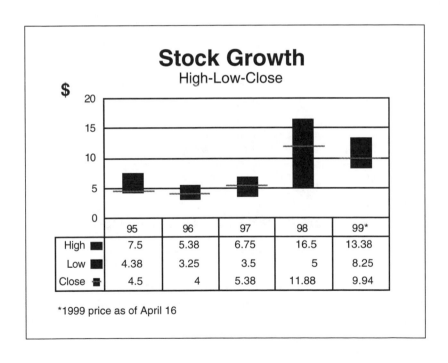

Stock Growth
High-Low-Close

$	95	96	97	98	99*
High	7.5	5.38	6.75	16.5	13.38
Low	4.38	3.25	3.5	5	8.25
Close	4.5	4	5.38	11.88	9.94

*1999 price as of April 16

94
Michael Baker Corporation

Baker

Airport Office Park, Bldg. 3
420 Rouser Road
Coraopolis, PA 15108
412-269-6300
www.mbakercorp.com

Chairman:
Robert L. Shaw
President and CEO:
Charles I. Homan

Earnings Growth	
Revenue Growth	
Stock Growth	★ ★ ★
Consistency	★ ★
AMEX: BKR	**5 points**

Michael Baker is an engineering and construction company that handles a wide range of major construction projects, from buildings and bridges to telecommunications and wastewater systems. Most of its work is done in the United States, although about 10 percent of its revenue comes from projects outside the United States.

The Coraopolis, Pennsylvania operation has several key corporate units, including the following:

- *Building.* The firm does general construction, project management and building design, architectural and interior design, and construction inspection. The firm builds hospitals, corporate headquarters, data centers, correctional facilities, schools, airports, and entertainment facilities.

- *Civil.* Michael Baker handles civil engineering and water resources projects, including telecommunications systems, pipelines, resources management, water and wastewater systems, and facilities operations and management. One of its leading customers is the U.S. Department of Defense, which uses Michael Baker for surveying, mapping, geographic information systems, planning, design, construction management, and total program management.
- *Energy.* The firm offers a variety of services for the oil and gas, utility, and petrochemical industries, including turbine overhauls, mechanical services, and training services for energy producers.
- *Environmental.* The company offers a combination of engineering and consulting services, such as bioremediation of petroleum-contaminated soils, evaluation and redevelopment of brownfield sites, and compliance for oil and gas production platforms in the Gulf of Mexico.
- *Transportation.* Michael Baker is involved in the planning, design, and construction of highways, bridges, airports, busways, and other transit facilities.

The firm was founded in 1940. It has about 4,000 employees and a market capitalization of about $62 million.

EARNINGS PER SHARE GROWTH

Loss of $.30 per share for 1998.

REVENUE GROWTH

Past four years: 19 percent (4 percent per year)

STOCK GROWTH   ★ ★ ★

Past three years: 95 percent (25 percent per year)
Dollar growth: $10,000 over the past three years would have grown to about $20,000.

CONSISTENCY   ★ ★

Increased earnings per share: three of the past four years
Increased revenue: three of the past four years

MICHAEL BAKER AT A GLANCE

Fiscal year ended: Dec. 31
Revenue and net income in $ millions

	1994	1995	1996	1997	1998	4-Year Growth Avg. Annual (%)	Total (%)
Revenue ($)	437.2	354.7	418.4	446.4	521.3	4	19
Net income ($)	−7.94	2.9	4.18	4.95	−2.42	—	—
Earnings/share ($)	−0.95	0.35	0.50	0.60	−0.30	—	—
Avg. PE ratio	—	14	11	15	15	—	—

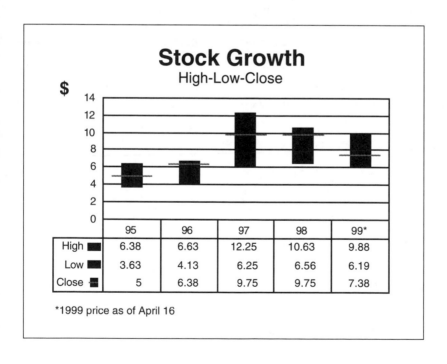

Stock Growth
High-Low-Close

	95	96	97	98	99*
High	6.38	6.63	12.25	10.63	9.88
Low	3.63	4.13	6.25	6.56	6.19
Close	5	6.38	9.75	9.75	7.38

*1999 price as of April 16

Anixter International, Inc.

4711 Golf Road
Skokie, IL 60076
847-677-2600
www.anixter.com

Chairman:
Samuel Zell
President:
Robert Grubbs, Jr.

Earnings Growth	★
Revenue Growth	
Stock Growth	
Consistency	★ ★ ★
NYSE: AXE	**4 points**

The nerve center of the 21st century economy would seem to be the end-less miles of cords and wires that link the World Wide Web and all of its users and hosts together. Anixter International is a long-established sup-plier of wire, cable, and related networking and Internetworking products for computers, video and voice systems, and other electronic products. It claims a client base of more than 100,000 customers around the world.

In all, Anixter sells more than 60,000 products, including a broad range of copper and fiber-optic cable, electrical wiring systems, military and commercial cable, networking and Internetworking systems, and a massive array of lugs, splices, connectors, cable ties, and tapes.

The Skokie, Illinois operation does not manufacture any of its own products. It serves as a distributor for more than 1,000 manufacturers and other suppliers, including Lucent Technologies, Siemens, Triangle/Royal, General Cable, Essex, and Alcatel.

Anixter has a worldwide sales and distribution network, including about 90 locations in the United States, 22 in Canada, 14 in the United Kingdom, 36 throughout Europe, 17 in Latin America, 16 in Asia, and 4 in Australia.

Its clients base is made up primarily of end users from corporations, government agencies, small businesses, manufacturers, communications operations, financial institutions, schools, hospitals, and utility companies.

Increasingly, the company has been shifting from being merely a product supplier to a supplier and service provider. For Anixter, it is a natural shift in its marketing strategy, as its client companies look for some assistance in designing or upgrading their complex computer network systems. Anixter's technical specialists can help an organization with assessment and planning of the computer network, design, installation, and ongoing technical support.

Anixter's increased emphasis on the service end of the business could bode well for future sales. As its client companies expand and upgrade their computer network systems, Anixter should have the inside track on providing the additional products and technical services.

Anixter was founded in 1957. It has about 6,300 employees and a market capitalization of about $821 million.

EARNINGS PER SHARE GROWTH ★

Past four years: 56 percent (12 percent per year)

REVENUE GROWTH

Past four years: 69 percent (14 percent per year)

STOCK GROWTH

Past three years: 9 percent (3 percent per year)
Dollar growth: $10,000 over the past three years would have grown to about $11,000.

CONSISTENCY ★ ★ ★

Increased earnings per share: three of the past four years
Increased revenue: four of the past four years

ANIXTER INTERNATIONAL AT A GLANCE

Fiscal year ended: Dec. 31
Revenue and net income in $ millions

	1994	1995	1996	1997	1998	4-Year Growth Avg. Annual (%)	Total (%)
Revenue ($)	1,732	2,194	2,475	2,805	2,920	14	69
Net income ($)	46.2	39.1	36.1	45.3	52	3	13
Earnings/share ($)	0.72	0.71	0.73	0.95	1.12	12	56
Avg. PE ratio	21	28	23	17	16	—	—

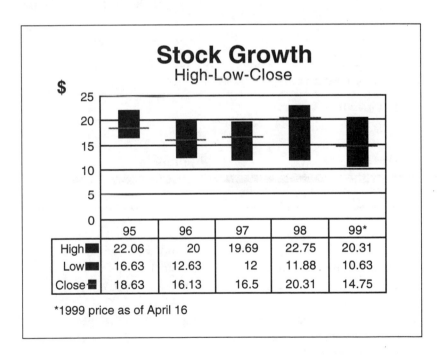

Stock Growth
High-Low-Close

	95	96	97	98	99*
High	22.06	20	19.69	22.75	20.31
Low	16.63	12.63	12	11.88	10.63
Close	18.63	16.13	16.5	20.31	14.75

*1999 price as of April 16

Dan River, Inc.

Dan River Inc.

2291 Memorial Drive
Danville, VA 24541
804-799-7000

Chairman and CEO:
Joseph L. Lanier
President:
Richard L. Williams

Earnings Growth	★ ★ ★
Revenue Growth	
Stock Growth	
Consistency	★
NYSE: DRF	**4 points**

Dan River is trying to sneak into your bedroom. Founded in 1882, the company is a leading manufacturer of bedroom items, including comforters, bed sheets, pillowcases, shams, bed skirts, decorative pillows, and draperies.

The Danville, Virginia operation also makes a broad range of woven cotton and cotton-blend apparel fabrics. It is the leading supplier of men's dress shirt fabrics in North America.

Dan River's bedding products account for about 54 percent of total sales revenue, while apparel fabrics make up the other 46 percent.

The firm popularized the complete bed ensemble with its Bed-in-a-Bag product for retailers that includes a comforter with matching sheets, pillow cases, shams, and dust ruffle.

Its bedding products are sold through department stores, specialty home fashion stores, direct marketers, national chains, mass merchants, and regional discounters. Among its leading retail customers are Kmart, Wal-Mart, Federated Department Stores, J.C. Penney, and May Department Stores.

Its apparel fabrics are used primarily for the manufacture of men's, women's, and children's clothing. Dan River's yarn-dyed and piece-dyed woven apparel fabrics include oxford cloth, fancy broad cloth, seer-suckers, denim, twills, and chambrays. The firm also makes apparel fabric for uniform manufacturers and for use in decorating and crafts. It also makes cotton fabrics for the furniture market.

Among its leading fabrics customers are Arrow, Brooks Brothers, Liz Claiborne, L.L. Bean, Land's End, J.C. Penney, and Sears.

The company has grown in recent years through marketing expansion and some key acquisitions of smaller textile operations.

Dan River went public with its initial stock offering in 1997. The firm has about 5,500 employees and a market capitalization of about $193 million.

EARNINGS PER SHARE GROWTH ★ ★ ★

Past four years: 168 percent (28 percent per year)

REVENUE GROWTH

Past four years: 39 percent (8 percent per year)

STOCK GROWTH

Past one year: −28 percent
Dollar growth: $10,000 over the past year would have declined to $7,200.

CONSISTENCY

Increased earnings per share: two of the past four years
Increased revenue: three of the past four years

DAN RIVER AT A GLANCE

Fiscal year ended: Dec. 31
Revenue and net income in $ millions

	1994	1995	1996	1997	1998	4-Year Growth Avg. Annual (%)	Total (%)
Revenue ($)	371.5	384.8	379.6	476.4	517.4	8	39
Net income ($)	3.53	0.258	5.68	13.3	15.8	46	348
Earnings/share ($)	0.31	0.02	0.40	0.90	0.83	28	168
Avg. PE ratio	—	—	—	18	18	—	—

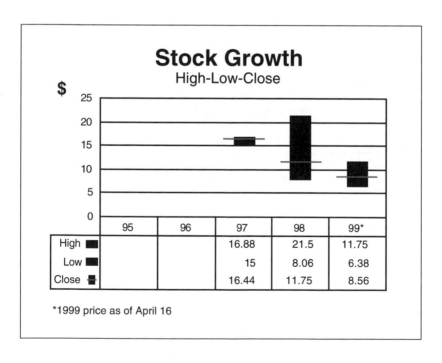

Stock Growth
High-Low-Close

$	95	96	97	98	99*
High			16.88	21.5	11.75
Low			15	8.06	6.38
Close			16.44	11.75	8.56

*1999 price as of April 16

Interface, Inc.

2859 Paces Ferry Road
Suite 2000
Atlanta, GA 30339
770-437-6800

Chairman and CEO:
Ray C. Anderson
President:
Charles R. Eitel

Earnings Growth	
Revenue Growth	★
Stock Growth	
Consistency	★ ★ ★
Nasdaq: IFSIA	**4 points**

With a name like Interface, you've got to be thinking high tech. But Interface is definitely low tech—floor level. The company makes carpeting and other floor coverings that it markets worldwide.

Interface claims to be the worldwide leader in the "modular carpet" segment, which includes both carpet tile and two-meter rolls. Its Bentley Mills, Prince Street, and Firth brands are strong sellers in the designer-oriented sector of the broadloom segment.

The Atlanta-based firm not only manufactures carpet and floor covering, it also provides installation and maintenance through its dealer network, and specialized carpet replacement services through its Renovisions, Inc., subsidiary. Its Interior Fabrics Group is a leading manufacturer of panel fabrics for use in open-plan office furniture systems.

Interface's specialty products operations also manufactures raised/access flooring systems, antimicrobial additives, adhesives, and various other chemical compounds used in the installation and maintenance of floor covering.

The firm markets its products in more than 100 countries. Its internal marketing and sales force includes more than 1,000 people in more than 100 offices in 35 countries.

About 70 percent of its sales are generated in the United States. Other leading areas include Western Europe (23 percent of revenue) and the Asia-Pacific region (7 percent). Interface is aggressively expanding into new markets, such as China, Southeast Asia, South America, and Eastern Europe.

Traditionally, much of the company's business has been in the renovation market. But with the new building boom in the U.S. commercial office market, Interface expects to see a greater share of its income derived from that segment.

Interface has expanded its business in recent years through a series of acquisitions. Among its leading acquisitions over the past decade were Heuga Holdings in Europe in 1988, Bentley Mills in 1993, Prince Street in 1994, and Firth Carpets in 1998.

The company has 7,300 employees and a market capitalization of about $470 million.

EARNINGS PER SHARE GROWTH

Past four years: 37 percent (8 percent per year)

REVENUE GROWTH   ★

Past four years: 77 percent (15 percent per year)

STOCK GROWTH

Past three years: 9 percent (2 percent per year)
Dollar growth: $10,000 over the past three years would have grown to about $11,000.

CONSISTENCY   ★ ★ ★

Increased earnings per share: three of the past four years
Increased revenue: four of the past four years

INTERFACE AT A GLANCE

Fiscal year ended: Dec. 31
Revenue and net income in $ millions

	1994	1995	1996	1997	1998	4-Year Growth Avg. Annual (%)	Total (%)
Revenue ($)	725.3	802.1	1,002	1,135	1,281	15	77
Net income ($)	16.5	20.3	26.4	37.5	29.8	16	81
Earnings/share ($)	0.41	0.51	0.62	0.79	0.56	8	37
Avg. PE ratio	17	15	14	16	28	—	—

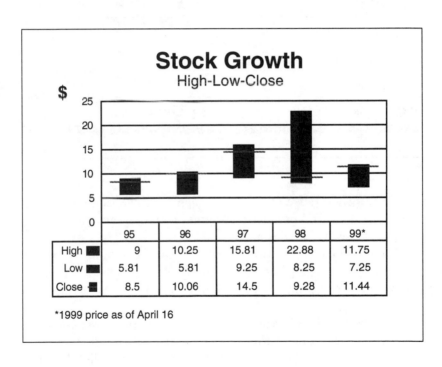

Stock Growth
High-Low-Close

	95	96	97	98	99*
High	9	10.25	15.81	22.88	11.75
Low	5.81	5.81	9.25	8.25	7.25
Close	8.5	10.06	14.5	9.28	11.44

*1999 price as of April 16

98

Schawk, Inc.

1695 River Road
Des Plaines, IL 60018
847-827-9494
www.schawk.com

Chairman:
Clarence W. Schawk
President and CEO:
David A. Schawk

Earnings Growth	★ ★
Revenue Growth	
Stock Growth	
Consistency	★
NYSE: SGK	**3 points**

Schawk offers a wide range of prepress graphic services and digital imaging for advertising and product packaging, including everything from soup cans and cereal to cookies and candy.

The firm is involved in the production of color separations, electronic production design, film preparation, and platemaking and press proofs for the three main types of printing processing: lithography, flexography, and gravure processing.

The Des Plaines, Illinois operation specializes in preparing color images and text for high-volume print production runs of consumer packaging. Schawk does not do the actual printing but serves as a link between the companies, their creative designers, and their printers. It handles such prepress operations as art production design, digital photography, retouching, and color separation and platemaking services.

Schawk works with some of the nation's leading consumer products companies. In fact, the firm has on-site consultants to help expedite the print preparation process at a number of leading foods companies, including Pepsico, Pillsbury, Quaker Oats, Nabisco, Keebler, Campbell Soup, and Stouffer Foods.

About 70 percent of Schawk's total revenue comes from prepress processes relating to packaging. The balance comes from prepress services for point-of-sale displays, advertising, and direct mail.

Schawk maintains both digital and analog data archives of product package layouts and designs as a value-added service for some of its customers. In marketing its services the company stresses its strengths, including high-quality customized imaging capabilities; rapid turnaround; up-to-date knowledge of the printing process; digital imaging asset management; art production; and the ability to serve its clients' global prepress requirements through its U.S. operations and international alliance partners.

Schawk was founded in 1953 by Clarence W. Schawk, who still serves as chairman of the board. The company has about 900 employees and a market capitalization of about $280 million.

EARNINGS PER SHARE GROWTH   ★ ★

Past four years: 84 percent (16 percent per year)

REVENUE GROWTH

Past four years: 40 percent (8 percent per year)

STOCK GROWTH

Past three years: 29 percent (9 percent per year)
Dollar growth: $10,000 over the past three years would have grown to about $13,000.

CONSISTENCY   ★

Increased earnings per share: two of the past four years
Increased revenue: three of the past four years

SCHAWK AT A GLANCE

Fiscal year ended: Dec. 31
Revenue and net income in $ millions

	1994	1995	1996	1997	1998	4-Year Growth Avg. Annual (%)	4-Year Growth Total (%)
Revenue ($)	103.9	87.2	90.8	116.1	145.4	8	40
Net income ($)	12.3	6.3	5.53	12.1	17.7	9	44
Earnings/share ($)	0.58	0.26	0.22	0.56	1.07	16	84
Avg. PE ratio	19	34	37	19	13	—	—

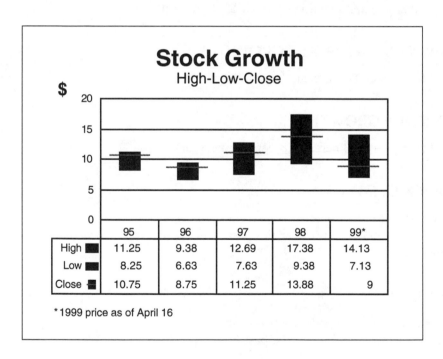

Stock Growth
High-Low-Close

	95	96	97	98	99*
High	11.25	9.38	12.69	17.38	14.13
Low	8.25	6.63	7.63	9.38	7.13
Close	10.75	8.75	11.25	13.88	9

*1999 price as of April 16

99

Opinion Research Corp.

23 Orchard Road
Skillman, NJ 08558
908-281-5100
www.opinionresearch.com

Chairman, President, and CEO:
John F. Short

Earnings Growth	
Revenue Growth	★
Stock Growth	
Consistency	★ ★
AMEX: OPI	**3 points**

Opinion Research helps companies analyze the effectiveness of their marketing and advertising programs through customer satisfaction surveys, market demand analysis and forecasting, corporate image consulting, competitive positioning, and telemarketing.

The Skillman, New Jersey operation collects customer and market information through computer-assisted telephone interviews, personal interviews, mail questionnaires, and specialized techniques such as business panels.

Opinion Research serves a wide range of industries, but its major focus is on automotive, financial services, telecommunications, retail and trade, and health care companies. About half of the company's revenues come from projects that require periodic updating and tracking of information, offering the potential for recurring revenues.

The firm offers assistance to its customers on a wide range of issues, including:

- *Customer loyalty and retention.* Opinion Research assists clients in quantifying customer loyalty and increasing customer retention. Through a series of surveys, the firm helps clients with information on the elements of products and services that are most important to their customers; on how well these products and services compare to the competition; and on which customers will continue to purchase and recommend such products and services.

- *Corporate reputation and branding.* The firm works with clients to manage their corporate and brand images, and identify and achieve optimal positioning in the marketplace.
- *Market demand analysis and forecasting.* The company helps customers gauge the market demand for new products and services.
- *Advanced analytical and data modeling.* The firm uses advanced market research techniques and predictive segmentation learning models to help client companies improve their teleservices success rates.

Opinion Research also helps client companies with employee survey programs and data collection and processing through telephone interviews.

Founded in 1938, Opinion Research went public with its initial stock offering in 1993. The company has about 360 employees and a market capitalization of about $25 million.

EARNINGS PER SHARE GROWTH

Past four years: Loss in 1998

REVENUE GROWTH ★

Past four years: 84 percent (16 percent per year)

STOCK GROWTH

Past three years: −12 percent
Dollar growth: $10,000 over the past three years would have declined to $8,800.

CONSISTENCY

Increased earnings per share: two of the past four years
Increased revenue: four of the past four years

OPINION RESEARCH AT A GLANCE

Fiscal year ended: Dec. 31
Revenue and net income in $ millions

	1994	1995	1996	1997	1998	4-Year Growth Avg. Annual (%)	Total (%)
Revenue ($)	39.8	44.1	47.3	56.7	73.2	16	84
Net income ($)	1.29	−1.67	0.808	1.15	−0.020	—	—
Earnings/share ($)	0.31	−0.39	0.19	0.28	−0.01	—	—
Avg. PE ratio	21	—	27	16	18	—	—

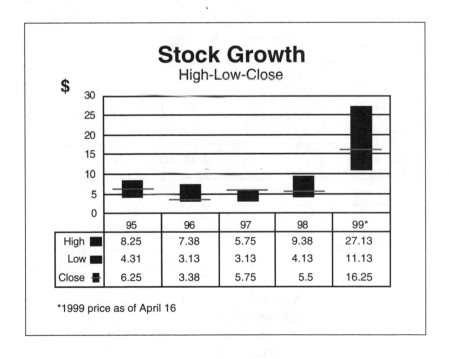

Stock Growth
High-Low-Close

	95	96	97	98	99*
High	8.25	7.38	5.75	9.38	27.13
Low	4.31	3.13	3.13	4.13	11.13
Close	6.25	3.38	5.75	5.5	16.25

*1999 price as of April 16

100
Griffon Corporation

100 Jericho Quadrangle
Jericho, NY 11753
516-938-5544

Chairman:
Harvey R. Blau
President:
Robert Balemian

Earnings Growth	
Revenue Growth	★
Stock Growth	
Consistency	★ ★
NYSE: GFF	**3 points**

Griffon is a diversified manufacturer with operations in the building products, specialty plastic films, and electronic information and communications systems markets.

Griffon's subsidiary, Cloplay, is the nation's leading manufacturer of residential garage doors and one of the leading makers of commercial garage doors. It sells a broad line of both steel and wooden garage doors. Its Atlas Roll-Lite Door subsidiary makes heavy duty rolling steel doors, grilles, and counter shutters for the industrial and commercial markets. Griffon also operates a service company that installs and services manufactured fireplaces, garage doors and openers, and a range of related products.

The firm markets its residential garage doors to home centers and other retailers throughout the United States, such as Home Depot, Menards,

Lowe's, and 84 Lumber. It also markets its doors directly to a national network of professional installers.

Building products account for about 62 percent of the company's annual revenue.

About 21 percent of Griffon's revenue comes from its specialty plastic films division. The firm makes plastic films and laminates for use in disposable diapers, adult incontinent products, and sanitary napkins. Most of its sales are to Procter & Gamble Company.

Griffon's other key segment is electronic information and communications systems, which account for about 17 percent of revenue. Through its Telephonics subsidiary, the firm specializes in advanced information and communications systems for government, aerospace, civil, industrial, and commercial customers.

Telephonics makes maritime surveillance radars, air traffic management systems, advanced military communications systems, IF equipment, transit communication systems, command and control systems, microwave landing systems, and avionics for commercial airlines. About 50 percent of its revenue comes from projects for the U.S. government.

Based in Jericho, New York, Griffon has about 5,500 employees and a market capitalization of about $320 million.

EARNINGS PER SHARE GROWTH

Past four years: 22 percent (5 percent per year)

REVENUE GROWTH   ★

Past four years: 103 percent (19 percent per year)

STOCK GROWTH

Past three years: 18 percent (5 percent per year)
Dollar growth: $10,000 over the past three years would have grown to about $12,000.

CONSISTENCY   ★ ★

Increased earnings per share: two of the past four years
Increased revenue: four of the past four years

GRIFFON AT A GLANCE

Fiscal year ended: Sept. 30
Revenue and net income in $ millions

	1994	1995	1996	1997	1998	4-Year Growth Avg. Annual (%)	Total (%)
Revenue ($)	451.2	506.1	655.1	770.2	914.9	19	103
Net income ($)	29.4	23.2	28.1	33.2	29.3	—	—
Earnings/share ($)	0.79	0.69	0.88	1.06	0.96	5	22
Avg. PE ratio	10	13	11	13	13	—	—

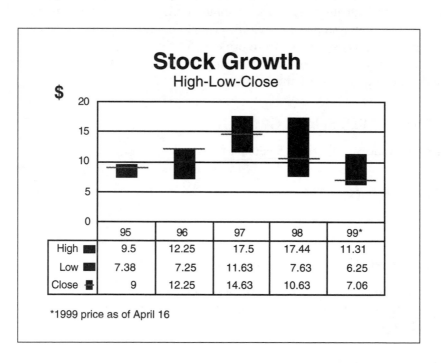

Stock Growth
High-Low-Close

	95	96	97	98	99*
High	9.5	12.25	17.5	17.44	11.31
Low	7.38	7.25	11.63	7.63	6.25
Close	9	12.25	14.63	10.63	7.06

*1999 price as of April 16

The 100 Best Stocks Under $20
by State

State	Ranking
CALIFORNIA	
Applied Signal Technology, Inc.	44
Cattellus Development Corporation	56
CBT Group, PLC	60
Ducommun Incorporated	22
Hall, Kinion & Associates, Inc.	51
Hot Topic, Inc.	48
ICU Medical, Inc.	65
Ingram Micro, Inc.	36
Newport Corp.	68
PFF Bancorp, Inc.	87
Southwest Water Company	45
Standard Pacific Corp.	28
Summa Industries	19
ViaSat, Inc.	49
Xylan Corporation	55
COLORADO	
Mail-Well, Inc.	13
Vari-L Company, Inc.	78
CONNECTICUT	
NFO Worldwide, Inc.	74
Trex Medical Corporation	52
FLORIDA	
AmeriPath, Inc.	64
Equinox Systems, Inc.	57
FDP Corp.	30
Recoton Corporation	86
Technisource, Inc.	27
GEORGIA	
CryoLife, Inc.	38

State	Ranking
GEORGIA, continued	
Interface, Inc.	97
K&G Men's Center, Inc.	61
Melita International Corp.	4
ILLINOIS	
Anixter International, Inc.	95
LINC Capital, Inc.	71
MYR Group, Inc.	10
Schawk, Inc.	98
Stericycle, Inc.	29
Technology Solutions Company	11
INDIANA	
Brightpoint, Inc.	21
Made2Manage, Inc.	82
MARYLAND	
Integral Systems, Inc.	14
RWD Technologies, Inc.	15
MASSACHUSETTS	
American Science & Engineering, Inc.	34
Chase Corporation	42
Lawrence Savings Bank	62
Litchfield Financial Corporation	39
Maxwell Shoe Company, Inc.	92
Mercury Computer Systems, Inc.	72
Thermo Ecotek Corporation	91
MICHIGAN	
Gentex Corporation	9
MINNESOTA	
Funco, Inc.	25
Ontrack Data International, Inc.	79
Techne Corporation	54
NEVADA	
DBT Online, Inc.	35

State	Ranking
NEW HAMPSHIRE	
PC Connection, Inc.	23
NEW JERSEY	
Intelligroup, Inc.	18
Opinion Research Corp.	99
Pure World, Inc.	17
RCM Technologies, Inc.	24
NEW YORK	
Actrade International, Ltd.	2
Astronics Corporation	37
ATEC Group, Inc.	31
Compass International Services Corporation	41
Del Global Technologies Corp.	33
Global Payment Technology, Inc.	40
Griffon Corporation	100
Hauppauge Digital, Inc.	1
Interstate National Dealer Services, Inc.	8
Medialink Worldwide, Inc.	70
Richton International Corporation	6
TSR, Inc.	7
Vicon Industries, Inc.	73
Winfield Capital Corp.	80
NORTH CAROLINA	
Embrex, Inc.	46
OHIO	
Century Business Service, Inc.	69
Chart Industries, Inc.	20
Corrpro Companies Incorporated	75
Essef Corporation	32
Seaway Food Town, Inc.	47
OKLAHOMA	
TV Guide, Inc.	3
Webco Industries, Inc.	77
Xeta Corporation	66

State	Ranking
OREGON	
Timberline Software Corporation	16
PENNSYLVANIA	
Ansys, Inc.	81
Cable Design Technologies Corp.	58
Michael Baker Corporation	94
Prophet 21, Inc.	89
STV Group, Inc.	67
UBICS, Inc.	63
SOUTH DAKOTA	
Daktronics, Inc.	93
TENNESSEE	
Covenant Transport, Inc.	76
Goody's Family Clothing, Inc.	59
TEXAS	
Advanced Neuromodulation Systems, Inc.	90
American Oncology Resources, Inc.	50
AmeriCredit Corp.	5
Capital Senior Living Corporation	26
Dawson Geophysical Company	83
RF Monolithics, Inc.	85
Tandy Brands Accessories, Inc.	88
UTAH	
Mity-Lite, Inc.	43
Nature's Sunshine Products, Inc.	84
USANA, Inc.	12
VIRGINIA	
Dan River, Inc.	96
WISCONSIN	
Gehl Company	53

The 100 Best Stocks Under $20
by Industry Group

Industry	Ranking

AEROSPACE AND DEFENSE

Ducommun Incorporated	22

APPAREL AND ACCESSORIES

Dan River, Inc.	96
Tandy Brands Accessories, Inc.	88

BUSINESS SERVICE

Cattellus Development Corporation	56
Century Business Service, Inc.	69
Compass International Services Corporation	41
Corrpro Companies Incorporated	75
Daktronics, Inc.	93
Interstate National Dealer Services, Inc.	8
NFO Worldwide, Inc.	74
Ontrack Data International, Inc.	79
Opinion Research Corp.	99
Schawk, Inc.	98
STV Group, Inc.	67

COMMUNICATIONS

Brightpoint, Inc.	21
Cable Design Technologies Corp.	58
Medialink Worldwide, Inc.	70
Melita International Corp.	4
TV Guide, Inc.	3
ViaSat, Inc.	49
Xylan Corporation	55

COMPUTER
Networking

ATEC Group, Inc.	31

Industry	Ranking

DISTRIBUTORS

USANA, Inc.	12
Xeta Corporation	66

ELECTRONICS

Anixter International, Inc.	95
Applied Signal Technology, Inc.	44
Gentex Corporation	9
Recoton Corporation	86
RF Monolithics, Inc.	85
Vari-L Company, Inc.	78
Vicon Industries, Inc.	73

ENERGY

Dawson Geophysical Company	83
Thermo Ecotek Corporation	91

FINANCIAL

Global Payment Technologies, Inc.	40
Lawrence Savings Bank	62
LINC Capital, Inc.	71
Litchfield Financial Corporation	39
PFF Bancorp, Inc.	87
Winfield Capital Corp.	80

MANUFACTURING

Astronics Corporation	37
Chart Industries, Inc.	20
Chase Corporation	42
Essef Corporation	32
Gehl Company	53
Griffon Corporation	100
Interface, Inc.	97
Mail-Well, Inc.	13
Maxwell Shoe Company, Inc.	92
Mity-Lite, Inc.	43
Nature's Sunshine Products, Inc.	84
Newport Corp.	68

Industry	Ranking
MANUFACTURING, continued	
Pure World, Inc.	17
Summa Industries	19
Webco Industries, Inc.	77
MEDICAL PRODUCTS	
Advanced Neuromodulation Systems, Inc.	90
American Science & Engineering Inc.	34
Del Global Technologies Corp.	33
Embrex, Inc.	46
ICU Medical, Inc.	65
Techne Corporation	54
Trex Medical Corporation	52
MEDICAL SERVICES	
American Oncology Resources, Inc.	50
AmeriPath, Inc.	64
Capital Senior Living Corporation	26
CryoLife, Inc.	38
RETAIL	
Funco, Inc.	25
Goody's Family Clothing, Inc.	59
Hot Topic, Inc.	48
K&G Men's Center, Inc.	61
Seaway Food Town, Inc.	47
TRUCKING	
Covenant Transport, Inc.	76
UTILITIES	
Southwest Water Company	45
WASTE SERVICES	
Stericycle, Inc.	29

Index